Race, Culture, and Schooling

Identities of Achievement
in Multicultural Urban Schools

Race, Culture, and Schooling

Identities of Achievement in Multicultural Urban Schools

Peter C. Murrell, Jr.

Center for Innovation in Urban Education
and Northeastern University

Lawrence Erlbaum Associates
Taylor & Francis Group

New York   London

Cover design by Kathryn Houghtaling Lacey.

Lawrence Erlbaum Associates
Taylor & Francis Group
270 Madison Avenue
New York, NY 10016

Lawrence Erlbaum Associates
Taylor & Francis Group
2 Park Square
Milton Park, Abingdon
Oxon OX14 4RN

© 2007 by Taylor & Francis Group, LLC
Lawrence Erlbaum Associates is an imprint of Taylor & Francis Group, an Informa business

Printed in the United States of America on acid-free paper
10 9 8 7 6 5 4 3 2 1

International Standard Book Number-13: 978-0-8058-5538-8 (Softcover) 978-0-8058-5537-1 (Hardcover)

Library of Congress Cataloging-in-Publication Data

Murrell, Peter C.
    Race, culture and schooling : Identities of achievement in multi-cultural urban schools / Peter C. Murrell, Jr.
        p. cm.
    Includes bibliographical references and index.
    ISBN-13: 978-0-8058-5537-1 (cloth : alk. paper)
    ISBN-13: 978-0-8058-5538-8 (pbk. : alk. paper)
    ISBN-13: 978-1-4106-1748-4 (e-book)
        1. Education, Urban--United States. 2. Minorities--Education--United States. 3. Academic achievement--United States. 4. United States--Ethnic relation. I. Title.

LC5131.M875 2007
370.9173'2--dc22   2006037736

Visit the Taylor & Francis Web site at
http://www.taylorandfrancis.com

This book is dedicated to my daughter Anya,
whose presence in my life has
been a joy and
inspiration

Contents

Preface

Can you imagine situations or kinds of activity where you feel very smart? How about situations where you feel just barely competent enough—maybe only sort of smart? Finally, can you imagine situations or certain kinds of activity that you prefer to avoid because you feel kind of dumb? These are three statuses of learning achievement educators face with their students on a daily basis. We teachers try to maximize those circumstances in which our students experience themselves as smart because we know that this experience figures prominently in their engagement, commitment of effort, and subsequent achievement success. As educators, we also try to minimize for our students the school experiences in which they feel "kind of dumb" as we know that this diminishes effort, commitment, and achievement performance.

According to self-efficacy theory (e.g., Bandura, 1986), there is a reciprocal relationship between students' beliefs about their capacity and the effort they put forth leading to achievement success. When the effective effort put forth by students results in achievement success, this elevates their sense of efficacy (belief in their own capacity) that, in turn, elevates their effort. This cycle, which constitutes the relationship between achievement and beliefs about one's own capability, also works in reverse. Students who lack confidence in their ability to achieve on school-related tasks diminish their effort and subsequently perform less well.

This book is about the complex interplay between sense of self (identity) and achievement performance and the factors that mediate both in the complexities of race, culture, and poverty in urban U.S. schools. As important as students' belief about their capacity is, however, we know that achievement is more than a matter of boosting confidence. With all due respect to the *Little Engine That Could,* school achievement is more than just "thinking you can." Achievement success is mediated by one's beliefs in one's capability, but also by the quality of school experiences and social interactions with others in school settings in which those beliefs play out. How people experience and actively represent themselves in any given school context has everything to do with their effort, performance, scholastic development, and school success. My core proposition is this: *Identity is our agency in activity; who we are is a matter of what we choose to do and how we choose to invest in that doing.*

Let's try a thought experiment. Think about a time when you were doing something where you felt smart. Try to form a mental image of how you were able to bring about this feeling of being smart. This can be any episode or routine experience in which what you do or what you have done leads or led you to feeling intellectually robust. You might imagine a lecture demonstration, or something simpler like carrying on a conversation on a subject in which you are exceptionally conversant. For example, for myself the introduction of a course on the first day of class of a new semester is a situation that comes to mind as a setting in which I feel smart. Now, once you have the image of the experience in mind, ask yourself this: What was the basis of your feeling smart? Can you imagine specifics of what you did in realizing this feeling of smartness—this sense of being smart? Can you imagine things you might have done to make the feeling of smartness last? Can you imagine things that seemed like the "typical" you, or perhaps most like the "untypical" you? Can you imagine a distinction between feeling smart and being smart?

To continue the exercise just a bit further, now try to imagine your "feeling smart" episode from another perspective—from the perspective of those who might have been observing you and interacting with you in that episode. What do you suppose others observing you in the episode might have noticed about you and your actions in achieving your sense of being smart? Can you imagine them drawing their own conclusions about whether you were smart or not based on how you presented yourself in the episode? As the third and final part of this exercise, think now of a time or episode when you were observing someone who seemed to be acting as though he or she was smart. What were the visual signs? Which of those signs struck you as "frontin'" or putting on airs? Which of these signs or behaviors were off-putting?

The point of this exercise is to demonstrate that the experience of being smart is not a single state of mind or emotion, but is, rather, a complex social construction. It is not just what you believe about yourself or your capabilities that determines being smart, or just how you project your sense of self, but also what others believe about you and what they make of your actions. In addition to your self-presentation and others' interpretations of your presentation in a given social setting, there is a set of social factors that mediate identity and performance. These factors are embedded in the shared meaning systems constituting the social and cultural fabric of the setting in which teaching and learning occur. These factors include the nature of:

- Audience, its interaction with you, and what the people constituting the audience believe about you and how they respond to you.
- Impression management, the impression you seek to create in the setting with a given audience, either consciously or unconsciously.
- The confluence between the impression you make and the impression others take of your demonstration of smartness.
- Your actual proficiency demonstrated by you as the actor or speaker in the episode.
- How you value the activity and setting of your performance (even if it is merely a conversation on a given topic).
- The specific context of people and the relationships, shared understandings, assumptions, and bias that are put into play.

There are both psychological dynamics of cultural cognition and sociological dynamics of human communication that mediate the social identities of learners. The core argument here is that if we could get a handle on these factors—both of identity and social practices that mediate identity—we could re-create experiences of both feeling smart and being smart for every learner. We significantly diminish, if not eradicate, achievement gaps by creating social learning environments that develop identities of smartness, accomplishment, and achievement for anyone. In short, we would have the means to promote identities of achievement.

Human beings are motivated to maximize the moments and episodes during which they feel smart. Human motivation and symbolic forms of self-expression are therefore major ideas in the analysis. The motivation animating identity formation and identity expression may operate largely out of awareness, but nonetheless impels people to act in ways that sometimes undermine their actual learning achievement and other goals. Part of what I advocate in these pages is improving schooling by making both learners and their adult teachers more aware of their motivations regarding their identity, social positioning, and status in the significant human exchanges in which they participate both in and out of school. It does not take much for people who are motivated to be smart to engage with others in ways that actually work against them—positioning them as not smart. This is why improving achievement is never simply a matter of raising self-esteem, because people who actually are motivated to achieve can still operate in ways that diminish their likelihood of reaching that aim.

THE AIMS OF THIS VOLUME

An understanding of how identities of children and youth support school success and social development is vitally important—both in terms of the challenges of urban education and as a matter of public interest. There is a small body of research that explores the relationship between academic identity—roughly defined as individuals' sense of affiliation with school life, school work, and school experience (Nasir & Saxe, 2003)—and scholastic performance (e.g., Carter, 2005; Gibson, Bejínez, Hidalgo, & Rolón, 2004; Mehan, Hubbard, & Villanueva, 1994; Ogbu & Davis, 2003; Stanton-Salazar, 2004). This book investigates the critical developmental and social processes mediating students' academic identities in those settings posing the greatest challenges to their school achievement and personal development. It looks specifically at the acts of identity—namely, self-representation (identity expression), positioning (positionality), and improvisational self-determination (agency)—as the primary factors mediating school success.

To properly address the issue of underachievement of African American children and other children of color, we need to view schooling as the socialization of our young people in ways that help them work successfully through the parallel and intermingled developmental tasks of academic achievement and identity realization. We need to look at the problem more critically by asking different questions. Instead of asking what is wrong with the children or what they are *missing*, we need to ask what children are *not finding* in schools that they need to identify with to learn, achieve, and develop. In short, we need to examine not just the child and not just the school environment, but also the child-in-context as the unit of analysis to understand how both mutually constitute each other in the social and cultural practices of schooling. To do this, I propose a situated-mediated identity theory and use it as a conceptual framework to explain the relationships between schooling processes on the one hand and the psychocultural and sociocultural processes experienced by youth growing up in ethnically, racially, and linguistically diverse urban communities on the other hand. The result is the articulation of a system of practice that educators and other committed adults can apply to promoting healthy social and emotional development of children and youth in association with their school achievement.

Situated-mediated identity theory is a cultural psychology of school achievement based on a relatively new conception of identity called *situated identity* as the critical dimension of school experience that mediates achievement and scholastic success. The theory is based on six premises:

1. Self, and realizations of self (identity), are socially constructed through various forms of relational activity in human interaction, especially communication.
2. Identity is best understood as situated and fluid, not static and fixed, and is seen in the representations of self that individuals put forth to the wider social world.
3. The situated representations of self taken on by an individual (role or positionality) are situated roles that individuals assume and express (consciously or unconsciously) in any given setting or social environment.
4. The positionality or set of roles assumed in school settings profoundly shapes achievement and ultimately determines school success.
5. Shared situated identities created and mediated by common experiences in school settings (which some theorists have referred to as *academic identities*) form a local culture that shapes school performance and sense of self.
6. Finally, this local culture—the structure of the immediate cultural-social context of instructional activity settings together with the situatedness of a learner's performance—can be shaped to mediate positive and productive academic identities in ways that ultimately lead to school success.

This volume develops an explanatory framework for each of the processes based on these six premises, and then works it into an applied psychology of identity and agency development among children and youth, as well as their teachers, striving together for academic achievement in diverse school settings. The framework is a theoretical and practical account of the relationships between healthy identity realization on the one hand and the barriers and resources that exist in the social and cultural contexts of school settings on the other hand. Using this theory, I develop a working framework of achievement by addressing the following questions:

1. In what ways does identity matter to achievement and scholastic development among children and youth, particularly those of color?
2. What should educators and other responsible adults know about identity processes and the social settings in which they occur to promote school success for everyone?
3. How should we structure the social environments of schools to promote identity development and achievement processes among all children?

Situated-mediated identity theory is the name I have given the framework for addressing these questions. This volume, therefore, offers a system for understanding how teachers and other caring adults recognize and draw on cultural legacies and identity projections of young people in the design of a new common culture of achievement. The purpose of this system is to guide those concerned with how identity, achievement, and instructional practice interrelate in school practices for children and youth, especially in diverse and urban school settings. The framework is based on an emerging research literature on cultural development and cultural psychology, incorporating what we already know about the social and cultural contexts that maximize learning, cognitive development, and identity formation. The theory of social identity charts an action agenda for culturally relevant practice, including guidance and clinical intervention.

Situated-mediated identity theory is the product of more than 25 years of research and instructional practice in culturally, linguistically, and ethnically diverse schools and communities. This new account of identity and agency development emerges from a critical reinterpretation of developmental theory and from an appropriation of ideas from a diverse array of disciplines in cognitive science such as cultural sociology, cultural psychology, semiotics, cognitive psychology, and educational anthropology. It is also informed by an emergent, vibrant literature on the situated and socially mediated nature of racial and cultural identity development among youth (cf. Carter, 2005; Flores-Gonzáles, 2002; Hunter & Davis, 1992, 1994; Nasir & Saxe, 2003; P. Perry, 2002; Sadowski, 2003; Stevens, 2002; Yon, 2000).

The decidedly educational flavor of this volume is intentional for several reasons. First and most important, this is a work emphasizing the animation of theory into practice. Theorizing about racial identity development and agency is one thing, but I want the value of the cultural practices theory to be tested in the crucible of real work in real settings with the young people who need it most. The value of the theory is based on whether it enables teachers, parents, and counselors to work effectively with young people in light of the structural barriers that threaten their academic success. Second, school is the site in which young people spend a considerable amount of time—negotiating relationships, interacting with adults, and engaging in purposeful activity. Finally, schools are institutions that are supposed to promote secondary socialization. I mean to provide an action theory for teachers, guidance counselors, social workers, school psychologists, and other practitioners who work on a daily basis with children and young adults to fulfill the function of secondary socialization.

ORGANIZATION OF THE VOLUME

Part I of the volume (chaps. 1–3) constitutes the theory portion of the situated-mediated identity framework that provides a deep analysis of identity development in cultural and social context and its relationship to well-being and academic performance in diverse settings. As will be seen (see Table 1–2 in chap. 1), the theory posits three distinct forms of identity development (i.e., situated identity, positionality, and agency), three distinct settings for this development (i.e., the cultural community, the cultural-symbolic community [or figured world], and the community of practice), and three processes that relate the forms of identity development to the settings (viz., primary socialization, secondary socialization, and improvised self-determination). I believe that this concurrent analysis of *processes, settings,* and *forms of identity* is necessary for a full understanding of school achievement in today's diverse world.[1] I believe such an analysis is necessary for realizing and addressing the critical factors influencing young people's development as learners, as citizens, and as empowered adults, and for connecting these factors to their school performance.

---

[1]Stevens (2002) modified Spencer's person-process-context formulation positing processes of intersubjectivity as the mediator between person and context. Spencer's (1995) framework is termed a *phenomenological variant* of the ecological systems theory of Brofennbrenner (1979, 1986). Similarly, the work of Côté and Levine (2002) posits a person-interaction-social structure framework linking individual to context, as well as for synthesizing psychological, sociological, and constructivist accounts of identity.

Chapter 1, "Dilemmas of Diversity in Urban Education: Race, Culture, and Underachievement," situates the specific problem of underachievement in the larger dilemma of urban education with respect to how schooling should be organized to account for the special social and educational challenges found in culturally, racially, ethnically, and linguistically diverse settings. Chapter 2, "Overview of Situated-Mediated Identity Theory," is the general overview of the theory. The framework is situated in contemporary conceptions of identity development and of racial identity development. The chapter presents the basic tenets and arguments for the situated-mediated identity approach to youth development and education, making the case for the importance of providing the needed social, cultural, intellectual, and moral supports for children and youth. Chapter 3, "Cultural Practices Inquiry: Culturally Reading Individuals-in-Settings," articulates a simpler working version of the situated-mediated framework. It summarizes the working form of the framework as a kind of *syntax*, a rule system that characterizes how to read individuals in relation to practices of cultural learning that adults create in learning communities that promote achiever identities and agency for young people. Chapter 3 concludes the first part of the volume on the theory.

Part II of the book (chaps. 4–7) is the practice part of the framework that illustrates how to arrange a rich symbolic world that provides young people with the necessary cultural capital to grow into capable, healthy, and empowered citizens. The second part of this volume is devoted to applying the method of cultural practices inquiry (MCPI) using illustrative case examples from elementary school, middle school, high school, and professional settings. The purpose is to provide clear and concrete applications of the cultural practices theory in different settings. Through the illustrative case examples, readers are able to make meaningful connections between the theory and their own teaching practices. Chapter 4, "The Construction of Academic Identities: Situativity, Positionality, and Agency in Intellectual Life," begins the application section of the volume with an explanation and application of situated-mediated identity theory of human development for young children. The three dimensions of identity—situated identity, positionality, and agency—are illustrated for instructional practice. Chapter 5, "Communities of Achievement as Culturally Configured Worlds," explains more fully the notions of a cultural community and a cultural-symbolic community and community of practice (COP). This discussion uses cultural practices inquiry as a framework for determining which cultural variations matter in the achievement identities and performances of children in school settings.

Chapter 6, "Acquisition of Cultural Practices of Achiever Identities as Learners," is an analysis of relationships between an individual's cultural contexts and his or her acquisition of abilities that are required and valued in school settings. Learning achievement is conceptualized as the acquisition of academic practices and cultural tools. I also examine the critical concept of cultural competence—among both learners and teachers—and what it really should mean in the creation of identities of achievement for both children and adults in a school environment. Chapter 7, "The Cultural Practices of Achiever Identities of Teachers," examines in greater detail the development of academic proficiency in terms of cultural practices and situated identities of teachers, providing more illustration as to how secondary socialization of particular cultural practices results in scholastic and academic proficiency. Finally, the epilogue summarizes the application of the theory by looking at the social context and cultural mediation that take place in urban locations. I briefly contrast the default context of the culturally mainstream American-figured world extant in contemporary schooling with the Black-figured world of achievement. Drawing most on the example of African American culture, I discuss how cultural practices such as improvisation, perspective taking, signifying, and double voicedness/vision become the substrates for competency in advanced scholastic skills such as literary interpretation, empirical investigation, and text analysis.

ACKNOWLEDGMENTS

I am especially indebted to my mother, Eva Ruth Greenlee Murrell, who read the manuscript and offered valuable suggestions on form and content. I want to express my appreciation to my wife, Terry Meier, for her support and valuable comments on the manuscript, as well as her patience in enduring my obsession with completing the project. I want to express special thanks to my dear friend and colleague Micky Cokely, who read and advised me on earlier drafts of the manuscript. Finally, I want to thank Northeastern University for my sabbatical leave despite my responsibilities to the Center for Innovation in Urban Education during my year-long absence to complete work on the project.

I

Theoretical Framework

1

Dilemmas of Diversity in Urban Education: Race, Culture, and Underachievement

We assume that the most fundamental objective of education is the development of individual human dignity, or self-realization within community. The next step lies not in a more concrete plan, but in a *search for a group of people*, some "missing community," with the courage and energy to re-examine how education, most broadly conceived as the interaction between reflection and action, can invigorate the lives of all of its citizens.

— Newman & Oliver (1967, p. 61)

CRISIS IN EDUCATION: STRUCTURAL INEQUALITY ALONG COLOR LINES

By now, most readers are aware of the public concern over the shortcomings of public urban schooling in the United States and the persistent structural inequality in the educational experiences and opportunities of poor children and children of color. Public schools, particularly those in large metropolitan school districts, are dramatically less successful in educating working-class, urban, African American and Latino children and youth than their White, middle-class counterparts. For example, only 12% of African American fourth graders reach proficient or advanced levels and 61% have not been taught even the basic level in reading or mathematics. Similarly, 61% of African American eighth graders fall below the basic achievement level compared to only 7% who reach the proficient level or above (Education Trust, 2002).

Black and Latino students, who constitute the majority of students in virtually every urban school system, are disproportionately expelled, suspended, adjudicated as criminals in zero-tolerance expulsions, and relegated

3

to special education programs. Many urban school districts also host large communities of recent émigrés from other countries, whose children's struggles with school pose still another dimension of the so-called achievement gap. The disparities in financial and instructional resources between urban school districts and their more affluent suburban counterparts are a national disgrace (Anyon, 2005; Kozol, 1991, 2005; Noguera, 2003).

One reason the underperformance of children in underresourced school systems is not addressed more successfully is that we persist in using an optic that looks primarily at the symptoms (i.e., differential test score performances) of structural inequality and too little at the root causes that are the shortcomings in our social and professional practices, as well as our economic and educational policies. A case in point is the one-sided characterization of systemic racial inequality as the result of an "achievement gap," a term used frequently by the educational research and policy community to refer to the persistent differences in aggregated high-stakes achievement test performance between ethnic minority learners and White learners. The characterization is one-sided to the extent that it implies that the disparities of student performance are mainly a matter of deficits and shortcomings of the ethnic minority school population, without an honest appraisal of how the other gaps—disparities in educational, financial, and material resources—contribute to the degradation of achievement performance. This characterization obscures the fact that there are significant gaps in many other factors that mediate school success. For example, Gordon (Gordon, Bridglall, & Meroe, 2004) makes the case that access to social and cultural capital, such as that provided to inner-city school children in the form of supplementary education as after-school enrichment and youth development programs, could alone close the achievement gap. Hence, characterization of the issue as a gap leads to an incomplete picture of differentiated school performance because it overlooks the underperformance of our systems of education. Considering the individual side without the systems-context side will always yield an incomplete picture of school achievement.

The test score discrepancy is a symptom of a much more deeply entrenched system of privilege and educational disenfranchisement that is a major factor in academic underperformance (Hilliard, 2004). Eradicating the achievement gap requires, therefore, concentrating our efforts on at least two fronts: (a) elevating the quality of teaching and learning for the population of underperforming students (at the microlevel), and (b) eliminating the structural inequalities such as fewer and less experienced teachers, fewer materials and financial resources, and absence of supplementary programs that develop young people (at the macrolevel). Too often, we have allowed a performance outcome (i.e., differences in aggregate test score performance between groups) to be treated as though it were the problem to be solved instead of focusing on the deeper issue of the quality of teaching and learning processes and practices. The challenge now is to not allow this unbalanced picture to lead us into still another round of "blame the victim" policy dressed in different garb. Both popular and policy views tacitly assume that the gap is merely a matter of personal shortcomings of minority and poor children and their families, instead of being grounded in our systems of schooling and the ways they fall short of providing students what they need to perform, achieve, and develop.

RACE, CONTEXT, AND ACHIEVEMENT

What accounts for differences in standardized achievement test performance of the achievement gap data, generally between African American, Latino, and central-city school children on the one hand, and White, culturally mainstream, and suburban children on the other hand? What is in the schooling environment that might produce differential achievement outcomes? There is a general acknowledgment among educational researchers that there are a multitude of such contextual factors embedded in the schooling experiences and subsequent achievement outcomes for children of color that need to be accounted for. In other words, context counts, but it is not clear just *how* it counts, for whom, and under what circumstances. For example, a number of educational researchers (Comer, 1998; Delpit, 1988; Fordham, 1988, 1996; Foster, 1989; Hilliard, 2004; Hollins, 1996; Kunjufu, 1985; Ladson-Billings, 1994; Murrell, 1994; Reid & Henry, 2000) have examined the nature of this growing disparity in school performance between African American children and their White counterparts. What this body of work has shown is that culturally mainstream White school settings often pose a number of social, cultural, political, and developmental impediments for African American children that go unrecognized by teachers and school personnel, but that nonetheless have significant adverse impacts on students' adjustment to school life. That is, there are material, social, ideological, and cultural aspects of life in contemporary school environments that are inimical to Black achievement (Murrell, 2002).

Even though much educational research has examined race in relation to the achievement gap, differences in discipline patterns, and disparities in achievement outcomes, this work does not begin to capture the reality of race as both a *product* and *process* of schooling practices. The contemporary body of work fails to ask a critical prior question: What does one's ethnic or racial identity mean in school settings where race is a subtle determiner of social and cultural relationships? There is a lot that goes on in urban schools in the daily practices involving racial stigma that goes unrecognized. As we have seen, the practices of racial victimization and racial privilege are often quite substantial, but can be quite invisible to those in those contexts.

THE INCREASING SIGNIFICANCE OF RACE

Contrary to popular belief, there is an increasing, not a decreasing, impact of race in school practices and policy. This, in turn, profoundly impacts the schooling experiences of African American students in particular, and also White students and other students of color. For example, the work of Orfield and others has demonstrated that there is a greater segregation in U.S. schooling now than there was prior to the landmark case of *Brown v. Board of Education* in 1954. Hence, whatever educational benefits we imagined would result from a heterogeneous population of African American and White students will not be realized because most Black students now go to school in predominantly Black schools, and most White students go to school in predominantly White schools. However, of greater concern than the social segregation is the continuing presence of racism in the day-to-day pedagogical practices and policies in schools. DuBois (1903/1989) famously said that the problem of the 20th century is the problem of the color line. In the 21st century, the problem persists—including in schools (Bush, 2004; Lewis, 2003; Pollock, 2004; Van Ausdale & Feagin, 2002). This makes the project of reconfiguring schools to reflect the lived experiences, cultural legacies, and political realities of the communities served one of great importance and also one of great difficulty.

The difficulty of appropriately dealing with race and racism in schools is partially based in the mistaken, but widespread, view that race no longer matters in the opportunities and fortunes of African Americans and other ethnic minorities. Because many still think of racism in Civil Rights-era terms—that is, as acts of overt racial discrimination or preference—they are not prepared to see its impact all around them. Because most people are not used to thinking about racism as a system of social, economic, and cultural privilege, they are prone to regard it only as visible and overt acts of individual discrimination. As is true with any deeply embedded social system, racism's declining visibility in the public mind does not mean it has disappeared, only that it has taken a different form. The racism of the 21st century is not based in overt acts, but in the continued covert projections of Black inferiority and White supremacy in the American psyche. The "old racism" was clearly based on entrenched notions of genetic inferiority. In contrast, the new racism is often clothed in the vestments of *cultural difference* (Connolly, 1998). As Yon (2000) describes it:

> "New racism" is a term that was coined to describe the shift from crude forms of scientific racism based on biologically determined social hierarchy to racism premised on the belief in immutable cultural differences. The newer form of racism is couched in the language of "values," "incompatible cultures," and "complex differences," effectively discriminating without even using the word "race." (p. 11)

The new racism exists in everyday practices that occur right under the noses of teachers and adults charged with the care of young people. The new racism inheres in a generalized assumed racial stigma.

What happens to children of color in both integrated and segregated contexts is a more entrenched version of what we refer to in the literature as *institutional racism*. Institutional racism refers to the maintenance of various racial privileges in our society and social institutions. The newer, more deeply entrenched form of institutional racism is referred to as the new racism by several scholars—a cultural racism that is dyed in the fabric of U.S. cultural, social, and political life. Cultural racism inheres in those practices and policies that outwardly intend to deal with issues of equity and difference, but end up maintaining or increasing the disadvantage of the subordinate group. Recent works of several sociologists and educational scholars have articulated this new form of racism in *discourse practices*—the social practices of communication and everyday human interaction in which culture is most frequently and deeply expressed (e.g., Alton-Lee, Nuthall, & Patrick, 1993; Bush, 2004; Lewis, 2003; Pollock, 2004; Tatum, 1997; Van Ausdale & Feagin, 2002). This body of work documents the new racism in the form of racialized discourses and practices in school settings.

Time and again, under the noses of adult caregivers and teachers (despite diversity training and multicultural awareness), there is a discourse of Black inferiority and White privilege that damages the development and educational opportunity of African American students and other ethnic minority students in school settings. For example, researchers Van Ausdale and Feagin, observing a multiracial group of children, aged 3 to 5, over an 11-month period in a preschool setting located in the Southern United States, found that children as young as 3 in this setting were not only aware of racial differences, but also clearly understood the power of racialized talk and deliberately used this power in negotiating their relationships with peers. In one of many instances of such behavior found in their study, Van Ausdale and Feagin (2002) described the behavior of a 4-year-old White girl who on one occasion reduced an African American schoolmate to tears by insisting that he could not take a white rabbit home because he was "Black." In another incident Van Ausdale and Feagin describe, three children (two White and one Asian) were pulling one another across the playground in a wagon. When the Asian child picked up the wagon handle one of the White children admonished her, "No, no. You can't pull this wagon. Only White Americans can pull this wagon" (p. 37). At that point, the Asian child started to cry and ran to find a teacher. In their taunting of classmates about skin color and their use of racialized language to get their way, the study showed that preschool-aged White children are as capable as White adults of drawing on popular cultural representations of race embedded in the social fabric of everyday American life. The many taken-for-granted assumptions supporting the ideology of Black inferiority and White privilege are accessible to anyone—they are even available in the social fields of children in school settings through words and actions they see and hear in the adult world.

Contrary to being merely a stain on an otherwise unblemished U.S. social tapestry, cultural racism is dyed in the wool of America's discourses of merit and achievement, and therefore invisible to those who share that "culture of power" (to use Delpit's term characterizing this shared ideology). The capacity to inflict racial violence in this manner—through the slightest discursive turn, gesture, or decision—exists on multiple levels—personal, social, and institutional. Suffice it to say at this point that racist practices exist on multiple structural levels of schooling. Often they are hidden in the meaning systems of a school community, such as when, for example, the ideology of color-blindness shapes schooling practices and policies in ways that place children of color at a disadvantage with respect to their White peers.

Lewis (2003) documents the embeddedness of this form of color-blindness in the discourse and school practices of a predominantly White suburban school community she investigated in California. According to Lewis, the color-blind ideology assumes a race-neutral social context, a stance that race does not matter in the setting. Furthermore, she demonstrated how it operated as a *meaning system*—an ideology[1] that is enacted in a community's day-to-day conversations, interactions, and practices—in a way that stigmatizes any attempt to raise questions addressing racial inequality in daily life and labels attempts to raise legitimate questions as "playing the race card" or as resorting to "identity politics" (Lewis, 2003, pp. 33–34). This color-blind ideology plants the assumption that any person raising questions about racial inequality in a setting is simply trying to bring in race where it does not belong. This ideology clearly inhibits honest, systemic, and deliberative interrogation of racialized practice in educational settings (Comer, 1998). Use of this ideology is part of what constitutes the new racism, cultural racism, discussed earlier.

Another feature of the color-blind ideology that is damaging to academic identity development for children of color is its implicit definition of educational equality as that of *equivalent treatment*. The equivalent treatment concept of equality suggests that equal treatment of, for example, African American students with respect to their White counterparts, achieves educational equity. As noted earlier, rarely is there actually equivalent treatment (Anyon, 2005; Kozol, 2005; Noguera, 2003) in the first place. Even if equivalent treatment were to be achieved, this popular notion of equity does not take into account differences in the *cultural capital*—the cache and quality-of-life chances that accrue differently according to social, racial, and economic status. The reduction of differential impacts across racial categories is not the same as creating equal educational opportunity (Crenshaw, 1997; Murrell & Borunda, 1998) because it does not begin to address structural inequality in terms of cultural capital.

The color-blind ideology operates on the institutional level. The color-blind ideology in predominantly White communities threatens to become the new substitute for the genetic inferiority and biologically based explanations of Black inferiority of times past. In its assertion of a "race does

---

[1]McLaren (2003) states that *ideology* refers to the production of sense and meaning. This makes it a meaning system that individuals use to interpret the world and themselves in it. Ideology is "a complex of ideas, various types of social practices, rituals, and representations that we tend to accept as natural and as common sense" (p. 79).

not matter" point of view, the color-blind ideology masks the fact that race still functions as a source of power and privilege for White people. The color-blind ideology is powerful at protecting the status quo because virtually everyone would prefer that race did not matter. Acts of racism in the present day are much more covert than they were in the Jim Crow era of discrimination or in the Civil Rights era. The work of Lewis (2003), Van Ausdale and Feagin (2002), and Pollock (2004) is important because they document the way that the undercurrent of color-conscious practices and discourses creates a toxic social and cultural climate for children of color. The inscription of generally low expectations for African American and Latino students, and other students of color in urban school settings, is one unfortunate result of the color-blind ideology. It is not unrelated to ideologies of meritocracy and racial privilege.

The disparities in school quality are compounded in school settings that are populated predominantly by students of color in relatively underresourced urban districts. For example, consider the well-documented phenomenon of scholastic alienation, meaninglessness, and what sociologists call *anomie*[2] experienced by African American boys the longer they are in school (S. H. Holland, 1996; Kunjufu, 1985). Young African American children, energetic and enthusiastic when they enter school in kindergarten, by third or fourth grade lose their enthusiasm, interest, and motivation. As I have researched this phenomenon in my own work, the most significant factor turns out to be an absence or loss of sense making and meaning making in the design of learning environments for children and youth. In school settings that do not maintain a sense of purpose, intellectual verve, and sense of identity, the African American children who are academically successful are, all too often, merely the ones who learn to endure the tedium and lifelessness of the curriculum and the setting, even though they experience them as devoid of meaning or connection to what matters in their lives. Urban school goers in particular all too often experience this form of schooling, what Haberman (1991) described as the *pedagogy of poverty*. In this instance, the successful children are those who learn to steel themselves for this existence—to comply with, and perhaps become adept at meeting the litany of demands, routines, and

---

[2]Anomie is not just an experience of African American children, but is an issue for many young people. For example, it is a factor in the phenomenon of rampage school shootings, like the one that occurred at Columbine High School. Rampage shootings tend to take place in rural and suburban settings, rarely in urban areas, and rampage shooters are predominantly White males, among whom a lack of meaning is a common denominator. Some have proposed, for example (Pollack, 1999) that there is a negative male youth culture in the United States—a "boy code"—that prevents the formation of positive social relationships and intimacy.

rituals. These are the students who simply forgo any expectation that schools will make sense or substantially connect with real life, and those who do not steel themselves are the ones that gradually disengage entirely.

This division between students who persist and those who fall away is an important phenomenon. For the sake of rigor and for the illustration of how the situated framework offers a remedy to this problem, I diverge for a moment with an example to elaborate on three categories of students: (a) those who persist in enduring schooling even though it has ceased to make sense to them; (b) those who fall away and eventually check out of schooling activity; and (c) those who persist because they find meaning, purpose, and academic identity. I argue that these categories constitute three critically important forms of situated identity called *positionalities* (a concept that is developed more fully in subsequent chapters) that mediate not only the actions and decisions the students make, but also how others—especially teachers, aides, and other adults in the instructional space of the students—respond toward them. The separations between those in the "fallen away and checked out" category and those in the two "keep trying" categories are accelerated by how the adults respond to them in the everyday life and discursive practices of school. These three categories constitute student positionalities that influence how they are regarded as achievers by teachers, aides, and other adults (e.g., college student volunteers). The smallest of the three categories is that constituted by those "keep trying" students who have found meaning, purpose, and, most important, an identity of achievement (Murrell, 2006) in their school experience.

The "keep trying" positionality receives positive regard; the "checked out" positionality is disregarded, dismissed, and eventually written off. For example, I notice in the field reports of my student volunteers working with inner-city African American children clear indications of how they prefer working with children displaying the "keep trying" category and have nothing to say about those occupying the "fallen away and checked out" positionality. More disturbing than their articulated preference for "keep trying" students is the way in which the "fallen away and checked out" students become invisible and unmentionable in the volunteers' reflective writing. One of the student volunteers wrote:

> I would like to pursue either third or fourth grade. I feel as though by that age [sic] the students have some interest in learning and as a teacher I would like to keep that interest going. I feel that with [student's name] even though she does not like math a whole lot and she thinks it's hard she is still willing and actively learning it. I feel as though I help her through the problems and when she understands it both she and I feel happiness and relief. (Student paper, November 2005)

As noted earlier, third and fourth grade is when the fall away and checking out effect becomes apparent, so the pupil being written about is deemed to be persisting with "some" interest in learning. Although this young teacher-to-be, like many others like her, may be dedicated and perhaps will be a good teacher some day, the issue of accomplished practice goes beyond committing only to those students who merely try hard. At stake here is the subtle formation of a racial stigma that legitimates writing off those students who do not try hard, or, in the words of teachers, "do not want to learn." Not only are the children in this written-off category disproportionately children of color, but children of color begin to represent children who do not want to learn in the minds of future teachers. The issue at hand is the racial stigmatizing of the images of African American students, of what constitutes mathematics learning in an African American context, and the roles of the White teachers already occurring in this individual's very first tutoring experience in the Black community. What is missing for this student in teacher preparation is an awareness and interrogation of this subtle effect—one where the standard of excellence for children of color among urban teachers is gradually reduced to an expectation that children merely "not give up" regardless of there being any intellectual gain or reward.

In terms of my framework, the pupil's positionality of not yet giving up and trying hard is already becoming the model of the good student in an African American context for this young, White future teacher. The image of mathematics is already becoming the "hard task to be overcome," consistent with Haberman's pedagogy of poverty, in which the learning outcomes are viewed not in terms of new understanding or mastery, but in terms of being a cause for relief for having accomplished a task. Urban educator Howard (1990) refers to this image of school achievement as an instance of the "get over" standard, a negative cultural practice in urban schools and communities where academic accomplishment is seen in terms of getting over or getting by a task, a test, or a course as if it were some obstacle. The get over standard results in mediocre academic performance because the goal is to meet the minimum requirements. The emerging teacher positionality of this future teacher, unless it is challenged, is likely to incorporate this get over standard, where the tacit role of the teacher is one of helping students get over as opposed to one who sees himself or herself as producing changes in the child's capacity as a mathematics learner. There is a danger of young White future teachers adopting pedagogy of poverty positionalities that carry low expectations of Black students and other students of color before they even begin teaching. Here then is an example of the subtle manner in which race and class preference can enter into teacher thinking. It takes the form of a teacher candidate's emerging preference for children who embrace the get over standard, coupled with a dismissal of students who do not want to learn but who most need the best teachers.

The crisis in urban education, especially the continuing significance of race and racism in these subtle forms, is a crisis of meaning requiring a deeper interrogation of the meaning systems by which schooling is organized. Racism's continuing impact is due to our collective inability to get a handle on all forms of symbolic violence. In addition to the cultural racism deeply entrenched in U.S. cultural practices, there are also exclusion practices based in social class bias (e.g., Connolly & Healy, 2004a, 2004b), homophobia (e.g., Kimmel, 1994, 1997), and sexism (e.g., Gilligan, 1982/1993, 1992; Kimmel & Messner, 1992; Sadker & Sadker, 1986, 1994). The analysis of race and racism is key in this project, but no less so than these other forms of symbolic violence. Our challenge is to recognize the meaning systems in the social spaces young people inhabit that tend to reinforce exclusion and inhibit more ethical and humane impulses in social dynamics. The conditions that permit the other forms of symbolic violence to emerge in school communities—such as expressions of class privilege, homophobia, sexism, and ethnic hatred—need to be understood and examined as impediments to promoting social and academic development of children and youth, especially in urban schools and diverse settings. This requires an examination of the meaning systems that define and shape the experiential worlds of children and youth, as well as looking carefully at how we organize the sociocultural environments in school settings.

Determining what happens to children of color in White contexts is therefore more than a matter of unpacking what we have termed institutional racism, but requires an analysis of cultural racism deep in the fabric of U.S. cultural, social, and political life. Unlike racism in the form of individual discriminatory acts, cultural racism is injurious to both perpetrators (i.e., White educators, students, and parents) and victims (i.e., children, youth, and their families of color). The cultural racism embedded in contemporary schooling practice is like carbon monoxide, a highly lethal colorless and odorless gas; by the time one detects its presence, it is already too late. There are two ways to fail children who face the toxicity of racism and racist practice daily: by what we (hopefully inadvertently) *do to them* and what we *fail to do for them*.

The work of several educational researchers examining racialized discourses in school contexts have documented how they operate as a form of symbolic violence against African American people and other people of color (e.g., Lewis, 2003; Pollock, 2004; Van Ausdale & Feagin, 2002) in school settings. As mentioned earlier, symbolic violence in the form of racialized discourse may be taking place on a daily basis right under the noses of adult caregivers and teachers in uses of racial discourse by White students in ways that go unnoticed and unchecked. The capacity to inflict racial violence discursively exists on multiple levels of human interaction, much of which is outside the ken of adults in the unseen and unnoticed social networks formed by children in school settings.

The injury done to the sensibilities of children and youth because of racialized discourse may not always be a matter of what happens to them, but what fails to happen for them. Here is an example involving a classroom practice that is familiar to many elementary educators. This discursive practice is common in primary grades and goes by different names—such as morning circle and sharing time—but the basic idea is for the teacher to lead the entire class of students in a sort of town meeting to address issues and build community. When the practice is used by accomplished teachers to intentionally enrich children's capacity for engaging in public talk and building community, it is a good idea. But when, in a pedagogy of poverty, round-robin sharing time absorbs huge amounts of instructional time with no particular aim, it accomplishes little more than to reinforce the lack of meaning and purpose of school activity. Too often I see this round-robin report-out conducted in ways that cause children to become indifferent to the reports of other children and oblivious to any of the community-building value of the collective assembly. Much worse than this are the hard lessons that this activity setting can teach children about the callousness and indifference to human suffering in the adult world. In her ethnography of three schools, Lewis (2003) observed this feature in the morning circle ritual in the urban elementary school. In this brief excerpt from her field notes she recorded:

> Sally: "My mom's friend and her kid got run over by a car. Her two-month-old baby and her daughter and her got run over. They're dead." Mr. Ortiz asks how the car is. She doesn't know. Thompson: "On Saturday we went to a city park and Sunday went to a mountain." Lisa: "Yesterday, her big dog ran out the door and bit a small puppy and the little dog was bleeding on its back." (Lewis, 2003, p. 46)

According to Lewis, Mr. Ortiz then proceeded to go around the rest of the circle with no further commentary on student reports. Although I have seen countless similar episodes of this morning ritual in my work, none were as striking as Mr. Ortiz's seeming callousness in asking about the car in the child's narrative instead of expressing any kind of regret or sadness about the people who lost their lives. Yet, given how little attention we give to how we organize school life in urban schools, this lapse is not quite so surprising. Given the many challenges and distractions of urban teaching, it is perhaps not so unexpected that teachers in the United States have momentary lapses like the one reflected in Mr. Ortiz's failure to appropriately process the content of the children's narratives. Sadly, I work with many teachers who have become so desensitized and unaware of the emotional life of the children in their classrooms that they too fail to respond appropriately to children's narratives about loss, injury, and death. These teachers probably do not intend to do harm, but regardless of the teacher's intent, the effect on the children is the same. Without taking seriously the meaning children make of their schooling experience, we may be diminishing their opportunities for development.

My point is not to indict teachers, but to argue that bad things happen for children when we do not deliberately and systematically attend to the meaning systems, the cultural values, and the quality of relationships in the social environments we shape for them. As we have seen, the adoption of rituals like morning circle without an understanding of the kind of social and cultural world we are trying to create can actually be emotionally damaging to children. In instances like the foregoing, children will not necessarily acquire a sense of community and caring by the ritual of the morning circle unless it includes deliberate practices of community and practices of caring. What they may well be learning instead are chilling lessons about the coldness and indifference of the adult world.

The point here is that there is a cultural integrity that is currently missing in the educational experience of many African Americans and other children of color in our schools. How do we construct this integrity and offer it as an enriched social environment in school contexts? What vitally important aspects of African American culture, for example, have been overlooked in the intellectual and social environments of so many predominantly Black inner-city schools? What new understandings about intercultural existence in urban life among scores of ethnic, racial, and linguistic groups should be available and accessible to our children? What would the social environment in schools be like if they were to eliminate the everyday toxins of racism? These are questions we need to address to improve contemporary public schooling. These are the issues I tackle in Part II of this volume using the situated-mediated identity theory.

BEYOND CULTURALLY RELEVANT PEDAGOGY

There has been a growing consensus among educational researchers and practitioners that learning is enhanced when it occurs in contexts that are socially, culturally, cognitively, and linguistically familiar to the learner. In other words, learning achievement is improved for individuals who are participating meaningfully in a culturally familiar and supportive social setting (J. S. Brown, Collins, & Duguid, 1989; Lave & Wenger, 1991; Tharp & Gallimore, 1991). However, at present, the whole concept of culture in the current and contemporary educational literature on achievement is problematic because it does not suggest how teachers, educators, and other professionals apply cultural knowledge to teaching and learning.

A case in point is the domain of scholarship addressing culturally responsive teaching. This body of work is viewed as the leading approach to address questions of "teaching to diversity" and working successfully with African American children and other children of color. Culturally responsive teaching is also referred to as culturally relevant teaching (e.g., Ladson-Billings, 1994), culturally compatible teaching, and culturally synchronous teaching (e.g., Irvine, 1990). Although an important advance in educational thinking regarding the role of culture in schooling, there is a troubling limitation to an approach that purports to reduce the mismatch, incongruity, or asynchrony between mainstream and ethnic minority cultures. First, there is an arbitrary bifurcation of dominant culture and subordinate culture. Although this division might have utility in the abstract discussion of social relations, the discussion of culture in this way reinscribes the old deficit notion of the educationally advantaged versus disadvantaged groups. With no sense of how the two groups in question actually differ in terms of cultural forms and practices, how do teachers work with the concept without it merely stereotyping kids?

Second, when people talk about the cultural incongruity in reference to the experience of, for example, African American children in culturally mainstream U.S. public school, they are operating only with an indexical sense of culture—one that offers no information beyond an individual's membership in a static category. *Oppositionality* or *oppositional culture* is one way in which Black culture is reduced, so as to fit a Black culture versus mainstream culture dichotomy. In the absence of knowing the academic-relevant cultural forms and practices, it is easy to think of Black culture and Latino culture as categories in opposition to the category of White culture. It is also easy to think of Black culture or Latino culture as merely being incompatible with, or incongruous to White mainstream culture that reduces their main defining features as difference. The problem with this dichotomy is that opposition becomes the key feature of difference between cultures. Imagine, now, an educational intervention that seeks to reduce opposition—working with a dichotomy without having the vaguest sense or appreciation of what Black culture or Latino culture really consists of or might mean to participants. The result is that people often end up interpreting the term *culture* as merely another indexical category— a symbolic substitute for White versus Black, mainstream versus non-mainstream, or normal versus atypical. Obviously, this is not going to be a very useful paradigm for appraising our practice, nor is this dichotomous notion of culture something we want to embrace. This direction threatens to return us to the previous era of a deficit model of urban education.

The original value of the body of work on cultural incongruity theory (e.g., Ogbu, 1981, 1983, 1988, 1992; Ogbu & Davis, 2003) was in explaining how the differences in achievement between African American learners and their White counterparts flowed from the social, historical, political, and cultural fabric of their educational experiences. Now, however, we are confronted with the challenge of digging deeper into teaching practice, which requires a more sophisticated conception of culture and cultural difference. The problem with cultural congruity as a framework is that it merely positions the children on the down side of the achievement gap as "the other." Worse than that, it forecloses the interrogation of culture in the critical social and academic settings of school. Without interrogating the deep-rooted cultural values and practices that are antithetical and inimical to development of agency and achievement, we will not know how to organize the social, cultural, and intellectual life of children in schools to counter the intellectually, culturally, and spiritually toxic environments.

In fairness, multicultural education, from which the cultural congruity and culturally responsive framework derives, is not a single approach. It is more appropriate to think of it as an educational philosophy constituted by a number of approaches to transforming contemporary educational practice toward greater diversity, equity, and social justice (Banks & Banks, 2004; Sleeter & Grant, 1988). In general, it is an educational philosophy of change toward aims of democracy and social justice. As a reform effort, multicultural education not only addresses curricular content integration and what is valued in the processes of knowledge construction, but it also entails equity pedagogy, prejudice reduction, and antiracist practice. However, a number of writers have rightly criticized multicultural education as it is applied in curricular and instructional practice because of its emphasis on the surface aspects of culture instead of the deep structure of social inequalities in social stratification (Murrell, 1991; Olneck, 1990, 2000). As it currently is applied in instructional practice, it is an approach that does little to challenge people's understanding of race, culture, and difference, yet it gets accepted as a social justice curriculum and the solution to structured inequality in education. Variants of traditional multicultural education that more critically question school practices in relation to school outcomes (e.g., critical multicultural education) come closer to what is needed, but their implementation is just as problematic because school communities are not at all disposed to adopt a framework that would force them to think systematically and analytically about how race and class operate to privilege some and disadvantage others (Lewis, 2003).

This book develops an action theory for building culturally relevant practice from the ground up, so to speak, by locating the inquiry in the cultural practices and by making the creation of a cultural community the meta-goal of our professional activity. This is an alternative to the approach of providing educators with aspects of multicultural education frameworks or diversity training with the hope that this will improve their capacity to interrogate their practice. The cultural context of a school community is complex—too complex to expect changes in practice without ever dealing with practice. I argue that the tack of encouraging an entire community of professionals to adopt a critical framework is less productive than the tack of actually doing the cultural interrogation as part of their professional practice.

This is why I advocate going directly to examination of the social and cultural practices—starting with those that injure individuals, perpetuate injustice, and degrade the quality of teaching and learning, and then moving to those that are socially, intellectually, and spiritually enabling. Then by linking practices with evidence of greater well-being among the young people, there is a better chance that the educators and caretakers will recognize and revise those practices found to be detrimental to development and achievement. The focus of this volume is the location of student proficiency development in the cultural practices in which they participate (in which the teacher plays the pivotal role), not in the characteristics of the individual student. This permits the specification of what is culturally relevant not just in terms of individuals, but in terms of contexts of human interaction that reflect the lives, cultures, and histories of the people involved (cf. Pease-Alvarez & Schecter, 2005).

A NEW DIRECTION FOR CONTEXTUALIZING
THEORY AND PRACTICE

I am certainly not alone in suggesting that successfully addressing the achievement gap requires recognizing it as the much larger problem of structural educational inequality deeply rooted in the practices, policies, and pedagogy of the U.S. education industry. Nor am I the first to focus attention on the contexts of schooling as critical to children's scholastic and personal development. What is unique here is a framework for reformulating how teachers and students co-construct their social selves and academic selves in school settings. The framework shows how we can elevate school achievement by understanding the mutually constitutive relationship between the processes of social identification of teachers and students on the one hand, and the social-cultural practices of schooling on the other hand.

This volume offers a new perspective on how to promote children's agency and identity as achievers through the examination and reshaping of instructional, social, and cultural practices in school settings in ways that promote, not degrade, the academic performance and development of all young people. This perspective places human activity at the center of the critical examination of social identification and academic learning. My approach stresses the importance of looking at achievement performance specifically as activity—as jointly constructed and enacted learning practice and teaching practice—in social and cultural context occurring over time.

This volume presents a system for understanding the contribution of identity processes (of both learners and teachers) to school performance, and the ways that our social and cultural practices in school settings can be reorganized to promote positive identity development and agency among young people. The system shows how by developing identities of achievement, students develop their school success, intellectual development, and personal agency. The system consists of a theoretical framework and approaches to instructional practice to illustrate the psychocultural processes and the sociocultural conditions that promote academic achievement and personal development of children and youth in diverse urban schools. The framework accounts for the cultural forces at play in schools, the patterns of social and cultural activity in school contexts, and the development of performance and proficiency of children—all through the lens of concept called *situated identity*. It is an approach urging a much deeper analysis of cultural practices and cultural learning in school settings.

I focus on cultural practices and cultural learning because the most significant forms of human learning, especially those that are the foundations of scholastic proficiency, are actually acquired through socialization in rich cultural communities. People's lives are shaped by their symbolic worlds, as well as by their material circumstances, in a process that sociologists have termed *socialization*. This volume focuses on those cultural practices consonant with learners' social and cultural identity, their sense of history, and the sense of belonging to their people.

The cultural legacies of a people can provide resources for both character development and intellectual development of students, but only if they are represented in the social and cultural environments of the school. This is needed to revitalize urban schools. For example, one meaning system that could be evoked for a predominantly African American school and community could be the theme of African Americans' historic struggle for freedom and literacy as the foundation for value placed on education in the contemporary Black community. A knowledge and application of this cultural legacy would be valuable to those who are trying to help students make connections among literacy, humanity, and the ability to deal in the real world. It is possible to recapture the meaning system embedded in the powerful, community-based commitments to education in the symbolic world of preintegration Black schools in the South (Murrell, 2002; Perry, 2004; Siddle-Walker, 1996).

Symbolic world and figured world (see D. Holland, Lachicotte, Skinner, & Cain, 1998) are terms used to refer to the meaning systems and values contained in those historical and cultural legacies of a people and culture. Reconstituting figured worlds becomes the foundation for enabling children's access to their own cultural legacies of educational values and learning capital, as well as opening new worlds of meaning and value. In short, what diverse people acquire as *primary socialization*—rich and varied abilities of communication, self-expression, creativity, and thought—may be made available to them through *secondary socialization* as well. We can, in fact, structure the social foundations for children's acquisition of school proficiencies, as well as social competence, by deliberative attention to the form, content, and practices of the social learning environments in school. It is through considering what modes of secondary socialization will be beneficial to our students that we engage in building a nurturing and enabling school culture. Cultural learning and cultural practices are the foundation for bridging gaps of experience, ability, sensibilities, and meaning systems among children seeking to benefit fully from their school experience.

Traditionally, meaning systems are created by family and society for the individual in a process of primary socialization. However, in current times, fewer and fewer young people may have access to the cultural resources of the symbolic world of their people—resources that sociologists now refer to as *cultural capital* (Bourdieu & Passeron, 1977). Put simply, cultural capital is the cultural material available to individuals that provides them advantages in the world. For example, we assume that getting along with people in a wide variety of contexts and situations is an advantage in the world. Parents who teach their children manners, for example, impart through primary socialization cultural tools for getting along with others in a wide variety of settings.

One strand of the analysis in the following pages examines contextual and racial factors as framed by this question: How is it that those who believe they operate righteously regarding socially just practice become the chief proponents of racist ideology and the continuation of racist practice? The answer lies in exposing the meaning systems in, and ideologies of, school communities and then by analyzing whether they inhibit or support whole-person scholastic development. The answer also depends on a well-developed sense of identity formation and identity processes young people experience in school settings. The method for doing this work is called *cultural mapping*. It is a method for exposing the symbolic terrain and those meaning systems adverse to the scholastic and personal development of children of color (e.g., the ideologies of meritocracy and color-blindness). It is also a method, for examining the uses that young people make of those symbols and meaning systems as they position themselves as learners. Using this method, it will be possible to examine competition, color-blindness, and meritocracy as new racial formations that, over time and through a variety of school practices, can serve to disadvantage children of color.

This cultural mapping method involves three phases: an analysis of the identity profile of the individual learner, an analysis of the meaning systems and cultural practices in a given school environment, and finally, the positioning that the individual does within a social setting. The processes of positioning are a critical part of our explanation of the processes of identity-in-activity. The general theory for the identity profile analysis is presented in chapter 2, and the theory for the cultural practices analysis is presented in chapter 3. Cultural mapping is the method by which to uncover the ideologies and meaning systems that play a significant role in shaping cultural practices and how young people position themselves in relation to those practices. For instance, cultural values such as individualism, meritocracy, or competition are not necessarily harmful to any particular ethnic or racial group in the abstract. However, a school program based on these values, with no sense of the larger impact on the developmental opportunities for children, can produce negative differential impacts. The emergence of new racial formations occurs when values are applied in practice in unexamined ways. The quintessentially American cultural values of meritocracy and competition may become racialized ideologies embedded in the meaning systems that shape relationships between racial groups. Chapters 3 through 5 offer a more detailed illustration of this key concept of cultural mapping by doing cultural practices inquiry.

SUMMARY AND CONCLUSIONS

The dilemma of diversity is based in race and racism, as well as culture. It is based on the fact that as a society, and as professionals, we have not been addressing (and are currently not prepared to address) racialized practices directly in the schooling experiences of children and in the educational practices that are supposed to serve them. Our social and institutional environments are rife with racially coded messages, practices, and patterns. However, rather than recognizing them and the ways they distort justice and destroy opportunities in education, we embrace ideology that keeps them out of sight and out of mind. The race-neutral political agenda of conservatives cannot be blamed for the existence of this all-American ideology. That agenda would not explain the disproportionate rhetoric about an achievement gap when there are so many other profound ways that the schooling experiences of the educational haves and have-nots differ. Both are the public and political expression of the color-blind, race-does-not-matter ideology that most Americans tacitly hold and explicitly practice. This ideology is what prevents a deeper reading and understanding of culture. This is the reason why difference has been superficially recoded in terms of culture instead of race.

Dilemmas are different from problems. Dilemmas involve choices in which each alternative has both positive and negative aspects. Resolving the dilemma of diversity is not a matter of coming up with a solution, as one would do solving a problem. Resolving a dilemma is a matter of determining whether your favored choice has enough of the positive such that you can live with the negative. The dilemma of diversity in the United States is one in which the desire for the positive—to reduce adverse educational outcomes for poor children and children of color—is being inhibited by aversion to the negative. The negative is the unwillingness or inability to seriously acknowledge and challenge the role that race continues to play in the public life of the United States.

Creating culturally reflective learning communities in practice has proven a difficult challenge. Multicultural education in teacher preparation seems stuck on the agenda of cataloging the necessary qualities of the caring, competent, culturally responsive teacher, without necessarily developing these capacities in practitioners or in their practice. Candidates learning to teach in school settings where people are not prepared to talk about how race operates in their day-to-day practice and experience are not going to benefit from either traditional or critical multicultural education. Rather, focusing on the practices—the means, requirements, and aims of human learning and development that currently exist in a school community—teacher preparation taken as a whole seems stuck on specifying in advance the qualities that people and communities need to have.

The diversity dilemma comes down to this question: Are we going to fully recognize what happens to people in the real, day-to-day fabric of their lives and look to change that? Or, alternatively, are we going to continue to compare outcomes across systems we already know to be unfair? I think that dilemma is resolvable as we turn to the social fields of life in school communities, which is what the remainder of this book does. In the course of presenting a theoretical framework keyed on situated identity, I explain the dynamic relationship of identity with the frames of social life in schools, and will show these are inimical to Black achievement and identity development in so many urban schools. Using the situated identity framework, I show how the continuation of racialized practice is toxic for all children. In later chapters, I also articulate the new frames of reference constituting the figured worlds we need to create in those school settings to promote identity development.

Why focus on identity in this framework for intervention and rethink the achievement of children and youth in diverse contexts? It is because identity is the key to human motivation, self-understanding, and agency. What we refer to as *identity* is a powerful—perhaps the most powerful—meaning system by which individuals interpret their experience. Identity—one's sense of being—is precisely what is being assaulted in socially and culturally toxic environments of public schools. Why focus on the social and cultural practices in this framework? These are what either support the development of children or tear it down. In the next chapter, I articulate a cultural psychology of school achievement and performance that by necessity includes a deep analysis of cultural context. The theoretical overview and the method of cultural practices inquiry will provide the analytical tools necessary to reveal the critical factors influencing young people's development as learners, as citizens, and as people.

2

Overview of Situated-Mediated Identity Theory

Contrary to popular misinterpretations of identity development theory, identity is not the culmination of a key event or series of events … In fact, it is not the culmination of anything. It is, rather, the lived experience of an ongoing process—the process of integrating successes, failures, routines, habits, rituals, novelties, thrills, threats, violations, gratifications, and frustrations into a coherent and evolving interpretation of who we are. *Identity is the embodiment of self-understanding.*

—Nakkula (2003, p. 7, italics added)

In the course of writing this volume, I have had occasion to note how people react to the phrase "identities of achievement" in the title. When people first hear in the title something about identity and achievement, typically they are listening for one of two familiar categories in the educational and psychological literature: racial-cultural identity or culturally responsive teaching. When they ask what the book is about, they typically have a ready-made dichotomy in mind: Is it about culturally relevant teaching strategy and pedagogy, or is it about the processes of racial and cultural development? What they are not prepared to understand is that the answer to the question is both, but in a more comprehensive way—and it puzzles people because they cannot imagine these two aspects studied simultaneously. My situated-mediated theory brings these two aspects together. In my framework, the study of cultural practices and the resulting outcomes in terms of human development and achievement are essentially codependent. Most people are still not accustomed to thinking about teaching and learning practice and student identity realization as codefining each other, even though it is absolutely critical that they do so. This is true even though this relation is expressed in our professional discourse all of the time—as in the ubiquitous phrase "teaching and learning" in reference to schooling.

This chapter is an overview explanation of the grounded, interdisciplinary developmental theory for promoting identities of achievement and is called *situated-mediated identity theory*. I have developed this theory out of years of practice dedicated to promoting academic proficiency, identity, and agency among children and youth in culturally, linguistically, and racially diverse school settings. The theory explains how young people, especially children and youth of color, develop the agency to psychologically inoculate themselves against the ubiquitous assaults on their identity in the everyday social practices in schools shaped by ideologies of racial inferiority and White privilege. Based on this work, I am convinced that successful academic attainment, especially among young people of color, requires that students develop critical awareness of themselves in cultural, social, and historical context, as well as the local contexts in school settings. Their success as students depends on their capacity to develop the personal agency needed to maintain identity integrity in an increasingly complex and contradictory symbolic world. As discussed in the previous chapter, achieving academic self-efficacy often is much more difficult for African American adolescents, and other students of color in public school settings, than it is for their White peers, because it is complicated by institutional racism. The challenge of creating identity-enabling environments for all young people in diverse school settings requires a deeper and more extensive understanding of human development than presently exists in contemporary schooling practice, especially as it is situated in linguistically, culturally, racially, and economically diverse social contexts. Identity is the key construct in this deeper analysis.

Situated-mediated identity theory provides the conceptual framework for a deep reading of the intersections of identity, race or ethnicity, culture, and achievement. The theory examines identity socialization of individuals within the varied contexts of their learning activity and social surroundings in school settings. It is meant to be an interpretive tool for practitioners in urban education, grappling with the issues of race, culture, identity, and achievement. Before describing the situated-mediated identity theory as an analytical tool for understanding school achievement as culturally shaped activity, a bit of background is in order.

MOVING FROM TRADITIONAL IDENTITY THEORY

In recent years there has been an increasing interest in the general notion of identity in educational psychology and the professional literature on education. Identity is already an important concept in teaching, learning, and human development, as well as a research interest in the social sciences. The concept appears in a growing interdisciplinary research literature that draws widely on the social sciences and humanities, including psychology, cultural studies, sociology, and anthropology (Côté & Levine, 2002). Hoffman (1998) suggested that for those researchers who draw on this literature, "identity has become the bread and butter of our education diet" (p. 324, quoted in Sfard & Prusak, 2005). Although I would not go so far as to argue that identity is *the* analytical lens for educational research as some do (e.g., Gee, 2001), I certainly consider it to be essential for culturally, socially, and historically contextualizing learning achievement. I concur with Sfard and Prusak (2005) who wrote:

> We believe that the notion of identity is a perfect candidate for the role of "the missing link" in the researchers' story of the complex dialectic between learning and its sociocultural context. We thus concur with the increasingly popular idea of replacing traditional discourse on schooling with the talk about "constructing identities." (p. 15)

According to the traditional body of work on identity, particularly the pioneering research of Erickson, identity formation is an important developmental task of young people moving from childhood to adolescence. Most current theory draws on this traditional body of work, where the central idea is that a stable identity results from a stage-wise process of psychosocial development that is more or less completed in adolescence. In this view, the psychological task of the adolescent is to come to terms with a myriad of competing roles, expectations, and self-images to establish a coherent sense of self. In this sense, identity is an achievement of healthy psychosocial development—the result of a successful completion of this developmental task of adolescence. Contemporary theory in human development and developmental psychology has been only somewhat less dominated by the "storm and stress" (G. S. Hall, 1904) conception of adolescent development in recent years. Our own experiences as teenagers are apt to further reinforce our commonsense notion of adolescence as a time of identity confusion, self-doubt, and self-consciousness.

Although this traditional body of work remains an important foundation in human development, it has limited generalizability when applied to promoting the academic achievement of children of color in the racially, culturally, and linguistically complex social environments in urban schools and communities. The issue here is that this traditional theory is primarily grounded in cultural norms of White, middle-class, and relatively affluent

families and societies. This raises questions about the applicability of traditional theory to experiences and cultures of children in an increasingly
racially, culturally, and ethnically diverse social world. In particular, the
dynamics and organization of family and neighborhood structures for
people of color in diverse urban communities, as well as their definitions
and ascriptions of adulthood, differ dramatically from the culturally and
racially homogenous social settings in the suburban United States and the
norms of contemporary theory. For example, single-parent families and
families in which the adolescent may frequently be in a parental role to
siblings is a strikingly different portrait of adolescence than you find in
either textbooks or the contemporary experiences of White, culturally
mainstream America. It follows from this that the developmental tasks of
children and youth from diverse cultural communities cannot be assumed
to fit the model prescribed by traditional theory. Because the developmental tasks of young people today are much more culturally, materially,
and situationally determined than traditional theory suggests, we need a
theoretical framework that accounts for diversity and the currency of
youth culture.

Another issue of this traditional body of work that I address in my
framework is the tacit assumption that identity is a static, stable, and
unchanging entity, once successfully achieved in adolescence. In contrast
to this view, I argue for a situated identity—where the identity of an individual is best understood as located in human activity, and mediated
through the human dynamics of the social setting as well as by the social,
cultural, and historical contexts of their social activity in and out of
school. I introduced the concepts of mediated identity and situated identity to explain identity as a process of increasing participation in specific
cultural settings of activity in and around school. According to my framework, the primary developmental task of adolescence is not just acquiring
a new status of relatively stable self-awareness, but movement through a
developmental process of achieving agency, proficiency, and positionality in
relation to the many and varied reference groups and activity settings experienced through life.

OVERVIEW OF SITUATED-MEDIATED
IDENTITY THEORY

Situated-mediated identity theory proposes successful social identification
in school (or any endeavor for that matter) as a developmental progression
of three phases, as one moves from (a) situated identity awareness, to

(b) awareness of one's positioning and positionality, to (c) agency. The first phase of developing an awareness of oneself as situated is the realization that one is a different person in different contexts. The second phase of developing awareness is one of realizing how one actively positions oneself in his or her interactions with others to present the desired persona to others. Here I draw heavily on the legacy of work by Goffman and his dramaturgical articulation of identity. The third phase is agency, a critical conscious understanding of both one's situation and positionality in any given setting or context.

The thesis of my situated-mediated identity theory is that the most important developmental achievements—self-efficacy, intellectual agency, and emotional resiliency—result from, and are mediated by, the acquisition of cultural practices. Moreover, I argue that these cultural practices need to be recognized and appropriated by both adults and youth in conjoint processes of teaching, learning, and developing. Think of it as a theory of identity and agency development of children and adolescents in culturally, linguistically, and ethnically diverse settings.

Before continuing with the overview of the situated-meditated identity theory, I must state two caveats. The first concerns the scope of my identity theory. I am not proposing a new grand, all-inclusive theory[1] of identity formation in the tradition of psychoanalytic developmental theorists (e.g., Erikson, the father of the identity concept; Freud, 1959), social identity theorists, or racial identity theorists (e.g., Cross, 1991; Helms, 1990). That is, I am not seeking to explain identity as a phenomenon as much as I am providing working explanations of the critical processes of identity and agency (self-efficacy) development in the settings where this knowledge is least understood, but most needed—schools. Neither do I attempt to construct a new theory of identity formation or theorize racial identity or cultural identity as the prime focus. Rather, the theory offers a mediated and situated identity interpretation of both racial-ethnic and cultural identity as they are situated in activities of teaching and learning, and related to achievement and school success.

The second caveat concerns the uniqueness of my identity theory. Situated-mediated identity theory draws from and builds on a number of theoretical ideas coming from sociology, anthropology, psychology, and critical theory. The proposition that identity is embedded in social processes

---

[1]Actually, the more appropriate and useful distinction is between what Glaser and Strauss refer to as "formal theory" versus "substantive theory"—where the latter, when conducted as a process of theory generation, aspires to yield a formal theory.

and the notion of a multiplicity of social identities grounded in and bound together by social practice are not new ideas (Burke, 1937; Coulter, 1981; Mead, 1934). Both ideas also occur in relatively recent work in sociology in the form of critical theory and cultural studies (e.g., Bauman, 1996; S. Hall, 1996, 1997; S. Hall & du Gay, 1996) as well as in role-identity theory, the latter of which views identity as a collection of internalized role identities (Marks, 1977; Marks & MacDermid, 1996; Stryker, 1987; Wiley & Alexander, 1987). More recently, the idea of identity embedded in particular social processes of communication has emerged in a tradition viewing identity as constituted in discursive interaction (cf. Carbaugh, 1996; Sfard & Prusak, 2005; Wortham, 2003, 2006). This idea that social action, especially in the form of communication and discourse practices, produces situated identities is well represented in a multidisciplinary set of research literature that I build on in my theory.

Analogously, the notion of identity having multiple strands is not a new idea. The multivalenced view of identity is examined thoroughly in the work of Côté and Levine (2002), who developed a powerful framework for incorporating three levels of identity—social identity, personal identity, and ego identity. They use in their framework *social identity* to designate the individual's position in a social structure and the term *personal identity* to denote the concrete aspects of individual experience rooted in interactions. The term *ego identity* in their framework retains its traditional meaning in the psychodynamic and personality theory of classical psychology—referring to the more subjective sense of continuity that undergirds personality. What is important here is the understanding that we can think of identity as a description of an individual's unique characteristics and traits, as well as a social entity constructed in social interaction and cultural processes of socialization.

What is also of importance here is that theorizing academic identity must take account of social identification as a dynamic between the individual and the social world of schooling and intellectual activity. One example of this is Stevens' (2002) work, which offers a persons-in-context framework for interpreting the unique socialization experiences of African American girls in inner-city communities. She posits processes of intersubjectivity as the suture between societal mandate and individual self in the definition of identity. Other researchers have looked at the social construction of academic identity in relation to both school practices (e.g., Flores-Gonzáles, 2002) and learning processes (e.g., Wortham, 1994, 2001, 2006). Flores-Gonzáles (2002) set out to show how students become school kids as opposed to street kids developing school-oriented identities. She offers a more sophisticated rendering of the idea of oppositional identity based in racial identity (Fordham & Ogbu, 1986) or social class identity (MacLeod, 1995; Willis, 1982).

In any event, social identity is important for analyzing identity development-in-context and refers to a person's position in a social structure (Côté & Levine, 2002; Stevens, 2002). It differs from the commonsense notion of social role in that it is situated—having more to do with the meanings ascribed to the role by self and others in an actual setting of activity and interaction. Stevens's (2002) coinage of the term "cultural anchorage" (p. 23) is a useful way of thinking about the concept of social identity. A particular social identity is realized when social roles (e.g., father, fraternity brother, activist, professor) are legitimated in the individual through meaning-making actions of everyday life. Social identity is a product of the individual's interaction in social and cultural worlds and unique systems of human activity, affiliation, and meaning (D. Holland et al., 1998; Mead, 1934).

This multidisciplinary body of work supports my contention that identity formation, identity expression, and identity development are important processes for young people in culturally diverse contexts, because identities can embody entire cultural meaning systems, termed *figured worlds*. The nature and degree to which culture figures into social identification, human performance, development, and well-being has a great deal to do with the individual's capacity to act on self-knowledge—that is on agency. The distinctions between the situated-mediated identity theory and conventional identity theory are summarized in Table 2–1.

I synthesize these psychological, sociological, and anthropological takes on identity to develop an applied cultural psychology—an applied (grounded theory) understanding of racial and cultural identity for promoting the academic achievement and social development of students in diverse educational settings, especially those marginalized and historically underserved by the structural inequalities of U.S. schooling. The focus is particularly on identity processes of young people in school settings, and how these mediate, and are simultaneously shaped by, academic learning experiences.

An important issue this multidisciplinary body of work brings up is the existence of social types—models of identity that can be ascribed to or assumed by individuals. This underscores processes of social identification—those that are a construction of the self by the self, and those that are shaped by prescribed roles. As we shall see later, both are important. If we viewed the formulation of social identities exclusively in terms of these

TABLE 2–1

**Comparison of Traditional and Situated-Mediated Identity
Theories of Identity Development**

Traditional Theory of Identity Development	*Situated-Mediated Identity Theory*
Identity is defined as the set of characteristics that somebody recognizes as belonging uniquely to himself or herself and constituting his or her individual personality for life.	*Identity* is defined as our agency in activity—who we are is what we choose to do and how we choose to invest in that doing.
Identity is a status a relatively stable self-images, values and roles—achieved in adolescence.	*Identity* is a work in progress, not necessarily achieved in adolescence but the "work" continuous through adulthood. It is a *continuous composition that is enacted* depending on the social setting and situational context of the individual.
Identity is discrete construct.	*Identity* is a *continuous composition that is enacted* depending on the social setting and situational context of the individual.
Identity achievement occurs as the cumulative result of the degree of "success" in transitioning sequentially through a number of psycho-social developmental stages.	Identity is *situated* in symbolic, social and historical context. *Identity* is mediated by variety of situationally determined self-referencing and self-representing processes characterizing who the individual is in relation to the social setting.
Individuation is the differentiation of self within parental bonds and the context of family relationships.	*Individuation* is both differentiation and appropriation of different roles, actions, personas, and activities in the contexts of social relationships.
Contemporary theorists define self-efficacy in terms of *"beliefs"* or as a *"sense of self"* instead of as a process. Bandura (1997), for example, defines self-efficacy as "beliefs in one's capabilities to organize and execute the courses of action required to produce given attainments" (p. 3).	I define self-efficacy in terms of *activity* and *performance*. Rather than self-efficacy being referred to as an individual's belief, I assert a definition of self-efficacy that has three components: (1) the individual's competence or capability in a culturally and socially recognized and valued area; (2) the individual's awareness of his or her competence that has come about from; (3) reasonable demonstration of that competence or proficiency.

TABLE 2–2
Framework for Situated-Mediated Identity Theory

Type of Identity Growth	Type of Social Context	Type of Cultural Practices
Situated Identity	Social-Cultural Community	Primary Socialization
Positionality	Social-Symbolic Community	Secondary Socialization
Agency	Community of Practice Activity Setting	Improvisational Self-Determination

social types or what Wortham (2006) would call models of identity, we would leave out the important contribution of ego-identity processes in the formation of the social self. For every instance, for example, where a teacher ascribes the mantle of good student or bad student, there is also an instance where the child seeks to uniquely define himself or herself despite the ascriptions, stereotypes, or prescribed expectations others place on him or her.

My theory is meant to account for the many possible, yet unrecognized, social identities that can be taken up by young people at different times and in different situations. Not only are there a variety of social identifications young people can take on, but models of "the good student" are construed differently by students and their teachers. For example, in my own work investigating middle school mathematics, it was clear that the behaviors and discourse patterns teachers thought constituted the good mathematics student and what students thought differed considerably. In the instance of the low-achieving group, the excessive degree to which they dominate talk during group work and large-group discussion was viewed by the students as success behavior but viewed by the teacher as a contributor to their mathematics underachievement (Murrell, 1994).

The major components of my theory are summarized in Table 2–2. Situated-mediated identity theory enters the uncharted waters of identity development in relationship to achievement efficacy in diverse school settings. It is a theory of practice that focuses on the growth of individuals in relationship to the social settings in which they grow, develop, and achieve. Grounded theories such as this typically have a pragmatic purpose. For situated-mediated identity theory, that purpose is to give teachers, counselors, school psychologists, and others who work with children and youth an interpretative framework for creating identity-enabling school environments to promote identities of achievement. Cultural practices inquiry is a way of making explicit and interpreting the types of settings, experiences, cultural material, communication patterns, and pedagogical strategies that promote the identity and agency development of young people in school settings.

Before moving to a detailed explanation of the components of the theory shown in Table 2–2, let me state two more of the organizing tenets of situated-mediated identity theory and illustrate the distinctions from contemporary theory that are summarized in Table 2–1. One of these is the importance of understanding schools and classrooms as cultural communities and social environments with particular cultural features, and then using this understanding as the basis for interpreting the developmental processes of young people. Situated-mediated identity theory is premised on the proposition that school success is achievable for all students when learning achievement is understood as the acquisition of a set of preferred cultural practices, and when teaching and learning are understood as the socialization of these cultural practices in educational settings. The theory accounts for the processes of identity and agency development that teachers, counselors, and other educators need to understand to work successfully with children of color in the educative process. The other organizing tenet of situated-mediated identity theory is that there are a variety of processes—academic and social—that mediate identity, processes that the individual influences and is influenced by. For example, there are a variety of self-referential activities that are acts of identity. These include narrativization (e.g., telling stories), dramatization (dramatic enactment), and symbolic self-representation (e.g., forms of dress, talk, etc.). These self-referential activities are forms of sense making that comprise the cultural tools that mediate identity and achievement.

I argued in the last chapter that the processes of identity realization—especially for children and youth of diverse backgrounds and especially in diverse settings—get distorted and stunted in ways that go largely unrecognized and unnoticed by adults. Because sense making, especially about race, class, and gender, is not a customary part of educational practice, adults typically have no systematic way of recognizing and dealing with the conflicts posed by racism and racial oppression to student social settings. Hence, the hidden discourses of racism go unrecognized by adults, yet are available to children as a tool against other children. As I also noted in the last chapter, children as young as 3, 4, and 5 years of age often hold a solid, applied understanding of the dynamics of race and use racialized talk to control others right under the noses of their adult caregivers (Van Ausdale & Feagin, 2002). If, as situated-mediated identity theory advocates, we focus on what promotes identity realization at the same time we track development of academic talent and scholastic proficiencies, we might have the means to create identity-affirming learning communities that serve all children in the public schools. Beyond this, we might also have the means of creating learning communities that foster the development of social competence, character, and the cultural tools to maintain personal integrity.

SPECIFICS OF SITUATED-MEDIATED IDENTITY THEORY

In the following chapters, I develop in greater detail the three categories of identity development as depicted in the first column in Table 2–2. I begin with a preliminary explanation with the first concept in Table 2–2—situated identity. According to traditional developmental theory, identity is a state that is achieved in adolescence. What I mean by traditional theory includes the canon of theorists typically taught in educational psychology and human development courses in teacher preparation programs. This canon usually includes the work of stage theorists—Piaget for cognitive development, Erikson for psychosocial development, and Kohlberg for moral development. According to contemporary theory, successful identity development is presumed to conclude in adolescence with the achievement of a relatively stable set of values, roles, and self-images that the adolescent arrived at through volitional choices (Erikson, 1968, 1980). Furthermore, according to traditional theory, unsuccessful identity development may be characterized by three alternative statuses (e.g., Marcia, 1994): (a) *identity foreclosure* is the situation in which the adolescent is supposedly committing to the goals, values, and lifestyles of others; (b) *identity diffusion* when individuals reach no conclusions regarding who and what they are or will be; and (c) *identity moratorium* is the status when the process of development—the choosing, the trying out of roles—is placed on hold.

Situated-mediated identity theory departs from traditional theory regarding what constitutes an identity (see Table 2–1). At the core of the distinction is the notion that identity is active, socially mediated, and determined (at least in part) by our intentional action. This is the core idea: Identity is our agency in activity—who we are is what we choose to do and how we choose to invest in that doing. Situated identity may not be an easy idea to grasp at first, because it seems counterintuitive to the way most people think about identity as being a stable self-image or self-concept. Moreover, readers may at first find this concept of identity more elusive and less concrete than the way it is defined in contemporary theory. However, I believe that the power of being able to explain the processes of identity development in relation to the richness of cultural and social contexts is worth the conceptual stretch.

Situated identity, in simple terms, means that our sense of self, or identity, is not merely a static, unitary entity. According to this framework, identity is multifactored, fluid, and situationally determined. The fact that an individual may seem to be different people in different social contexts is a manifestation of situated identity. Different situations or contexts mediate different representations and expressions of the self. This idea contrasts with the traditional view of identity as the culminating achievement of social-emotional maturation during adolescence. In the traditional view, identity is constructed by the individual as the result of successfully resolving a series of psychodynamic dilemmas (Erikson, 1963, 1968). Although Erikson's theory has been taken by many to suggest a unitary view of identity, the theory nonetheless is an important foundation for my approach, especially as the foundation for explaining the developmental task of identity formation.

There are interrelated dimensions of Erikson's work on identity formation that are the foundation for all theorizing on identity. These dimensions are (a) the subjective/psychological dimension, or *ego-identity*; (b) the personal dimension, or the social-behavioral repertoire and character of the individual that differentiates him or her from other individuals; and (c) the social dimension, or the ascribed and assumed roles within a given reference community. The first dimension, the subjective-psychological, refers to the intrapersonal character of a person that is continuous and consistent across different settings. The second dimension refers to an individual's unique set of skill and proficiency acquisitions necessary for participation in the social world. Taken together, these first and second dimensions constitute what people mean by the term personality. The third dimension refers to the interplay between an individual's self-projections and the social collective's projections of the individual. According to Erikson's theory, when these three components do not come together during adolescence, an identity crisis is evidenced. An *identity crisis* is characterized by a subjective sense of identity confusion, and perhaps evidenced by "behavioral and characterological disarray" (Côté & Levine, 2002, p. 15), or a lack of commitment to recognized roles and expectations in the social and instructional contexts of the adolescent.

In the situated identity framework articulated here, the third dimension of social identification concerning the tension between individual representations of self and the ascriptions made of the individual by wider society is called *positionality*. This dimension is developed most in my situated-mediated identity theory, where, according to the theory, identity is not seen as unified in a complete and unchanging self, but as an amalgam of identity roles and patterns. My situated identity perspective, in contrast to the traditional view, conceives of the individual as the composite of many, sometimes conflicting, self-understandings and self-expressions.

In this view, the locus of identity is not all confined within the psyche of one individual, but is distributed over a number of social settings in which that individual participates (i.e., the sense that you are not the same person in different social settings). These social settings mediate how individuals choose to self-articulate or represent who they are in a given setting. For example, consider two settings within an elementary classroom—morning circle and small-group reading instruction. Hakim, an African American boy, might present as an apt and able student during morning circle, because he is an entertaining speaker and storyteller, but present as a reluctant learner during reading instruction because he is not yet a fluent reader. This notion of a situated identity that is mediated by the immediate setting or social context might seem a hard notion to accept at first because it asks you to consider that identity is not all inside the individual but is mediated by what is going on around the individual. It is perhaps a different view of identity than the one you came away with from your professional training, which was probably dominated by a psychology-oriented, "inside-the-person" conception of identity. However, with a little reflection, you might begin to visualize the idea that identity is a product of both the person and setting in which the person operates.[2]

In truth, nearly all of the recent approaches to the study of identity have attempted to address, in one way or another, the tension between individual identity and social identity. For example, the contribution of an approach called role-identity theory—a research tradition from sociology examining identity—acknowledges the idea of different selves in different contexts (Hogg, Terry, & White, 1995; Markus & Nurius, 1987; Stryker, 1968). The role-identity approach suggests that children and youth are different people in different contexts, as a matter of different role identities coming to the fore in different contexts. One moment the serious student, the next

---

[2]Note that this is not the same as the tradition of role-identity theory, which is discussed further later.

moment the class cut-up, is a case that can be seen as the expression of two different role identities exhibited by the same young person. The limitation of role-identity theory is the difficulty in explaining which roles come to the fore at any given moment, and what accounts for the apparent change from one role to another. Situated-mediated identity theory would accept fully addressing all forms of self-representation in a situated context. In general, the rich fabric of the situational context is what determines the current identity a young person presents, and this context is immanently knowable. More is said about this in chapter 3, but for the present, the concept of situated identity permits our analysis of the interplay between individual identity representation and social context.

To synthesize at this point, it is useful to view identity as both an entity and a process. To the traditional view that identity is a stable entity, the situative view adds the notion that it is also a work in progress. Once again, situated-mediated identity theory does not consider identity to be merely an achievement of adolescence. On this account, identity is conceived as a situational composition of self. If you imagine the idea of identity as being something that is continuously refashioned given the situation or social context the individual is in, you have the key idea of situated identity. To put succinctly the new definition, identity is our agency in activity. Who we are is what we choose to do and how we choose to invest in that doing. If, as I argue, identity is neither static nor a conclusive achievement, but rather is a dynamic, situationally determined expression of self, it stands to reason that to know a person's identity requires knowing how that individual presents and represents himself or herself in different contexts. That explanation is the upcoming discussion on positionality.

Situated identity is represented in the first column of the first row of Table 2–2. Those of you who are familiar with the sociohistorical perspective (e.g., Vygotsky, 1978) know that there are still other ways that an identity may be situated—in historical time, cultural setting, and geographic location. That is, the cultural material available to individuals constructing their identity is a product of historical time, cultural setting, and geographic location. Consider how racial identification might differ for adolescents growing up prior to *Brown v. Board of Education,* compared to those growing up during the Civil Rights movement, and as compared to the present. What constitutes "being Black" differed in each of those time frames—in terms of both self-ascriptions of "being Black" and the ascriptions placed on individuals by others. Racial identity in particular is a process reflective of, and situated in, social and political struggles. The recognition that racial meanings shift across time and place does not mean that they do not matter in identity formation; it just means that identity formation is situational, and that historical time and setting are important to the situatedness.

IDENTITY WORK OF TEACHERS AND LEARNERS

Before moving to a more detailed explanation of the nine elements of the situated identity framework shown in Table 2–2, I first note what is perhaps the most conceptually important feature of the framework: The framework applies to the identity of both learners and teachers. It is keyed not just on the identity work of children and youth, but *concurrently on the identity work of teachers and other adults as they work with young people*. Recall from the earlier discussion my claim that identity realization is not something that is completed in adolescence, but may be fluidly refigured in adult experience. Every adult who has ever entered a new professional or social setting, be it the boardroom or the classroom, also engaged in social identification in that setting—situating his or her identity in much the same way an adolescent does when he or she enters a new school or classroom. In other words, individuals are continuously reconstituting their identity according to how they position themselves, and are positioned by others, as they establish themselves in a given social setting.

This fluidity of change is even shown in much of the work on racial identity (Cross, 1991; Helms, 1993) and race is just one such possible dimension of situatedness. There are other dimensions on which I focus in the coming chapters—such as social justice and participatory democracy—that, as is shown, are important aspects of teachers' positionality as they attempt to forge relationships and structure social environments in ways that promote development in social, intellectual, and spiritual terms. The point here is that the situated-mediated identity framework considers the simultaneous and conjoint situating of identities of both learners and teachers in settings of instruction.

It should be noted that psychological theories of racial identity actually focus on one aspect of identity—modes of identification. In the situated-mediated identity framework, we are interested in the modes of identification, not just of students, but of their teachers, as well as how the two interact in instructional discourse and activity. As seen in chapter 4, this analysis entails documenting the positioning skills and maneuvers humans acquire and use to manage impressions of themselves in social settings. I concur with D. Holland et al. (1998) regarding the situational and improvisational nature of identity, who state that:

Identities—if they are alive, if they are being lived—are unfinished and in the process. Whether they be specific to the imagined worlds of romance or the careers of mental illness, or generic to ethnic, gender, race, and class divisions, identities never arrive in persons or in their immediate social milieu already formed. They do not come into being, take hold in lives, or remain vibrant without considerable social work in and for the person. *They happen in social practice.* (D. Holland, et al., 1998, p. vii, italics added)

To summarize to this point, identities are socially situated and are mediated by what happens in social practice. This social *enactment perspective* on identity, more formally known in sociology as the theoretical perspective of *symbolic interactionism* (Blumer, 1969), is my theoretical framework of practice regarding identity, race, culture, and achievement in diverse contexts. Why? Because the identity work adults do as they teach or counsel young people is just as critical to the process of healthy identity development of young people in diverse settings. As we shall see, the road to healthy development, effective learning, and demonstrable achievement is definitely a two-way street.

In Part II of this book addressing practice, I show that creating caring cultural communities in schools requires just as much identity work among adults as it does for the young people in their care. This is the reason why I argue that contemporary theories, including that of multicultural education, are insufficient because they leave out the transactions of identity work between child and adult in given contexts. The focus of this work is not on the methodology of sociological and psychological investigation of identity, but rather on inquiry into the cultural processes of change to elevate the achievement outcomes of young people—particularly those in underserved urban school settings. This change process requires a clear articulation of how we (both adults and learners) regard identity and the simultaneity of the inner self with the social self. D. Holland et al. (1998) state that "Identity is one way of naming the dense interconnections between the *intimate* and the *public* venues of social practice" (p. 270, italics added).

The social interactional component of my situated-mediated identity theory makes explicit the working connections among the private, internal, and social self in the process of gaining competence. It also makes explicit the dynamic and interactive nature of both learner and teacher positionalities in the variety of social contexts in schools. These are represented in the second column of the first row in Table 2–2. How well do we understand the internal life of young people and their external expressions of self? I theorize that there is an explainable connection between the intimate (private) and the social (public) worlds of the individual that is important in the practice of those working with young people. The main purpose of this volume is to make these connections explicit and adapt them to successful practice—of teaching, of counseling, and of parenting. The notion of practice is, therefore, also critical to my theory, as I seek to fully explain the dynamic nature of identity development in the contexts in which it matters. I argue that to understand diverse individuals in diverse settings, it is necessary to conceptualize identity development as the codevelopment of the setting (and its social practices) with the individual. The individuals I focus on are children and adolescents. The settings I focus on are cultural communities—particularly the cultural communities in schools.

HOW THE 3 X 3 ELEMENTS FIT TOGETHER

Table 2–2 summarizes the mediated identity theory and shows how three forms of identity development relate to contextual settings and by what three processes identity realization primarily operates in these settings. Sense making, or meaning making, is a universal cultural practice extant at all three levels and should be considered one of the key cultural practices that provide the glue for the elements of the framework. Within this framework I explain other cultural factors (in addition to favored cultural practices) influencing young people's identity formation as learners, as school achievers, and ultimately as empowered citizens. The framework posits three distinct forms of identity realization development (reading down the first column in Table 2–2): situated identity, positionality, and agency. In addition, the theory posits three distinct settings or contexts of development: the social-cultural community, figured world, and the activity setting (middle column in Table 2–2). These factors, which include students' interaction with adults and adult systems of meaning, are at the root of an emerging capacity to deal in (and with) the crisis of meaning in U.S. education—identity, race, and signification. I address this in chapters 4, 5, and 6. Finally, also summarized in Table 2–2 (follow the third column down), my theory proposes three important sense-making processes in the formation of an empowered and vigorous adult identity: primary socialization, secondary socialization, and improvised self-determination. The third column of the framework is developed in more detail in chapter 6.

The 3 x 3 framework summarized in Table 2–2 constitutes my theoretical apparatus for addressing the cultural dimensions of identity development in the context of the discursive and cultural practices of schooling. As mentioned earlier, the concept of sense making is the core of this apparatus for linking culture and human development. Sense making is a huge part of young people's cultural identity work, and culture provides the symbolic tools for the process. As mentioned earlier, this is the one universal cognitive cultural practice that links modes of identity (column 1) to social-cultural context (column 2). Psychologically, all humans engage in sense making as the response to the dissonance they experience as newcomers to a cultural scene or a new community of practice. This includes a child entering a school, a classroom, or lunchroom for the first time. This might also include a teacher entering a school, a classroom, or a teachers' lounge for the first time. Most important, this includes any person entering a culturally unfamiliar social scene. In racially diverse settings, both child and teacher are constantly negotiating race and their own racial positionality—even if they are not consciously aware of it.

The first row of Table 2–2 characterizes the theoretical strand linking the concept of situated identity to context (sociocultural context) and process (primary socialization). It is this strand that illustrates why the traditional conceptualization of identity does not take us far enough toward understanding human identity formation in real contexts like schools. Traditional stage theory does not inform teaching practice very well because it lacks the mechanism for accounting for individual change with the dynamics of human interaction in diverse settings (I speak here from personal experience). Neither do traditional theories of identity address, in a systematic way, the interaction of the individual with the socializing cultural context. The situated-mediated identity theory presented here addresses the context of the social-cultural community and the process of primary socialization. I enlarge on the aims of contemporary theory by simultaneously addressing both the context and process of development, so that rather than merely defining stages or taxonomies of identity development, the empirical task becomes one of explaining the sense making young people engage in en route to realizing a full sense of self-efficacy and self-agency. It is possible to regard this entire first row as a strand of inquiry that applies the sociocultural approach to the enterprise of achieving the identity of a scholar, a learner in school. Table 2–2a represents this strand.

I want to turn now to the middle row of Table 2–2 to look at the concepts of positionality, social-symbolic or figured world, and secondary socialization. In some ways, this row of the table constitutes an entire domain of social psychology called social practice theory. It, too, represents a strand

TABLE 2–2a

Applied Sociocultural Tradition in Situated-Mediated
Identity Framework

Individual	Social/Cultural & Historical Context	Cultural Practices and Tools
Situated Identity	Social-Cultural Community	Primary Socialization

of inquiry, of social practice theory based on situated learning theory and activity theory. Social practice theory emphasizes the relational interdependency of individual, group activity, meaning, cognition, learning, and the gaining of proficiency. At this point, however, I want to keep my explanation and illustration of this strand simple and rely on the development of theory in the case study sections to follow to fully draw the relationships. This strand along the middle row of Table 2–2 consisting of the identity status of positionality,[3] the figured world as the context within which the positionality for the individual is established, and secondary socialization as the processes by which a community of practice socializes new members will require concrete illustration. This middle row (see Table 2–2b) constitutes the part of the theory that really stresses situated learning theory, which regards learning as the increasing participation of individuals in communities of practice (Cole, 1996; Lave, 1991; Lemke, 2000; Rogoff, 1994).

The strand in this middle row consisting of the concepts of positionality, social-symbolic context (figured world), and secondary socialization invites you to rethink how you view motivation in school settings. The default assumption of many teachers, at least in terms of how they organize classroom life, is that learners are motivated by getting good grades. According to my situated-mediated identity framework, human motivation in school is primarily determined by the investments young people make in creating and maintaining certain positionalities. This means two things. First, simply, one cannot assume grades or any measure of academic performance is the major part of young people's motive structure. Second, the inquiry into achievement motivation has to concentrate on how two things about positionality interact: (a) the nature and degree of investment

---

[3]This use of the term *positionality* is very similar to the notion of subject position as used by critical theorists, especially of the Frankfurt School. Both terms refer to the individual's social and historical location in his or her culture. The added meaning I wish to capture by the use of positionality is the situatedness of a subject position in a given frame or familiar setting.

TABLE 2–2b

Applied Situated Learning & Activity Theory
in Situated-Mediated Identity Framework

Individual	Structured Social, Cultural & Historical Setting	Cultural Practices and Meaning Systems
Positionality	Social-Symbolic Community (Figured World)	Secondary Socialization

in one's academic identity, and (b) the nature and variety of positionalities taken up in relation to that identity.

Note that in this framework, the inquiry into these two components is considered for both students and teachers in a learning setting. True to our analysis of symbolic exchanges between human beings as a way of interpreting their behavior, we will be just as interested in the positionality investments of teachers as those of the students. Moreover, it is our analysis of the conjoint investments in their respective positionalities that will yield the complete story of learning achievement, as we will be able to account fully for the contextual factors that have been difficult to get a handle on (e.g., teacher expectations, teacher beliefs).

As noted, because positionality is situational by setting, by context, and even by episodes within a conversation, there may be quite a variety of positionalities taken up by both learners and teachers in a given classroom. However, the challenge of understanding positionality is not quite so open ended as it might seem given this variety. The possibilities are narrowed by our understanding of other factors concerning the psychology of human interaction, youth culture, adolescent development, and, most important, the local culture of youth (e.g., hip-hop). For example, we know that a common dichotomy of social positioning young people face in the youth cultures of many schools is experienced as a forced choice: Do I want to be popular or do I want to be smart? We also know that other dimensions of positionality, such as gender, interact with this positionality and mitigate the dichotomy, as for example it tends to be easier for boys to be both smart and popular than it is for girls (Sadker & Sadker, 1986, 1994).

The point here is that these are aspects of the school's social and cultural environment that are within our control so that children do not feel that they are giving up something to be smart. It is also important to note that another factor that mitigates having to make the choice of whether or not to be smart is young people's ability to improvise new and innovative self-representations. That is, they can go beyond the given, obvious, and circumscribed roles of studentness in school settings through their own creative expression.

There are a variety of natural category positionalities—the most obvious being the student (P1) and the teacher (P2). Then there are positionalities that are more specific positionalities constituted by the common experiences and social realities of schooling for many people. Among these positions are the "school kid"–"street kid" dichotomy (Flores-Gonzáles, 2002) and oppositionality identity ascribed to African American students (especially males). Within the categories of school kid versus street kid and oppositional identity there are a variety of positionalities learners can improvise. Some of these improvised positions may not be to their advantage in terms of school achievement, despite the intent of the student. An example comes from the study I mentioned earlier in which I looked at mathematics learning achievement in middle school and what happened to young African American boys in a school setting that had figured a world of mathematics achievement. One of the discursive forms that resulted from the school's concerted effort at figuring the social-symbolic world of mathematics achievement was a school-wide emphasis on "math talk," a practice that involved thoroughly explaining one's mathematical reasoning and carrying on a productive mathematical conversation. Many of the African American boys capitalized on the school's valorization of math talk by verbally dominating both small-group and whole-class discursive activity. A group of African American students who already enjoyed the status as school kids or mathematics achievers began to lose that status in the eyes of the teachers, who increased their attempts to reduce the frequency and duration of the airtime for these students. These attempts of the teacher to curb the math talk of these students accelerated their fall from academic grace, because these attempts were experienced by the students as micro-aggressions designed to demean and diminish them. Thus, through their attempt to succeed academically in this setting, the group of African American students became oppositional. How would the situated-mediated identity framework address this problem? I return to this question following the discussion of the third strand consisting of agency, community of practice, and improvisational self-determination presently. First I want to briefly address the development of academic and scholastic proficiency through secondary socialization.

The notion of secondary socialization is where the framework addresses the development of academic skills and scholastic proficiency. Situated learning theorists' favorite example of such secondary socialization is their expanded notion of cognitive apprenticeship—the secondary socialization of skills between a master and an apprentice (e.g., Brown et al., 1989). Secondary socialization involves coparticipation between at least two individuals where one is more experienced and accomplished in the proficiency, talent, or ability being learned or used in the conjoint activity. Since the inception of the idea in learning theory in the early 1990s, cognitive psychologists have run with it in developing curriculum based on "apprenticing" learners to mathematical thinking (Schoenfeld, 1994), scientific problem solving (Anderson, 1993), and even reading strategies (Palinscar & Brown, 1984). This relationship between scholastic proficiency development and the coparticipation of apprentice and master will be revisited later.

The third row of Table 2–2 is depicted as the inquiry strand of applied culturally relevant education in Table 2–2c. This is the site of the working part of the theoretical framework. In the first cell is agency, the most highly developed form of self-awareness and achievement identity with respect to a well-defined and scholastically nurturing community of practice. There are a number of specific cultural practices exhibited by young people with identities of achievement. In particular, the cultural practices of self-narration, signifying, self-subscription, and improvisation are all cultural tools for those with the potential for achievement identities. This completes the overview of Table 2–2, but each column of the framework table is developed further in Part II of this book. More will be said about how the strands, represented by the middle and third rows of Table 2–2, actually operate in the following chapter.

Let me return to the earlier example of the problem of mathematics achievement among African American boys in middle school. How could so many pluses—a figured world of mathematics achievement, dedicated teachers, and students striving for success—equal a minus in the form of students (who were already good students) doing worse than they did at the beginning of the semester? In terms of this second strand and secondary socialization, the teachers and the school community were successful in communicating the value of the discursive practice of speaking mathematically, engaging in math talk. However, learners' participation in the desired scholastic practices is a necessary but not sufficient condition for mathematics achievement. The rest of the equation lies in the other cultural practices

TABLE 2–2c

Applied Critical Multicultural Education
in Situated-Mediated Identity Framework

Individual	Structured Social Organization	Shared Repertoire of Cultural Practices and Tools
Agency	Community of Practice Activity Setting	Improvisational Self-Determination

constituting a true learning community. For this we need the key concept from the framework that is the overarching cultural practice—that I call sense making—to which we turn next to show how it addresses the dilemma and pulls the entire framework together.

SENSE MAKING AS A CULTURAL
PRACTICE OF ACHIEVEMENT

Sense making refers to any attempt or process to determine the meaning systems in which one is operating. I use the term sense making as a specialized form of meaning making (Couclelis, 1995). Sense making is the interpretation of experience and the attachment of meaning to events, objects, activities, or anything taken as a sign.[4] The social practices, human interactions, and cultural productions through which signs become linked with concepts is the process of encoding, and the meaning is derived when a person interprets the relation in a process of decoding (S. Hall, 1980).

I am viewing sense making as a social form of semiotics—the formal study of meaning. Semiotics is the general study of signs in culture where culture is understood as the symbolic context within which meaning is constructed, coconstructed, and negotiated among individuals. It

---

[4]A sign that results from taking meaning from an object, event, activity, or symbol is a semiotic idea. In semiotics, taking meaning from an object makes it a sign. Additionally, commonly acknowledged signs are called *symbols*. A particular word or image stands for or symbolizes a concept, and thereby functions as a sign—a conveyer of meaning. The sign is not the carrier of meaning, however. Signs do not fix meaning because meaning depends on the socially mediated relationship between an idea and the sign used to index it. What carries meaning in the act of signing-signifying-and the difference between the sign and other signs? In Wittgenstein's (1953) words, "Meaning is the use to which we put signs." The socially constructed relationship between a sign and the idea it indexes is fixed as a code.

assumes that meaning is mediated through signs and sign systems, including language, texts, narratives, and discourses. I reserve the term sense making to refer to the meaning making people do in the presence of others. Meaning making always requires cognition, but an individual can make meaning on his or her own, as say, for example, interpreting an art object or processing the reading assignment in a textbook. However, there is meaning making that is individual interpretation, and then there is group meaning making that is a matter of coming to or constructing a shared sense or sensibility. As social actors, we use the conceptual systems provided by our culture and language to construct meaning through our communication with others.

According to my theoretical framework, the sense making that an adolescent does regarding his or her own identity is the primary developmental task of adolescence, but it is not a process limited to adolescence nor necessarily completed in adolescence. "Sense-making processes derive from ... the need within individuals to have a sense of identity—that is, a general orientation to situations that maintains esteem and consistence of one's self-conceptions" (Weick, 1995, p. 22). For all human beings, sense making is a prime motive of social behavior, as everyone strives to figure out who they are in relation to the world and their social and cultural environment.

Psychologically speaking, sense making is something everyone does every time they enter a new and unfamiliar setting. The process of sense making is a critical part of my theory development regarding identity of young people of color in predominantly White settings. The uncertainty in a new social scene gives rise to sense making employed by the individual to restore self-integrity—an internally consistent and positive-valenced self-perception (Steele, 1998; Weick, 1995). The dynamics of racialized discourse, culture, and ethnicity come into play as individuals attempt to restore self-integrity in settings that threaten that integrity. New social scenes or culturally unfamiliar settings can make it more difficult for young people to confirm an image of self or occasions of increased sense-making activity. Steele and his colleagues (e.g., Aronson & Good, 2002) have researched this process extensively—the reduction of dissonance between the new group's ascription of lower competence to the individual on one hand, and the individual's own (threatened) sense of efficacy on the other—the phenomena of stereotypic threat among ethnic minorities. The settings I focus on are primarily, but not exclusively, school settings.

At any rate, I regard sense making as the generic cultural practice that is universal to all humans, regardless of cultural, ethnic, linguistic, or historical background. There are different degrees and forms of sense making that are explored in the following chapters. For example, the collective sense making done by a community that shares values and meaning systems, called a figured world, can be deliberately created on behalf of young people—a discussion to which I return in greater detail in chapter 5. Similarly, there is the sense making of a community of practice, which essentially consists of the shared repertoire of interpretive and inquiry skills of the group. Sense making as a cultural practice does get particularized according to how cultural material is represented, made available, and used in the schools and communities. These processes are illustrated in the case examples in Part II of this book. Once these settings are described, we will be able to take a more detailed look at sense-making practices of children and youth.

As is also seen in the upcoming chapters, children entering socially uncertain settings are disposed to creative sense making regarding their own racial and cultural identity. In other words, in situations where an individual's persona seems to be under scrutiny—as it might when an African American child enters a school with clearly discernable racialized codes and practices—that individual might give a certain priority to sense making over other aims, such as the acts traditionally taken as markers of school achievement performance. Situated-mediated identity theory focuses on what individuals actually do to gain (or regain) a sense of self-worth, self-efficacy, or agency in such settings. The framework summarized in Table 2–2 allows me to map out the interactional and transactional components of identity formation.

One last proposition I state in relation to sense making is that it is both active and self-referential. In other words, the most significant sort of sense making children and youth do in school may well be self-referential meaning making—what I have previously termed identity work. Drawing on the aphorism from Wallas (1926):

> The little girl had the making of a poet in her who, being told to be sure of her meaning before she spoke, said "How can I know what I think till I see what I say?" (p. 23, cited in Weick, 1995, p. 12)

The situated-mediated identity theory rendition of this self-referential act of sense-making (identity work) summarizes my theoretical perspective this way: How do I know who I am until I determine what others make of what I do?

In my view, the reason contemporary identity theorizing to date is of such little use to practitioners is the fact that it takes little account of how humans make sense of their identity as it is defined in interaction with others. I take pains to demonstrate the reciprocal influence of identity projection and formative feedback from the group to the individual. This is consistent with the foundations of situated learning and the sociohistorical theory of Vygotsky (1978), Bakhtin (1981, 1999), and Wertsch (1985) incorporated in my action theory of teaching and learning (Murrell, 2002). People take cues for their identity realization from the conduct of others.

Without getting too technical regarding the issue of representation and other aspects of semiotic theory I draw on more extensively in the following chapters, I merely want to assert at this point a working proposition: Situated identity is (to use the semiotic term) signification. The term *signification* connotes an act of designation using symbols or signs. It is the active role of meaning in structuring the interaction between a person and a context so as to define the subjectivity of that person in a situation, as well as their positioning to certain discourses implicit in that subjectivity. Individuals compose their identity as an act of signification. Representing oneself might be thought of as an objectification of self, providing an audience with signifiers of oneself. An individual may be said to improvise this act based on the cultural material available to him or her in the setting. I discuss in Part II how adolescents do this by examining the various forms of narrating self.

In summary, sense making is an identity process that involves a capacity to read the cultural cues and signs that we perceive in reference to ourselves. I advocate and demonstrate an elaboration of this sense-making process, making it a part of professional practice. I also advocate strengthening the sense-making capacity of young people in Part II of the book, where I illustrate how the framework applies in practice.

THREE THEORETICAL FOUNDATIONS

To summarize, the situated-mediated identity theory framework is grounded in three theoretical foundations, each of which is represented by a row in Table 2–2, and by Tables 2–2a, 2–2b, and 2–2c. The first of these is *cultural-historical theory,* which posits that (a) culture is foundational in the development of consciousness and cognitive development, and (b) learning achievement and the development of cognitive and social proficiencies are cultural-historical in origin (Bruner, 1996; Cole, 1996; Scribner & Cole, 1986; Vygotsky, 1962, 1978; Wertsch, 1985, 1998). In this theoretical perspective, cultural practice is the logical unit of analysis for looking at the domain of proficiencies that young people attempt to acquire as they develop (see Table 2–2a). If you look at Table 2–2a, you will see the strand of situated-mediated identity theory as it applies to the Vygotskian sociocultural theory to identities of achievement.

The second theoretical foundation is situated cognition theory or situativity theory—a combination of social learning theory and activity theory. Activity theory posits that learning, teaching, and achievement are fundamentally social accomplishments that are shaped both by (a) the individual's participation in particular settings of activity, as well as by (b) the moment-to-moment interactions with activities and people in these settings (Beach, 1995; Brown et al., 1989; Chaiklin, Hedegaard, & Jensen, 1999; Engeström, 1987, 2001; Lave, 1988; Lave & Wenger, 1991; Lemke, 1997; Rogoff, 1994; Rogoff & Lave, 1984; Roth, 2004; Wenger, 1998). It is from this second theoretical foundation that the notion of situated identity is derived, as discussed earlier. This theoretical foundation is also the genesis of the notion of situated learning theory, which needs a word or two more of elaboration.

The situated learning perspective views learning in the context of our lived experience and participation in the world (Lave, 1997; Lave & Wenger, 1991; Rogoff, 1994, 2003). This view of learning as a situated activity runs counter to the commonly held connotation of learning as the internalization of knowledge that principally results from some deliberate process of teaching or instruction. It is my aim to move our thinking away from the conventional view of learning, as something that happens inside the head of the individual, to this situated perspective as a necessary condition for understanding and applying my situated-mediated identity theory. The conventional view of learning leads people to think only in terms of the information that children are able to internalize from school. Such a limited perspective does not take account of the vast amount of important cultural learning, identity work, and culturally mediated acquisition of new abilities that take place outside of institutionalized settings of teaching and learning. Adopting the conventional view would lead us to miss opportunities to understand how children grow into the social and academic world.

The conventional view of learning also leads to too much emphasis on measuring the individual's acquisition of information, and gives too little attention to developing the individual's capacity to do thoughtful things with newly acquired knowledge. For these reasons, the notions of situated learning and situated identity are important in the upcoming discussion. The situated-mediated identity theory contradicts the conventional view of learning as one kind of reified activity of content internalization and tends toward the view of learning as social and cultural practice—as participation in the social world. The situated-mediated identity framework inscribes the view that learning how to teach is a matter of increasing coparticipation of novice teachers in the culturally competent practice of more accomplished teachers, not the internalization of course content inside the head of the novice teacher. The notion of positionality, examined in the next chapter, animates this inquiry strand as depicted in Table 2–2b.

The third theoretical foundation is a cultural learning perspective on the development of practices in social context (Rogoff, 2003) and is the third inquiry strand depicted in Table 2–2c. Consider this strand the action theory to culturally responsive teaching and learning. The situativity of learning and instruction is perhaps the most significant cultural feature of distinction in the scholarship on Black achievement—Irvine's admonition that our considerations of cultural learning in teacher education should be guided by the differences that make a difference. The situated learning conception of practice is consistent with this admonition because the learning that matters is that which has significance in the world (or at least in the cultural milieu of instruction), not as the acquisition of an individual's mind. This shows up in practice when skillful teachers improvise. Improvisation is also an important part of identity work—a topic to which I return later as one of the key cultural practices linking identity work to scholastic proficiency, especially among members of hip-hop youth culture.

Let me expand a bit on this strand focused on applied critical pedagogy and critical multicultural education depicted in Table 2–2c. Accomplished teachers in diverse settings are not always expert in being able to articulate educational theory, but often are expert in the necessary intellectual performances and social practices that make for students' intellectual engagement and social development in school. More important, they are expert in figuring a social-cultural community of practice, which requires creating and maintaining a vibrant cultural life in the learning setting (Tharp, Estrada, Dalton, & Yamauchi, 2000; Tharp & Gallimore, 1991). They organize classrooms and the professional activity of adults in the setting in ways that promote children's learning achievement and development. The situated-mediated identity theory framework inscribes the idea that effective teaching in diverse settings is situated in this way, involving not only attention to the structure of the content to be learned, but also the structure of the contexts and cultural fabric of the social environment of instruction. Expertise, according to this situated learning view, is much more than the ability to transfer relevant knowledge from one context to the next, or to make appropriate selection of knowledge to a situation or assume appropriate roles in a field of participation. In addition, it involves the creation of a social-cultural community of practice.

According to the situated-mediated identity theory framework, accomplished teaching in diverse settings is less a matter of putting curriculum content across to learners, but rather more a matter of creating a social and cultural environment where this knowledge in use is distributed among participants and put to use by the common purposeful activity. The neophyte teachers' ability to understand accomplished practice depends not on their internalizing the same ideas as an exemplary mentor teacher, but rather in engaging in the ongoing practice of that teacher with students. Here the development of culturally and socially constituted knowledge is of greater value than book knowledge.

Many of you reading this may recognize these statements as the good old American philosophy of pragmatism—and the ideas of U.S. philosopher and educator John Dewey. Others of you may recognize these statements as the Marxist-influenced sociocultural or sociohistorical theory of Russian psychologist Lev Vygotsky. It is pretty interesting to realize the common ground—the preeminence of doing in learning and knowing—in both philosophical traditions. There are others that also share this common ground, but this discussion is developed elsewhere.

SUMMARY AND CONCLUSIONS

In this overview of the situated-mediated identity theory, I distinguished it from contemporary theory in development to present an activity-based and practice-based framework that captures the situational nature of identity development. The distinctions between situated-mediated identity theory and traditional theory are summarized in Table 2–2. In the next chapter I more fully develop the working parts of the theory, starting with the cultural practices of self-narrating, self-representation, and self-dramatizing as forms of signification.

3

Cultural Practices Inquiry: Culturally Reading Individuals-in-Settings

Race, gender, culture, politics, economics, and so on are not just abstractions or infrastructures or deep forces to be posited *a priori* in order to account for surface actions. Such things are figured in a social communicative way into the actual patterning of actual interaction processes themselves.

—Carbaugh (1996, p. 10)

WHY DO WE NEED TO ENGAGE IN CULTURAL PRACTICES INQUIRY?

Before introducing the use of situated-mediated identity theory in cultural practices inquiry, let me first explain why it is necessary to engage in cultural practices inquiry in the first place. Let us begin with a more specific form of the question: Why would we focus on situated identity when our educational challenge is to transform the practices, pedagogies, and policies of schooling to promote school success among all school goers? When it comes to considering diverse school settings, you might also be wondering why we should not instead be focusing on the cross-cultural issues between U.S. mainstream culture on the one hand, and on the other hand Chicana/Chicano, Puerto Rican, Somalian, Hmong and other cultural-ethnic populations? Certainly we should consider the cross-cultural issues in communication and other forms of meaning making as we work with diverse populations. However, as a general theoretical and practical approach to developing cultural competency for effective practice in diverse settings, this is absolutely the wrong tact. The cultural congruence approach tacitly assumes that our task is to assimilate the culturally and ethnically different, where the difference is from some imagined U.S. norm. This tacit assumption is precisely what is wrong with urban education in the United States. The issues of urban schooling and diversity are far too complex to reduce them to a matter of academic and social assimilation of one group or another into the so-called mainstream. This is why we need a cultural practices inquiry.

As I argued in chapter 1, the structural challenges to successful, culturally accomplished teaching in urban settings are complex. Consider the ecological model of Brofenbrenner (1979, 1986, 1998) that conceptualizes intersecting social spheres as a representation of the complexity—of micro-, meso-, and macroleveled spheres of experience. In urban education, there is a set of interacting structural challenges at each of these spheres. The macrostructural challenges such as racism and other ideologies of exclusion (e.g., the "sort and select" mentality of our assessment systems, sexism) intersect with the mesostructural issues of institutions (e.g., schools beset by limited resources, meeting annual yearly progress requirements, inexperienced teachers), which in turn intersect with the microstructural concerns (e.g., culturally encapsulated White teachers who are unsuccessful with children of color). Addressing the intersecting macro-, meso-, and microlevel structural challenges of urban education requires the appropriate lens that permits a simultaneous perspective at all three levels.

My framework is conceptualized as that lens that would allow simultaneous focus on academic identity development at these different levels. It is a means by which teachers may map out the discursive field wherein their identities, and the identities of their students, are made, unmade, contested, and remade. The situating of identity, adoption of positionality, and the assertion of agency are critical cultural practices at the nexus of educational attainment. I recap them now as a more specific statement of the knowledge requirements of cultural competence as six theory premises:

1. Self, and realizations of self (identity), are socially constructed through various forms of relational activity in human interaction, especially specific communication forms called discursive practices.
2. Identity is best understood as situated and fluid, not static and fixed, and is seen in the representations of the self individuals put forth to the wider social world.
3. The situated representations of self taken on by an individual (role identity or positionality) mediate roles that other individuals assume and express (consciously or unconsciously) in any given setting or social environment.

4. The positionality or set of roles assumed in school settings profoundly shapes achievement in performance and ultimately determines school success by mediating the individual's activity in the social setting.

5. Shared situated identities are created and mediated by common experiences in school settings (which some theorists have referred to as academic identities) to form a local culture that shapes school performance and sense of self.

6. Local culture—the structure of the immediate cultural-social context of instructional activity settings together with the situatedness of a learner's performance—can be shaped to mediate positive and productive academic identities in ways that ultimately lead to school success.

WHAT IS THE METHOD OF CULTURAL PRACTICES INQUIRY?

Put simply, the method of cultural practices inquiry is applied ethnography of the developing academic identity, scholastic positionality, and intellectual agency of young people. The method of cultural practices inquiry is the application of situated-mediated theory to the deep examination of young people's academic identity development in relation to specific school experiences and activities. The method of cultural practices inquiry is indebted to two conceptual formulations I have used to articulate what constitutes the users' version of my situated-mediated framework. One is the formulation of a communicatively determined personal identity offered by Carbaugh (1996). The other is a graphically sequenced explanation of sociocultural theory by Rogoff (2003). Let us briefly examine how each informs the method of cultural practices inquiry.

The method of cultural practice is perhaps best illustrated by the idea of using a *syntax*—a formal rule system—to make knowledge statements about what is going on with young people in particular contexts. Just as in the conventional sense of syntax as grammar, the elements of this system include a *subject* (i.e., situated self, positional role, agent) and a *predicate* consisting of a *verb* (i.e., self-expression, self-projection, impression management), and an element that acts as *modifier* (e.g., cultural scene, social scene, frame). I use the term syntax to characterize the method of cultural inquiry for two reasons. First, it is an efficient way of simultaneously considering the variety of forms of situated social identity (i.e., situated identity, positionality, and agency) as they are mediated by the discursive processes (i.e., primary socialization, secondary socialization, and improvisation) in particular interactional contexts (i.e., sociocultural community, social-symbolic community, and community of practice) over time. I express this syntax in propositional phrase or sentence form to show how it captures the complexity of the 3 x 3 system as depicted in Table 2–2. This syntactic structure also makes explicit the notion of positionality, which, as you recall from chapter 2, is not simply a role assumed by or assigned to an individual, but a dynamic location in a social setting. I modeled my syntax on the communicatively defined identity framework of Carbaugh (1996), which also specifies a subject (the individual or the group) and predicate (knowing and symbolizing).

The second value in using the syntactic structure to articulate the user's version of the framework is to avoid some of the inflexibility of contemporary theory (i.e., culturally relevant pedagogy) for expressing the relationships among identity, culture, race, and achievement in activity. As mentioned earlier, contemporary approaches tend to view culture categorically and hence, statically. In short, by using this framework we sidestep the problems of cultural determinism where cultural membership of an individual becomes an explanation of his or her performance. This is what Rogoff (2004) accomplishes in her sequenced discussion of the individual-in-culture from the sociocultural perspective by illustrating inquiry at the following levels simultaneously: (a) a focus on the individual as the object of study; to (b) the individual in social context influenced by peers and teacher; to (c) the individual in social and cultural context features that combine into meaning systems; to (d) the individual as transformed by activity—his or her participation with others. All four of these features are incorporated in the syntax of cultural inquiry in the next section.

Cultural inquiry requires a system that flexibly handles the dynamics of human interaction and symbolic exchange between a student and the wider social context, especially as situations vary for that student within the school context. The method of cultural inquiry, using the syntax structure just described, flexibly handles the complexity of the self-projections and the variety of settings and circumstances in school life. In short, it is a framework that avoids a simplistic cultural deterministic approach that dominates contemporary thinking about identity and achievement with regard to race, ethnicity, and culture. From this syntax formulation come the operating principles for the method of cultural inquiry by visually and graphically illustrating the working system. By conceptualizing it as a sort of syntactic structure, I hope to make clear the method of doing the cultural reading constituting deep inquiry into school achievement with regard to race, culture, ethnicity, and identity. I return to the more detailed articulation of the syntax presently. Let us first consider cultural practices inquiry as it examines culture and race, respectively.

CULTURAL PRACTICES INQUIRY ON CULTURE

Culture refers to the set of practices, ideas, beliefs, assumptions, and social norms that are widely and commonly shared by a group of people and that shape human interaction (Brislin, 1993; Geertz, 1973; Goodenough, 1971). The examination of culture in situated-mediated identity theory is activity based, focusing on the discursive practices that matter in the experiences of young people, rather than on categorical membership and treatment of the different forms and types of cultural representation extant in schools. In particular, this discussion keys on the cultural tools and practices young people use to project self, express self, and improvise self in the school contexts where identity and achievement intersect. This activity-oriented approach is a departure from the usual rendition of what has been called culturally relevant pedagogy (CRP) and culturally relevant teaching (CRT; Gay, 2000; Irvine, 2003; Ladson-Billings, 1994, 2001).

Elsewhere I have challenged the idea of culturally relevant instruction as a primary framework for educators working toward accomplished practice with children in underresourced communities. The limitation of the framework in application to practice lies not in the idea, but in the limited conceptualizations of culture when offered to teachers in professional development and in-service settings. The assumption that many individuals from White, culturally mainstream, and economically privileged backgrounds bring to the discussion of the topic of culture and CRP is the stance that culture is something other people have (Sleeter, 2000, 2001). As a result, their stance is typically not about locating themselves as cultural beings within the sociopolitical contexts of their work so that they can examine their own biases and assumptions. Rather, the stance becomes one of "tell me what I have to know about those people to work successfully with them." The critical self-assessment component of CRT and CRP often gets left off in practice, leaving teachers with the mantra of recognizing the cultural assets that children bring and the idea that getting better in their work in diverse settings is merely a matter of respectful engagement in a new cultural setting (Murrell, 2001, 2002; Sleeter, 1992).

It is because of this limitation that I have developed the situated-mediated identity framework to emphasize the processing and interpreting of cultural material that makes a difference to how human performance is socialized in a given setting—both in an immediate sense and a historical sense. The aim is the development of cultural learners. An effective cultural learner is able to appraise the cultured identity of individuals. In this framework, I want to evoke a deeper reading of culture when we look at the schooling experience of children and youth from diverse communities. I want to begin with challenging the assumed determinative power of culture.

What is problematic about our current approach to CRP and multicultural education is our propensity for a cultural determinism in our inquiry into student achievement. That is, we too often view culture (however we define it for or ascribe it to an individual) as being determinative of behavior, beliefs, motivations, needs, and wants of the individual. In short, we are giving culture too much credit for determining how individuals behave or respond to instruction in given settings. We need a finer grained analysis, so as not to move from racial stereotypes to cultural stereotypes of our own making. Culture is significant, but it is not a categorical determiner of performance, achievement, or identity, as is sometimes implied in the literature on CRT or culturally responsive teaching.

There are patterns and processes by which children and youth develop identities in relation to school that are far more sophisticated than the prefabricated categories we find in the literature such as working-class African American or middle-class Latinos or even school kids versus street kids (see, e.g., Flores-Gonzáles, 2002). Flores-Gonzáles's (2002) school kid versus street kid conception is somewhat more useful because it at least links identity stance with social-cultural context. She uses role-identity theory to propose that students are successful in school to the extent to which they are able to adopt and sustain a school identity and shows how school kid and street kid identities are socially constructed in the experience of schooling.

Although this framework is an advance over previous work, it ultimately is, for our analysis here, still too global and general. Why? Because we know that the street kid and school kid emerge at different times and in different contexts in the same individual. So we still need to account for the varieties in situated identities and performances of individuals across settings and not assume a permanent good kid versus bad kid ascribed role. Let us return now to showing how the situated-mediated framework could accomplish looking at the subtleties of experience that are informed by race in the immediate social scene. To extend this analysis from culture to race, I want to introduce three operating principles of the framework in regards to reading race and the impact of racism in examining school achievement.

CULTURAL PRACTICES INQUIRY ON RACE

There are three operating principles to the method of cultural inquiry for getting at a more nuanced analysis of race. These three principles parallel the three axioms Loury (2002) postulates as necessary to understanding racial inequality in the United States. The first principle is that race is best understood as a social construct, not a biologically determined category of membership (cf. M. K. Brown et al., 2003; Doane & Bonilla-Silva, 2003; Feagin, 2000; Moses, 2002). The corresponding cultural inquiry expected of those using the framework would be to examine and expose the ways in which members of a group naturally assume that race is a matter of skin color or ethnicity. Moreover, members of the learning community would need to understand the construction of race in at least two senses—in terms of ontogeny and phylogeny. That is, in both the development of the individual and the historical development of an ethnic racial group, race is a construct. Consider one instance of how "Whiteness" was constructed as a racial category in the history of the "Americanization" of the immigrants from Europe. For example, the experience of Irish emigration to the United States is a historical legacy that illustrates, and helped to define, the evolution of Whiteness (Ignatiev; 1996; Roediger, 1999). In the middle 1800s the newly arrived Irish in the United States, fleeing famine and destitution in their home country, were not considered White, but as belonging to a lesser category analogous to being Black. Through a complex intersection of processes in U.S. labor history, urban politics, and ethnic agency, the Irish Americans (who by today's sensibilities would have been clearly White owing to their Celtic coloring and features) gradually became White (Ignatiev, 1996).

The second operating principle for the method of cultural inquiry corresponds to Loury's (2002) second axiom for understanding the deep structure of racial inequality in the United States: the degraded status of African Americans in the U.S. institutions of school, the economy, government and so on, is not due to inherent or innate characteristics of Black individuals themselves. This anti-essentialist argument is important because it directly challenges the myth and the tacit assumption of Black inferiority. This tacit assumption is subtle, but certainly present in practices, discourses, and beliefs shared by many in the United States. If you were to, for instance, listen long enough and carefully enough to conversations at gatherings of educators talking about African American children, families, and communities, sooner or later you likely would begin hearing "Blackness" as the primary explanation for their underachievement or overrepresentation in special education.

The third operating principle corresponds to Loury's (2002) third axiom regarding the notion of racial stigma. He posits what I would consider a generalized positionality of racial stigma. His third axiom reads in full as:

> *Axiom 3 (Ingrained Racial Stigma):* An awareness of the racial "otherness" of blacks embedded in the social consciousness of the American nation owing to the historical fact of slavery and its aftermath. This inherited stigma even today exerts an inhibiting effect on the extent to which African Americans can realize their full human potential. (cited in Rowley, 2004, p. 16)

Loury compellingly argued for the existence of racial stigma. He argued that we need to understand stigmatized Blackness as a generalized degraded positionality of African American people in the United States. Consistent with the work of Goffman (1963), who applied the term *spoiled identity,* Loury asserts that a generalized positionality he called *racial dishonor* should replace discrimination as the key descriptor for characterizing the dynamics of racial inequality in the United States. This is a useful idea, consistent with the situated-mediated framework, because it historically frames the general positionality of African American children, youth, and families regarding race and achievement.

Based on this idea, my third operating principle is that this generalized racial stigma (GRS) of Blackness constitutes a positionality generated by the negative positioning of an entire group by an entire society. It is the stigmatization of an entire group by the entire majority (Rowley, 2004) that makes racial stigma a rarely recognized and rarely examined institution in U.S. social and public life. As a positionality, according to my framework, we understand that there are effects of racial stigma on the development of African American children. A stigmatized positionality is not just an ascribed role, but can also become an assumed role incorporating the dynamics of how individuals begin to see themselves in light of others and wider society. In other words, children's images of themselves can be influenced by how they experience the GRS.

As mentioned earlier, the work of Steele (1997) has experimentally shown how the degrading effects GRS positionality has on high-stakes standardized test performance can be attenuated. When conditions are set so that, for example, African American test takers neither assume nor are ascribed a GRS positionality (GRSP), they perform just as well as their White counterparts. Using this concept of GRS positionality, my third most important type of sense making for a learning community contesting institutional and cultural racism would involve understanding this process of positioning, and the GRS positioning that occurs in the social and public life of the learning community. I want to note one other important positionality that parallels the GRS positionality. It is the generalized assumption of White privilege (GAWP), which is the basis for GRS. People who tacitly assume that "White is right" and the White culture is the standard of quality naturally also project racial stigma.

THE METHOD: USING THE SYNTAX
OF CULTURAL PRACTICES INQUIRY

Let us return now to visualizing how the entire framework works as syntax using a basic propositional statement: *Who I am is who I symbolize myself to be in situated social scenes.* The formulation fits the definition of syntax—a rule system that allows for the production and interpretation of a very large variety of instances (utterances). Just like the language analog, the number of possible interpretations of identity is very large because of the combinatorially increasing possibilities of situations, contexts, and roles. With the variety of possible roles a person can take on, combined with the number of interpretations others may make of those roles, in turn combined with the number of settings that frame both roles and interpretations, the possible number of identity readings for a single child grows rapidly.

Let us look at the framework as a series of sentences developed in the manner that Carbaugh (1996) has done in his articulation of social identity with the following series of statements:

(S1) I *know* who I am, in part, by the way I *symbolize* myself in situated social scenes.

(S2) I *know* who you are, in part, by the way you *symbolize* yourself in situated social scenes.

(S3) You *know* who I am, in part, by the way I *symbolize* myself in situated social scenes.

(S4) We *know* who we are, in part, by the way we *symbolize* in situated social scenes. (p. 30)

These statements from Carbaugh (1996) represent the core propositional string of the syntax of reading identity. These propositional strings
have in common the same syntax: each with a subject, the *individual*, and
a predicate, *symbolizing self in a social scene*. Using this formulation I
can now restate the thesis of this volume: Academic achievement and
school success of individuals are functions of how successfully they
symbolize themselves in the cultural scenes that matter in school.

The success of self-symbolization in any structured setting or frame is
influenced by at least three things according to my framework: (a) how
well individuals know or understand themselves (as in Socrates' dictum
"Know thyself!"), (b) how well they read the social settings they find themselves in, and most important, (c) how well they read themselves *into* that
social scene. Recall from the previous chapter that this reading of self into
a social scene is called positioning, the symbolizing individuals do as they
read themselves into a social setting. Repositioning is the symbolic and
communicative activity that the group of people in the setting takes to challenge or modify the positioning of the individual. The identity of an individual that persists within this tension of positioning and repositioning in a
given episode is termed positionality. In this propositional description, you
can see how positionality is different than the notion of role or even role-
identity because it is situationally determined by the tension between what
the individual puts forth and what the group feeds back.

Now, you may be thinking that the notion of symbolizing self in a
social scene really needs to be unpacked in this framework because the
basic proposition, "Who I am is who I symbolize myself to be in situated
social scenes," hinges on the meaning of *symbolize*. It is complex and vari-
able, as suggested by the allowable substituted verbs *perform* and *participate*—both of which are allowable in my framework because it is activity
based. However, rather than define *symbolizing self* I am going to break it
down. In breaking down the notion of symbolize, I address several com-
plications. The first complication is that we are not really talking about
symbolizing in any one form, but in a multiplicity of forms that are taking
place simultaneously as the individual works to present the social identity
he or she wants others to take in. Recall Goffman's (1959) notion of
impression management as a very widespread form of self-symbolizing all
of us do. For example, in a job interview we attempt to manage the
impression of ourselves as capable, qualified, and suited for the position
for which we are applying.

Impression management is actually constituted by a number of symbol-izing acts requiring both performance and participation of the individual in a social scene. These symbolizing subacts include the individual's form of address to different members of the group, the tone of voice and cadence of speech, the posture and physical stance assumed within the group, the aggressiveness in turn-taking in the conversation, and so on. These are all acts of self-representation that could constitute an individ-ual's single effort to symbolize oneself as authoritative or as someone with leadership potential. Hence, symbolizing is not a single act, but an act that incorporates a number of subactions, postures, nonverbal commu-niqués, and so on, to position oneself.

This brings me to the second complication—the fact that symbolizing requires symbolic interaction with other people in a social context. Symbolizing is meaning making, and self-symbolizing is the meaning one makes of oneself (the image) for consumption by others. There is no symbolizing unless there is someone around to read the symbolization. People do not invest in a stylized projection of themselves unless there is someone else to interact with. This complication leads me to suggest that symbolizing really entails two actions. Young adolescents regularly, almost continuously, engage in impression management among their peers in a form known as "stylin'." As mentioned earlier, this process requires the impression-managing individual to engage in reading the audience—to actively interpret what other people make of the self-pre-sentation in the social scene. Once again, the predicate of the proposition (S1) *I know who I am in part by how I symbolize in situated social scenes,* actually has two verb elements in the sentence. These are the actions of (a) self-symbolizing, and (b) reading oneself into the social scene. Both are vitally important and, together, account for the sense-making activity one does for self-understanding and realizing of one's identity. This is the self-referential sense making described in chapter 2 illustrated by this phrase:

(S5)   How do I know *who I am* until I determine *what others make of what I do?*

What this means is that, in the propositions S1 through S4 articulating the situated-mediated framework, there are actually three verbs in the syntac-tic structure of the framework:

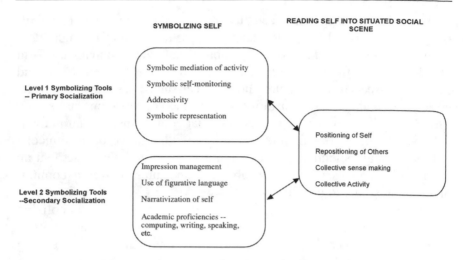

FIGURE 3–1 Syntax of cultural practices inquiry.

V1   Knowing (self).
V2   Symbolizing self.
V3   Reading self into the social scene.

V1 is an act of self-reflection and self-awareness. It relates to what psychologists refer to as self-concept. V2 and V3 together actually constitute the act of self-symbolizing—formally called positioning. So the situating of self as a component of academic performance, according to this framework, is constituted by three acts represented by V1, V2, and V3. We can now represent this graphically in Figure 3–1.

The third complicating factor in explaining self-symbolizing is that there are many ways to symbolize self. A major one has already been identified—impression management—but there are many other ways of symbolizing that I have represented as two levels in Figure 3–1.

In Figure 3–1, Level 1 symbolizing includes the skills of symbolic representation acquired through primary socialization. What are the symbolizing proficiencies or human capacities that emerge during the processes of primary socialization? According to Vygotsky (1962, 1978), what humans acquire in this primary socialization is the capacity to do things with words. In other words, children acquire the ability to represent objects, events, and relations of the external world by means of their developing capacity for using internal representations for the external world—most significantly, words. With words they can convey meaning abstractly, independent of the actual experience to the objects or events. The proficiency is evident in young children's penchant for naming things. This capacity or proficiency is called *semiotic mediation* and emerges in a number of other ways, including the following:

1. Symbolic mediation of activity—the use of signs, symbols, and language to constitute rules of engagement in a human activity.
2. Symbolic self-monitoring—the capacity to use symbols to organize and manage their own behavior and others' behavior, to monitor the performance of the group ("that's not how it is supposed to go").
3. Addressivity—the ability to direct intended meanings to intended recipients.
4. Symbolic representation—the ability to objectify or concretize other contexts of activity that are not immediately experienced. Narrativization is an example. (p. 280)

Vygotsky stressed that human play develops children's capacity for semiotic mediation. This capacity is practiced and strengthened through play. Play, therefore, is an important activity in the developmental tasks of young children. However, play is any symbolic activity—as in the connotation when we say to a colleague, "Let's play with that idea." Play is important developmental work because it permits children to internalize a system of representation that corresponds to the meaning systems of the wider world. That is, through play people acquire the cultural means to filter out the full array of stimuli in the adult world that bandy them this way and that. Rogoff (2004) notes of Vygotsky:

"[He] ... pointed out that children in all communities are cultural participants, living in a particular community at a specific time in history." This is another way of understanding why play is so important—it is the means by which children examine and explore the cultural nature of everyday life—situated as it is among the people, the culture, and the time they come from. (p. 10)

Level 2 symbolization concerns those communicative skills developed through secondary socialization. Symbolization at Level 2 is more a matter of social interaction and identity practices than is primary socialization. The social practices acquired in secondary socialization could include literacy and numeracy proficiencies as well as social and communicative proficiency known in the developmental literature as social competence. Other capacities might include impression management, signifying, and figurative use of language.

To summarize to this point, statements S1 through S5 are five ways of declaring the core articulation of the situated identity framework based on the act of symbolizing self in a social context. A core articulation is, *Who I am right now is what I am symbolizing myself to be right here and right now.* Using this framework educators engaged in reading the learner in setting, based on the performance and participation of that individual within the social scene, are doing cultural inquiry and being cultural learners.

So now we have in propositional form the syntax for doing a cultural inquiry that allows for the reading of individuals in situations. That core proposition may also be read as, *Who I am right now is how I am reading myself into the doings of this social scene.* I mean the notion of reading in the sense used by Freire (1970) and others as a broad, deep, and critically conscious sort of meaning making. *Reading* an individual in context entails simultaneously taking account of the historical, political, and cultural dimensions that make up the social scene as well as the individual's history. Doing cultural reads of students is a departure from the contemporary sense of culturally responsive teaching applied in schools, where the pedagogical agenda tends to be that of identifying individuals by cultural membership (or even by cultural displays) and then seeking to determine the qualities associated with the cultural category of membership. By contrast, the focus here is to locate the individuals in a social, cultural, and historical field of actual school settings, then interpret the individuals' field of meaning and intention according to how they choose to write their parts into the master narrative (as well as the local story). This means reading the discursive practices of the learner—the actual action and interaction of the individual.

As Carbaugh (1996) notes, the tentative nature of the phrase "in part" in statements S1 through S4 indicates that situated identity may draw on other determinative factors other than self-projection in a given social context. I touched on these in chapter 1—things like availability of reading material or after-school academic activity in the home or community. By playing with the pronouns and the verb *symbolize* in S1 through S4, we can appreciate the flexibility of this rule system in doing a cultural read of an individual achiever and acknowledge that teachers need to include themselves as a factor in the cultural read of the learner. Your actions, reactions, and dispositions are part of the context of the social scene your learners inhabit, and partly mediate how they situate themselves (situated identity), position themselves (positionality), and decide to act (agency).

The flexibility of the system is shown in the different perspectives of situating identity as illustrated by playing with the pronouns to produce the phrases (S1) *I know who I am;* (S2) *I know who you are*; (S3) *You know who I am;* and (S4) *We know who we are.* The common thread in each statement is the symbolization of self. The cultural learner is one who is able to, as he or she works with students, maintain an awareness of self-symbolization from each of these perspectives simultaneously: the *I* perspective expressed by S1, the *you-and-me* perspective expressed by S2 and S3, and the *we* perspective expressed by S4.

The flexibility of this rule system is also illustrated by playing with the verb *know.* Carbaugh (1996) plays with the verb *to know* in statements S1 through S4 by inserting the alternative verbs *show* and *constitute.* In my framework, these are allowable substitutions because they convey that knowing self or knowing others in a situated context are processes of identity realization. This is where the action is in the entire framework: the self-projective experience of self in situating one's identity. The other substitutions in Carbaugh's (1996) system for the term symbolize are *perform* and *participate,* indicating one's action in a group apart from the acts of self-representation.

In summary, the task of becoming a cultural learner addressing issues of identity, diversity, and achievement in urban schools is a matter of reading the individual as a cultural being. However, this read is not based on ascribed or assumed characteristics of the cultural-ethnic group, but rather upon an *interpretation of how that individual represents self in the world.* Cultural learners are reading the inscription of identity of participants in human interactions, including themselves and including multiple perspectives. I constructed this syntactic framework to narrow down the complexity of this task and focus on those elements of human psychology—meaning, motivation, experience of self—that matter most in learning achievement.

EGO IDENTITY AND EGO INVESTMENT IN SITUATING IDENTITY

Ego identity is an important concept in this theory of situated-mediated identity. Erikson's notion of ego identity is important because the ego capacity that develops as an individual passes from childhood to adolescence to adulthood is key to an individual's psychological well-being. This idea is relevant to considering how teachers can help students develop the capacity for self-awareness and agency. Just as important in my framework is Erikson's notion of *ego investment*, which is the force behind human beings' drive to represent themselves—position themselves—in a particular ways in given social settings. Ego identity refers to the psychological agency of an individual—the personality agency responsible for emotional, behavioral, and cognitive control. The points in time when this controlling agency loses integrity are the points at which the behavior, cognition, and affect of the individual become disorganized and erratic. The more important theoretical idea, however, is ego investment.

According to my framework, ego investment is fundamental to human development (Erikson, 1968), human motivation (Maslow, 1970), and is manifested in a generalized positionality of being. Recall the Reverend Jesse Jackson's mantra "I am somebody!"—this articulates exactly the thematic content of *generalized ego projection* (GEP). I theorize that the psychological ego investment of individuals, which manifests as the psychosocial projection as a GEP, is the basic positioning that all humans do regardless of context, social status, or state of mind. The GEP is represented discursively by the basic identity assertion: *I am, I am here, and I matter here.* My claim is that this basic positioning undergirds everyone's social interaction and animates all of the other possible positionalities or role identities an individual can take on in a particular cultural scene. They are disordered individuals indeed who deny their existence, their social presence, or their basic value in the way they represent themselves to others. In fact, as I show in a moment, the most common sort of ego disorder is the socially abrasive, egotistical overprojection of self (see Table 3–1). This basic positionality can be represented discursively at all three levels of situated identity (i.e., situated identity, positionality, and agency), as illustrated in both Table 3–1 and Table 3–2, where you will see the basic discursive expression for the GEP.

I should point out, as is a major tenet of Erikson's theory, that the ego investment may have either a positive or negative trajectory of growth. Let us look at the negative trajectory of growth first. In my framework, the basic identity assertion of "I am, I am here, and I matter here" in a negative trajectory of development becomes merely "I am special." Consider Table 3–1. The situated identity discursive representation in the first row of the table is "I'm special *and* you're not." The identity projection statement outside of the situated framework would simply be "I'm special," but this representative utterance containing the additional phrase "*and* you're not" reflects the presence of at least one other person and a social context.

The second row of Table 3–1 expresses the positionality or discursive representation of an egotistic self, which is "I'm special *because* you're

TABLE 3–1

Discursive Representation	Identity Representation
	Deficiency Situated Identity
"I'm special *and* you're not."	Differentiation of self in a socially situated context (a situated form of what Erikson termed *individuation*) at the expense of others and the valorization of self.
	Deficiency Positionality
"I'm special *because* you're not."	Differentiation of self as an act of positioning self higher at the expense of the others in the socially situated context (repositioning others as lesser than oneself).
	Deficiency Agency
"I'm special *because, as you can see, I'm the best one here at* (... conversing, problem solving, entertaining...)"	Differentiation of self by actions that valorize what one is good at— repositioning others by demonstrated capability at whatever shared activity is defining the social scene at the moment.

not." I should mention here that the emphasis on *because* in this statement more clearly shows the basic negative repositioning one person does of another. The essence of what I am terming egotistic ego investment and negative repositioning is summarized in this table. Speech acts that are analogous to "I'm special *because* you're not" constitute the hierarchical arrangement of self above others in a cultural scene. In children this negative form of generalized ego projection is developmentally appropriate. When it persists into adolescence and adulthood in forms not immediately recognizable, such as in ideologies of assumed privilege, racism, and entitlement, it is a problem.

It is also important to recall the discussion in chapter 1 regarding the availability of meaning systems in society that not only make this negative repositioning of one person to another unnecessarily frequent, but invisible. Race, for example, makes this negative positionality ubiquitous

TABLE 3–2

Discursive Representation	Identity Representation
	Actualizing Situated Identity
"I'm special and *so are you.*"	Differentiation of self in a socially situated context (a situated form of what Erikson termed *individuation*) in relation to others but not at their expense.
	Actualizing Positionality
"I'm special, *but in a different way than* you are."	Differentiation of self as an act of positioning self as merely distinctive among (not as better than) others in the socially situated context (no negative repositioning others as lesser than oneself).
	Actualizing Agency
"I'm special *because, as we all can see, I'm a part of something special!*"	Differentiation of self by one's role in the demonstrated capability of the group in the social scene at the moment.

in our society (Loury, 2002) as discussed earlier. Any White person that holds an innate belief in Black inferiority is likely to—by unnoticed gestures, forms of address, posture, turn taking, or any number of other discursive acts—communicate that he or she is better ("more special") than the African American person with whom he or she is interacting. As discussed earlier, a generalized racial stigma may, given the right social dynamic, animate this negative positioning even in individuals who see themselves as caring, compassionate, and ethical on issues of race.

Then finally, the last row in Table 3–1 is the discursive representation for a negatively developing agency, which is "I'm special *because, as you can see, I'm the best one here at* […]." This is the awareness and manipulation (mostly unconsciously when it is based on racial stigma) of one's positioning in the group—as to status, skills, and proficiencies—to serve the valorization of oneself. For example, consider a person who constantly steers a conversation to a topic area he or she knows the most about among the members of the current conversational group instead of toward a more productive turn, so that he or she can then position himself or herself as "the smartest one here" through his or her discourse and actions. A subtler example might be the positioning of a fourth-grade teacher who valorizes and spends time on the discipline areas he feels most proficient in, but tends to neglect those he does not feel proficient in (e.g., science and mathematics)—subjects that always get short shrift in depth, time on task, and expendability when the school day gets shortened.

The point is that cultural psychology of identity is intricately bound up in this basic positionality of ego projection—the generalized positionality I am calling GEP. My claim is that when well-meaning and otherwise capable teachers fail to achieve the same successes with their African American and Hispanic children, we need to look at the negative positionalities of both learners and teachers. We need to examine school environments and ourselves for the subtle ways negative positionality may be at the heart of adults' unsuccessful interactions with young people.

Next, let us consider the positive trajectory and, as we do, regard it as an aim in creating a culturally configured social environment for achievement identities. Consider Table 3–2, which contains the self-statements of a positive positionality deriving from psychosocial development in a cultural environment alternative to individualistic, zero-sum competitive values in U.S. popular culture (Comer, 1998). One such meaning system is readily available in the principles of Nguzu Saba, an African-centered worldview, and African American cultural values (Boykin & Bailey, 2000; Boykin, Coleman, Lilja, & Tyler, 2004; Murrell, 1997, 2002; Nobles, 1985). The key feature in these meaning systems is identity based in, and generativity toward, the group. The self-statements for situated self (row 1), positionality (row 2), and agency (row 3) in Table 3–2 are made in reference to the group, but not in contradistinction to the group. S1, *I am special and you are too,* is an affirmation of self and the other as a basic psychosocial stance, which develops in the individual throughout his or her psychosocial development. One additional twist to this positive GEP positionality concerns the improvisational variations that come into play due to ethnic identifications. This is what gives the GEP positionality the diversity and varieties of improvised identities that are visible in vibrant high school cultures, as when White high school students adopt hip-hop positionalities you might only expect from students of color (e.g., P. Perry, 2002).

What differentiates the positive, group-generative type of positioning from the negative, egoistic positioning? In lay terms we can describe this difference in terms of the degree of emotional maturity and character development of the individual. The more developed the person, the less reliance there is on the group to fulfill the being's needs. The more developed the individual, the less his or her needs structure is mediated by social context—for example, seeking the regard of other people. The framework for locating this level is the well-known hierarchy of needs proposed by Maslow (1970).

According to that framework, the human motive structure can be represented by a hierarchy of human needs based on two groupings: deficiency needs and growth needs. Among the deficiency needs are (a) belongingness and love as the need to affiliate with others and be accepted; and (b) esteem as the need to achieve, be competent, gain approval; and gain recognition. These needs at the lower level must be met before moving to the next higher level. Belongingness and esteem needs are key here. These are the needs in play in the generalized positionalities described earlier—as belongingness and being needs. Those who operate from deficiency needs are unlikely to invest in positive, group-generative positionalities, but instead are more apt to engage in needy ego investment—egoistic negative positioning of the sort summarized in Table 3–1.

According to Maslow, an individual is ready to act on the growth needs (listed later) if and only if the deficiency needs are met. Maslow's initial conceptualization included only one growth need—self-actualization. Self-actualized people are characterized by (a) being problem focused, (b) incorporating an ongoing freshness of appreciation of life, (c) a concern about personal growth, and (d) the ability to have peak experiences. Maslow later further differentiated actualization needs and named two lower level growth needs prior to the general level of self-actualization (Maslow & Lowery, 1998) and one beyond that level (Maslow, 1970). In sum, the baseline of positive positionality is whether the individual is acting on growth needs.

SUMMARY AND CONCLUSIONS

Thus far, in the method of cultural practices inquiry, I have asserted several generalized positionalities that can subtly affect student performance.

TABLE 3–3
Overall Situated-Mediated Identity Framework

Type of Subject	Type of Situated Social Scene	Type of Symbolization
Situated Identity	Social-Cultural Community	Primary socialization
Positionality	Social-Symbolic Community (Figured World)	Secondary socialization
Agency	Community of practice Activity setting	Improvisational self-determination

These include the GAWP, the GRS, and the generalized projection of ego shared by everyone. Generalized positionalities are not quite the same as roles, because what they incorporate are predictable expectations for human behavior. Their usefulness is in being able to enhance the interpretation of cultural scenes by identifying the source of influence on students as they are repositioned by adults. My framework is conceptualized as the lens that allows simultaneous focus at micro-, meso-, and macrolevels of experience. The method of cultural practices inquiry was explained as the application of a sort of syntax by which teachers may map out the discursive field wherein their identities, and the identities of their students, are made, unmade, contested, and remade. The situating of identity, the adoption of positionality, and the assertion of agency are the cultural practices that constitute the connection of urban education issues with actual human activity, decision making, and symbolic interaction. The general framework for this is shown in Table 3–3.

II

Application of the Framework

4

The Construction of Academic Identities: Situativity, Positionality, and Agency in Intellectual Life

People tell others who they are, but even more important they tell themselves and then try to act as though they are who they say they are.

—D. Holland et al. (1998, p. 31)

It is probably no mere historical accident that the word person, in its first meaning, is a mask. It is rather a recognition of the fact that everyone is always and everywhere, more or less consciously, playing a role .... It is in these roles that we know each other; it is in these roles that we know ourselves.

—Park (1950, p. 249)

In Goffman's (1959) famous study *The Presentation of Self in Everyday Life,* he distinguished between ego identity and positionality in a way that introduced action and performance as determiners of the individual self. In that work, one's personal identity (ego identity) existed behind a *persona*, a public and dramaturgical representation of self. The key idea is that one's personal identity is always inferred based on what one does or says. It has no content or structure per se, as it is an organizational feature of one's mentality. Personas, on the other hand, are public and shared. One's persona is expressed or presented discursively, and its uniqueness is recognized by how well it conforms to the roles and person types recognized by the large collective of people. It is this important distinction between the personal self and the public self that I take up in this chapter. Of central concern here is the nature of the dynamics of identity expression in relation to young people's performance and well-being in school settings.

Let me restate that the purpose of situated-mediated identity theory is to explain the relationship between young people's achievement motivation on the one hand and the shifting, complex social worlds they experience in school settings on the other hand. As stated earlier, mediated identity theory should not be regarded as a grand theory, but rather a starting point for understanding the social construction of learning achievement and academic proficiency as a process of mediated identity formation. In chapters 2 and 3, the basic conceptual apparatus of mediated identity theory was presented and summarized in Table 2–2 and Table 3–3. In this chapter I focus on the three dimensions of identity in the theory constituting the first column of that table—situated identity, positionality, and agency—and explain how they constitute three critical developmental tasks young people face as they struggle to make sense of themselves as academic achievers, cultural beings, and worthy human beings.

The first column in Table 2–2 depicts the three kinds of identity that already seem to have a psychological reality to everyday people. Recall that these included (a) the self or personal identity—one's sense of continuity and "me-ness" that has an integrity over time and through different contexts; (b) the selves that are publicly represented, in different ways at different times, as in the episodes of interpersonal interaction in the everyday world; and (c) the self of personal agency—in that one takes oneself as acting from a point of interest and intention located in or attached to the me-ness. These three types of selves—roughly speaking, ego identity, positionality, and agency—appear in various guises and forms in sociology, psychology, semiotics, and other disciplines. A thorough treatment of these three levels of identity as a formal integrated sociopsychological theoretical framework is available elsewhere (cf. Côté & Levine, 2002) and is not addressed here. Here I examine in greater detail those three elements—situated identity, positionality, and agency—to reveal school achievement as a social process of becoming a learner and an adult. What should become clear in this discussion is how identities of achievement are socially constructed across each of these levels of experience—the interpersonal level (micro), the institutional level (meso), and cultural level (macro).

SITUATED IDENTITY

Situated identity is the first element. I realized just how tricky it is to define situated identity on an occasion at a recent academic conference where I was explaining my work to a colleague there. She had asked me for a one-sentence definition of situated identity, which, surprisingly to me, I could not easily come up with. My explanation was uncomfortably wordy, but I managed to be clear enough by using concepts my colleague was familiar with, which included the notions of situated learning, sociocultural theory, ego identity, and an area of inquiry in sociology called role-identity theory. It troubled me, though, that my explanation seemed needlessly circuitous, and I forgot about this episode until later in the semester when I asked my students to do the same thing in my undergraduate course in learning and development. I asked students to define situated identity by telling me what their "take-away understanding" of the concept was from the course. Here is a sample of their written responses:

Student 1: Situated identity means that our sense of self (our identity) is not "fixed," rather, our identity is flowing and determined situationally by many factors. Our identity is formed through social practice. A person's identity is mediated by what is going on situationally. (April 2005)

Student 2: Situated identity is a combination of personal identity and social identity. In a particular situation those two senses of identity combine and the person takes on a situated identity. Also, in a particular situation the person is declaring their role in that social interaction, such as a student in a classroom is declaring that they are there to learn. By encouraging that as a situated identity the teacher can use that identity to secure the student's attention as a learner and encourage learning. (April 2005)

Student 3: Situated identity is an identity that is affected by where you are, whom you are with, and how they make you feel. Therefore teachers have a major influence on situated identity because it is their job to make a positive learning environment for their students. (April 2005)

Student 4: A person's situated identity (sense of self) is both the person and the setting the person is in. Our sense of self or identity is ever changing and is determined by the situation. It is mediated by what is going on around the individual and it is continuous throughout life. Understanding the concept of situated identity can lead a teacher to be more effective in promoting academic achievement by connecting with the families, the neighborhood, and the different cultures. Students are affected by their social context and cultural practices. (April 2005)

My students provided wonderful and accurate explanations, any one of which would have been more than adequate to satisfy my inquiring colleague at the conference a few weeks prior. Their definitions are all right on the money because of their semester-long intensive study using the concept as applied theory in children's learning and development during their field work in urban after-school programs. Many of my students used the idea to interpret children's motivation on a daily basis and saw how particular situations mediated children's senses of self, and how this in turn mediated their effort and investment in the learning activity. The notion of situated identity provided them with a way of actually responding to the admonition of "know your students and where they are coming from" to promote effective and worthwhile learning. In short, the notion of situated identity made sense to my students because of the framework that informed their practice as they worked with school-aged children in their urban field experiences. It also made sense to them because it helped them make sense of their daily successes and failures working with children from backgrounds very different from their own. It made sense to them because it provided a way of interpreting the relationship between self and learning, and seeing the importance of identity in mediating the teaching and learning process, both for their students and for them personally.

What these two experiences revealed to me is that the nature of understanding the concept of situated identity is itself an act of situating identity. The meaning of the term was more difficult to convey to my colleague than it was to my students who used it to grapple with the meaning of pupil motivation in their field experiences working with children of color in urban community centers. Many was the occasion in class debriefings when my students were able to reinterpret what first seemed to them willful and disruptive behaviors of children as expected and predictable acts of identity in particular situations in the settings where they worked. The key element in this understanding concerns a new situated understanding of human development and the different role identities that come into play as contexts and situations shift. In the next section I briefly examine how the issue of being a different person in different contexts has been dealt with in research literature.

The theoretical tradition of role-identity theory in sociology (e.g., Hogg, Terry, & White, 1995; Markus & Nurius, 1987; Stryker, 1968) has challenged the unitary status of identity, as has the work of Goffman (e.g., Goffman, 1967). In a similar vein, traditions of scholarship, such as Black feminist scholarship (e.g., Collins, 2000, 2005; Lorde, 1984) and situated learning theory (Lave & Wenger, 1991), also challenge the unitary notion of identity by emphasizing its dynamic social construction in a variegated cultural, racial, and gender politics. Role-identity theory emerged in the mid–1980s to address the nexus between the individual and the wider social world. According to this approach, individual identity is not viewed as a single entity, but as being composed of a number of role identities. A role identity is a self-ascribed definition—a self-definition or person schema that results from occupying a particular role or social category. Thus identity is viewed as a composite of self-definitions or self-schemas, each resulting from a particular role or social category (Hogg et al., 1995). This is a useful idea because it provides a means for accounting for the many stances young people present in academic settings. Role identities can emerge as social positions that individuals hold and value in varying degrees.

In role-identity theory there is presumed to be a hierarchy of role identities that are ordered according to their value to the individual. The role identities at the top of the hierarchy are more highly valued and therefore more likely to be enacted in social interaction than those at the bottom of the hierarchy (Callero, 1985; Flores-Gonzáles, 2002; McCall & Simmons, 1978; Stryker, 1968). In this formulation, role identities may be interrelated and consistent, such as being a parent, a spouse, and a Girl Scout leader; or they may be unrelated or inconsistent, such as being a rap artist, CEO of a major corporation, and a youth soccer coach. According to role-identity theory, *valences*, or the values an individual ascribes to his or her set of role identities, can change over time according to changes in social context or personal proficiency.

Role-identity theory attempts to explain the complexity of identity as it changes according to different social contexts, and to offer rules that determine which role identities come to the fore in any given situation. It is the pattern of enacted role identities that gives the individual his or her distinctive identity. A set of rules that accounts for the social identity that an individual projects in given settings is just what we would need for the work of promoting identities of achievement. However, when the finer details of human interactions are examined more closely, they appear more dynamic than role-identity theory can account for. There are several reasons for this insufficiency. First, the situated identities in play for children or youth in different settings are not all proscribed or known in advance, but may, in fact, be improvised (D. Holland et al., 1998; Stevens, 2002). In other words, the set of role identities a researcher or teacher believes may be operating for an adolescent may not be accurate and authentic. For example, Stevens (2002) argues that poor adolescents of color engage in identity exploration earlier than their White counterparts. She argues that for African American adolescents, an earlier exploration of identity is animated by the need to enhance self-efficacy in light of the social, economic, and scholastic stigma of being Black in U.S. society. Hence, not only are we likely to err in projecting which role identities might be in play in a given situation for the children and youth who experience social stigma in categories of race or ethnicity and socioeconomic status, but we lose sight of the improvisational nature of identity formation and the creative potential of young people for self-expression given their unusually difficult circumstances.

Second, there are limitations in the role-identity framework in regard to accounting for the dynamic, transactional, and improvisational nature of identity formation among children and youth, especially those from culturally, ethnically, and racially diverse backgrounds. Proponents of role-identity theory attempt to account for school achievement in terms of the pattern of more dominant and less dominant role identities in the collection making up the individual identity. Applying terms such as *salience* and *prominence,* the task from the role-identity theoretical perspective is to determine which role identities come to the fore and which are subdued. An investigation of school achievement would then, ostensibly, be a matter of determining and maximizing the prominence of, for example, the school kid identities over street kid identities (e.g., Flores-Gonzáles, 2002).

If we attempted to use role-identity theory in analyzing school performance of individual children, our analysis of school achievement would take the form of accounting for role identities that are inconsistent with one another for a given child. For example, for students in some contexts, the role identity as the popular student or cool student very much depends on the peer context. Consider that Majors and Billson's (1993) notion of "cool pose" among African American males contradicts the role identity of the the good student, and is therefore a positionality that is stigmatized by school adults. Consider also how the general positionality of the good student can be differentiated into a variety of subject positions such as the "hard-working" and the "serious" student, where the former does what he or she is supposed to do, and the latter exhibits both agency and promise. Both of these differ from a third possible positionality, the "bright" student, construed as the student who may get good grades despite being neither serious nor hard working. The role identities of being cool and being smart cannot easily coexist for some students in some contexts, and could account for underachievement. However, as we shall see, the positionalities created and improvised by young people are much more richly varied than would otherwise be suggested by role-identity theory. Therefore, the role-identity theory is too limited for our work here. What we can take from the role-identity approach is the idea that a person can assume, project, or be ascribed any number of role identities into patterns, termed positionalities in the theory presented here, in accordance with a given situation or context. According to role-identity theory, the presence of identity-enhancing events or identity-threatening events determines the situated identity an individual presents in a given situation.

To summarize, the problem with the role-identity approach is that it is not fine-grained enough to capture the rich experiences and interactions of social life in school. We noted two reasons. The first was that the positions young people take up are not all a matter of predetermined roles such as sister, feminist, school kid, street kid, jock, or poet. The second reason is that the role-identity explanation for how the individual composes himself or herself is too complicated, relying on an account of how different role identities are combined for an individual. Herein lies the limited applicability of the role-identity approach for linking identity development to school achievement: The notion of role accumulation depends on reinforcements for some roles and discouragement of others, and the total accumulation is to somehow account for the situated identity or pattern for the individual. The calculus of valences and reinforcements for particular roles is too cumbersome. The social environments in school settings are far too complex to do this sort of analysis situation by situation. Finally, role accumulation does not account for the unique expressions self-improvised by young people that are not based on any predetermined role. The concept of positionality is where I look to circumvent the shortcomings of role-identity theory as a way of explaining the processes by which people situate identity.

I take up in detail this notion of positionality in the next section. For the present I want to briefly address the critical component of situated identity that role-identity theory does not address sufficiently, namely, the meaning individuals draw on in their self-constructions.

Situated Identity and Meaning Systems

Meaning systems are both individual and collective. Individuals have meaning systems and communities share meaning systems. What we refer to as identity is a powerful—perhaps the most powerful—meaning system by which individuals interpret their experience. In my analysis, I concur with feminist scholar and poet Audre Lorde's (1984) assertions that (a) cultural material is composed of cultural-, racial-, ethnic-, and class-based roles; and (b) contributes to the gendered compositions of individuals constructed in historically, pragmatically situated activity settings of cultural communities. The challenge for us is how we will recognize these compositions in the developmental process of learners to become culturally competent teachers who promote identities of achievement. The core proposition regarding situated identity is that the individual does the composition of self—the individual composes himself or herself using the cultural material available.

The situated-mediated identity idea draws significantly on the work of Harré and Gillet's (1994) use of the term *signification* to indicate the active role of meaning in structuring the interaction between a person and a social context. The semiotician's notion of signification helps define the subjectivity of the person in a situation and their positioning with respect to certain discourses implicit in that subjectivity. Events and objects are given significance by the discourses in which they appear. These significations both arise from, and in part constitute, the subjectivity of an individual in relation to what is signified.

So the core proposition regarding the concept of situated identity is that the discursive act of situating of self in social context is the most important ongoing signification in which humans can engage. Individuals therefore compose their identity as an act of signification in each social setting they enter. Representing oneself might be thought of as an objectification of self—providing an audience with signifiers of oneself. An individual may be said to improvise this act based on the cultural material available in the setting. In any given setting, there are, of course, multiple significations, multiple interpretations, and multiple acts of meaning.

Summarizing Situated Identity

There are five propositions to carry forward in this discussion of situated identity to conclude this section. First, situated identity is a sense of self that is broader than the older concept of ego identity. The concept of situated identity refers to a self-status that places the older notion of ego identity (from the seminal work of Erikson) in the broader interactional social context of human activity. It is a construct that "combines personal identity with social identity" (Student 2) and is a sense of self incorporating "both the person and the setting the person is in" (Student 4).

Second, the concept of situated identity is more dynamic and culturally situated than the old ego identity construct. It is a construct that accounts for a sense of self that is not a fixed, static entity, but is "affected by where you are, whom you are with, and how these others make you feel" (Student 3). Third, situated identity is not merely the product of an individual's psychosocial developmental history, but also is a function of the legacy of social and cultural practices in which the individual engages with others. It draws on the Vygotskian principle that the experience of a coherent self is "formed through social practice ... [and] ... mediated by what is going on situationally" (Student 1).

Fourth, situated identity is improvisational, a conception that is of great value to teachers and others who want to understand students' behavior based on the personal agency they express as a component of identity. Realizing that young people act in ways that are declarations of identity is a means by which teachers can really know their students, giving them interpretive insight on behavior that may have seemed inexplicable before. As Student 4 writes, "the person is declaring their [sic] role in that social interaction, such as a student in a classroom declaring that they are there to learn"—students are fulfilling motives of being that may be, in that moment, more important to them than motives of academic achievement regardless of whether they are achievers or not.

The fifth and final proposition concerning situated identity is twofold: (a) Situated identity is constituted with both the individual's system of meaning and the meaning systems of the larger cultural group; and (b) situated identity is also one's connection to the meaning system of the wider social and cultural world of the individual. Situated identity implies the individual's composition of self in the broader social world. The dynamics of this latter process is what we turn to next in the section on positionality. In this way, situated identity is distinct from the notion of social identity, in that the latter concept does not imply an individual's active appropriation of the meaning systems in making up practices that define her or him.

POSITIONALITY

Positionality is the next dimension in the developmental trajectory of the situated-mediated identity theory. Positionality is attained when individuals intentionally situate themselves in a particular social setting. Referring back to my Table 2–2 in chapter 2 for a moment, I want to note again the three levels of identity indicated by the rows: Row 1 is situated identity, row 2 is positionality, and row 3 is agency—and each represents a succession in identity development in the situative framework. It is the second row content of positionality that I develop in this section, and the third row content of agency is developed in the next section.

Positionality is very much like a role identity, except that positionality is symbolically represented and socially enacted by the individual in accordance with the specifics of a given social scene. It is fair to say that all role identities are positionalities, but not all positionalities are role identities. In the language of social psychology, positionality is a role identity assumed by, or ascribed to, an individual that may either be factual (e.g., a mother, a female, an accountant) or discursively constructed (e.g., a loudmouth, a busybody, a hypocrisy-hater). Formally defined, positionality is the use to which individuals put the awareness of their operational selves, and how they locate their identity in the immediate social setting. Positionality is the operational awareness of the role identities the individual assumes, the role identities ascribed to the individual, and the significations of self that the individual draws on and projects in the social situation.

Personality Versus Positionality

Traditionally, personality is considered to be a relatively stable pattern of attitudes, responses, dispositions, motives, and so on. This is the psychologists' definition of personality, and as such the perspective is of the individual. This view of personality locates the variability of a person's behavior as a change in the pattern of attributes within that individual. For example, your mental schema of your friend as a person might include a marker of "is really into medical science and technology," which you ascribe to him or her as a relatively stable attribute of his or her personality. You then have the basis for explaining preferences in viewing television programs, selection of reading material at the newsstand, topics of conversation, and so on, based on this interest. So the behavior is interpreted according to a relatively stable set of traits within the individual and variations of behavior might be explained in terms of interest and investment according to situation.

Now, however, suppose that we look at the variability of the situation as our focus, rather than at attributes of individuals, as the source for accounting for differences in their level of motivation in different settings. If we did that, it might be possible to account for more than one attribute of individual interest at a time if we read situations as involving a pattern of any number of individual attributes that come into play. So, for example, we have the basis to predict or explain why our friend would accept an invitation to go to the science museum, but not to the museum of fine arts. What if our friend declines an invitation to accompany us to the science museum? Our explanatory framework or theory of personality has to be more sophisticated than one based on traits that match situations. My situated-mediated theory attributes the variability to the changes in patterns of individuals in situations. So, rather than basing explanations of individual motivation on something emanating from within the individual, I posit that these explanations are more appropriately derived from the situations in which people improvise the version of themselves they desire to put forth. Rather than grounding explanations of human motivation in situations within individuals, my theory grounds the explanations in situations. My theory posits that personality expression is less internally generated than it is situationally improvised. People are different people in different situations, not because different internal factors come to the fore, but because people improvise their being.

Now suppose we look at students' behaviors not just as explainable by the variability of situations, but also by the variability of individuals in situations. That is, suppose we consider the variety of social identities an individual has as based on his or her interaction with others in particular cultural scenes and settings. Now we are talking about positionality. Everyone desires a personal marker in a community of practice. Here a community of practice refers to a social setting for which there is a common enterprise and purpose, along with particular roles. I have stated this principle before—everyone inscribes his or her identity in a well-defined common enclave or new activity setting. This emanates from the "I am here" or the "I matter" primal motive. I have argued for the primacy of this motive based on Maslow's (1970) hierarchy of needs. As soon as humans develop a symbol system and as soon as we are able to reference self to others, we humans are capable of organizing our behavior according to this motive. Ideation of relations of self to others, is the principle meaning-making process for human beings. This cultural cognitive capacity is present in human beings at a very early age and is shaped by primary socialization, a topic to which I return in the next chapter.

The point here is that social scenes[1] invoke identities. Selves are fundamentally subjects of social presentations, with each of these self-presentations hinging on the ongoing strands of face-to-face interaction (Goffman, 1967). In this mediated identity framework I distinguish between ascribed identity and assumed identity.[2] The ascribed situated identity results from the positioning others do of the individual as they enter a given cultural scene, and an assumed situated identity in that scene is the positioning the individual does for himself or herself. According to my framework, positionality is the context of identity experienced and negotiated intentionally by the individual, based on his or her emerging awareness of the social world. In this way, at the meeting place of the individual with society, positionality is identity that is shaped by individuals' understanding and use of symbols of power, status, rank, and sense of privilege in a given social context. D. Holland et al. (1998) indicate that positionality is more than social situativity:

> [Positionality] … has to do with more than division, the "hereness" and "thereness" of people; it is inextricably linked to power, status, and rank. Social position has to do with entitlement to social and material resources and so to the higher deference, respect, and legitimacy accorded those genders, races, ethnic groups, castes, and sexualities privilege by society. (p. 271)

Positionality, therefore, is social situativity that is enacted by the individual operating within the constraints of the social frame.

Certain settings, such as schools, structure ready-made positionalities. For example, by the nature of classrooms, the positionality of the teacher is of one of authority and power. In every instance of a position of power, there is a position of subjugation and perhaps opposition, which are subject positions ready-made for students. However, within these obvious

---

[1] I use here Hymes's (1972) concept of scene or cultural scene, analogous to Goffman's (1959) use of the term *frame*, referring to an identifiable social setting and the set of communicative practices used in the setting, together with participants' senses of the communicative practices used there. Carbaugh's (1996) notion of cultural scene includes a second dimension—a kind of culturescape or the larger system of communication. He writes, "With these two senses, the concept of scene suggests a practical knowledge that is attentive both to a particular situation of communication practice, and to the cultural landscape in which that practice plays a creative part" (p. 16).

[2] This is similar to the distinction offered by Sfard and Prusak for the use of narrative approach to mediated identity, that of authentic identity and designated identity. Although their notion of designated identity is very close in meaning to my ascribed identity, their notion of authentic identity is theoretically problematic for reasons discussed by Côté and Levine (2002) and Harré and van Langenhove (1999). Briefly, the issue is that anything close to an ego identity ideal cannot be totally discursively determined, although they have simplified considerably the range of moves that constitute positioning.

overt subject positions are other possibilities of self-expression within particular contexts and situations. This subtler, finer grained improvisational process of self-definition is what needs to be explored more carefully. For example, consider the two categories of teaching styles or parenting styles that are presented as contrasting styles—authoritarian versus authoritative. Although these might be considered positionalities, there are still many different ways that authoritarian and authoritative parents and teachers can behave. What is of interest to us here are the ways in which identity may be deployed in different ways within the subject position of power as authoritarian, a positionality assumed by display of power and force of will, versus authoritative, a positionality assumed by qualities of social competence and intellectual leadership. I keep stressing the idea that positionalities are expressed in dynamic interplay between individuals because it is central to the situated-mediated identity theory. Right now, however, I would like to turn from positionality as an interpersonal phenomenon to exploring it further as an intrapersonal phenomenon.

Positionality is also the state resulting from one's positioning in a particular episode, frame, or conversation. When a young woman prepares herself for a job interview by attempting to project herself as confident and capable, that is an act of positioning. Similarly, when a high school freshman has to walk down a hall lined with upperclassmen he does not know, he likewise is positioning himself by attempting to appear cool (unruffled) and competent (tough). This type of positioning is also known as *impression management.* A person's positionality can, and does, change according to how others in the social setting behave toward that person. In other words, both the young job applicant and the high school freshman may be repositioned as not capable based on the actions of those they face. The impression they created can either be accepted or challenged. This challenge is known as repositioning—a notion that is further elaborated in the next section on positioning theory, from which the notion is derived.

Positioning Theory

Much of the original conceptualization of positionality we owe to the work of Goffman (1968, 1974, 1981) and the discursive account of human psychology by Harré and Gillet (1994) and Harré and van Langenhove (1999). According to Harré and van Langenhove (1999) the concepts of position and positioning were first introduced by Holloway (1984) in talking about subjectivity in the topic areas of heterosexual relations. She spoke of positioning oneself and taking up positions in the same manner as Harré and van Langenhove, especially the idea that discourses and settings provide positions for individuals to take up. According to these theorists, positioning is to be understood as the discursive construction of personal stories (narratives) and dramaturgical enactments (which I call dramatives) that make a person's actions intelligible, sensible, and relatively determinate as social acts and within which the members of the conversation have specific locations.

Once again, positioning is distinct from the notion of social identity because it requires action and interaction. Positioning is to be understood as the activity motivated to achieve a positionality. Individuals are positioned according to the storyline or script or frame of a particular situation. In a conversation, the storyline is much like the topic or theme that is the compendium of each participant's contribution to the stream. In other forms of close-order symbolic exchanges there may also be storylines. Initial positionings may be challenged and the speaker may thus be repositioned. The speaker may challenge an initial positioning and thereby reposition self. Positionality is situational because it depends on the recognition (by the individual or by others) of a particular role identity (or set of role identities) in given situation. Positioning theory assumes that in any given context, a person's authority, rights, and obligations are determined by particulars of that context. According to positioning theory, a position is:

> a complex cluster of generic personal attributes, structured in various ways, which impinges on the possibilities of interpersonal, intergroup and even intrapersonal action through some assignment of such rights, duties and obligations to an individual as are sustained by the cluster. For example, if someone is positioned as incompetent in a certain field of endeavor they will not be accorded the right to contribute to discussions in that field. (Harré & van Langenhove, 1999, p. 1)

Positionality is also a relational concept—as it may be both ascribed to the individual by others and assumed by the individual as a self-representation. Unlike the concept of social identity, positionality only has meaning in relation to a particular social context or frame. Positionality can be referred to as a role or set of roles that are particular to a social scene or situation:

> Not only what we do but also what we can do restricted by the rights, duties and obligations we acquire, assumed or which are imposed upon us in the concrete social contexts of everyday life. (Harré & van Langenhove, 1999, p. 4)

The concepts of positioning and positionality are adopted for my framework as an activity-based alternative to the more static notion of role identity. I have specifically formulated the concept of positionality from positioning theory (Harré & van Langenhove, 1999) for several reasons that are important to the overall situated-mediated identity theory. As I elaborate presently, the action of positioning is both an expression of self and an act of cultural inquiry[3] on the part of an individual working to fit into the immediate social context.

The adaptation of positioning theory to explaining the mediation of identity is useful here for three reasons. First, it is important to be able to move beyond a conception of selfhood based on static identity roles. People who work with children and youth have to know them, and have a sense of who they are—but not just on the basis of types (e.g., good student or serious student). The working knowledge adults need to be effective working with young people cannot be limited to typology— thinking of a young person as this type of student or that type of student. In fact, the ways in which we know students primarily as types is a trait of unnurturing school environments that yield acts of rebellion and school violence (Canada, 1998; Garbarino, 1999). The tendency to cat- egorize people as types is difficult to overcome. It is essential to move to a deeper understanding of human interaction in school settings and real- ize that children are different people in different contexts and to learn to understand people in relation to the immediate interaction, activity, and conversation in which they are participating.

The positioning theory of Harré and his colleagues is an important foundation of my framework for a second reason—it offers a way of explaining exactly how identity is constructed in a social constructivist framework by grounding it in the human activities that construct—princi- pally, discourse. To advance our understanding of achievement develop- ment, it is no longer sufficient to claim that good students are socially constructed without looking at just what those processes of socially con- structed achievement consist of. It offers a way out of the quandary posed by role-identity theory as discussed earlier—namely, its failure to account for the improvisation of self.

The third application of positioning theory to this situativity frame- work is that it allows for the multiple interpretation of young people's

---

[3]In the tradition of how sociologists do sociograms, an individual does a sociological read— discerning hierarchy by observing the interaction of individuals, forms of address, and order to talk.

behavior in instructional episodes in which proficiency figures into positionality (e.g., a reader response to a child's story), thus increasing the likelihood for a greater depth of meaning in understanding the child's experiential and symbolic worlds. The notion of position avoids the difficulties inherent in the use of the term roles or role identity as discussed previously.

The notion of positioning is an important conceptual tool for analyzing the most ubiquitous social practice among human beings—namely, conversation. Because positioning is a conversational phenomenon, it is necessary to draw on the methodological tradition of narrative analysis, the focus of which is to analyze discourse. Narrative analysis, used by ethnographers and other qualitative researchers, can be quite complex, a level of complexity that is beyond the scope of this work. However, the basics of analyzing discursive patterns in instructional settings are applied. Working with the basics of the situativity framework will require the definition of a few more key terms: (a) the speech act, (b) discursive practices, and (c) episodes or the social frames of positioning activity (including narratives and dramatives) that take place. Each of these is discussed in turn.

The notion of *speech act* comes from Austin's (1961) speech act theory, and was further refined by Searle (1979), Harré and Gillet (1994), and Harré and van Langenhove (1999). The beginning point in speech act theory is viewing conversation as a form of social interaction with a structure that can be systematically identified. The products of conversation are also social, and among these products are interpersonal relations, new relationships, and new positions and roles for individuals within the group. The notion of the speech act is an analytical concept for revealing the structure of conversations. In short, conversations are processed and decoded as a set of structured speech acts. This type and this level of analysis can include nonverbal contributions to the conversation. A speech act may have words as well as gestures and other significations. In any case, a speech act is defined by the social intention of the person who issued it. For example, no speech is necessary for a teacher to summon a student to her desk whose eye she has already caught. Without uttering a word and with the crooking motion of her finger, she can summon the student to her desk. This is a speech act of summoning because both sender and receiver understand the meaning of the communication, and because the act has *perlocutionary force;* that is, it has achieved the result of the student coming up to the teacher's desk. Perlocutionary force is that which is achieved in saying something (e.g., summoning, apologizing, or congratulating). A speech act may also have *illocutionary force*, meaning what is achieved by an utterance, such as embarrassment of a nemesis in a public forum. Those who use discourse analysis as a way of understanding meaning-making practices in social settings (e.g., Erickson, 2004) argue that a conversation unfolds through the joint action of all participants as they make (or attempt to make) their own and each other's actions determinate (Davies & Harré, 1999).

The second conceptual tool from this research tradition is the notion of *discursive practice*. According to the constructionist perspective represented in my mediated identity theory, selfhood is publicly manifested by a variety of discursive practices. These include self-narration, expressing an interest, declaring an intention, decrying the lack of fairness or justice in a situation, and so on. Discursive practice refers to all the ways in which people actively produce social and psychological realities. Discourse is defined as the institutional use of language and language-like sign systems. Discourse can also develop around a specific topic such as race or gender. Discourses can compete with each other and create distinct and contradictory versions of reality. The sense of discourse used here is a conceptual scheme in social theory.

These elements—speech acts and discursive practices (including dramatives and narratives)—are applied in the positioning theory of Harré and van Langenhove (1999) for analyzing the nature of identity mediation in social practices such as conversation and instructional interaction. I have adapted their positioning theory to create the notion of positioning activity—by which I refer to the set of ego-driven behaviors all humans engage in when interacting with others in a social setting or frame. If you doubt the primacy of the human motive to be noticed and be recognized, try being the guest story reader in a primary classroom sometime. In that setting with a new adult present, children see fresh opportunities for recognition and self-expression—as if the new adult presence is a fresh canvas to reflect back their self-projections into the ongoing social world by gaining the attention of the speaker for a few precious moments. Petitioning to get the teacher's ear or the speaker's ear is a form of positioning activity that teachers, if they are worth their salt, develop before the first day of class.

Positioning is discursive practice. Every social group employs any number of different forms of talk to achieve the end of situating oneself in the social setting in a particular way. These may even be ritualized in particular cultural forms such as boasting (woofin' and sounding) among young African American males or toasting at mainstream formal events (Smitherman, 1986). Positioning involves talk and other forms of close-order symbolic exchange (actions I call dramatives). For example, because I am an adult and frequent visitor to a school, there is always a determinative process that reveals my positionality in the school—as to whether I am positioned as a teacher (P1), or simply another adult other than a teacher such as a school visitor (P2). I discursively position myself as P1 when I issue a directive or corrective in the manner of a teacher— for example, "That's not how we leave our desks to line up, is it?" or "Hands to yourself!" Therefore, secondary positioning, although less determined by the initial storyline or set, is claimed by a speech act or other performance. On the other hand, I can position myself as benign adult visitor (P2) in instances where I do not assume the role of a teacher, such as allowing silly play and misbehavior to take place in front of me without saying something to the misbehaving children when no other adult is present. Those of you who work to prepare future teachers will recognize the classic difficulty student teachers have in trying to move from the second (P2) benign adult positionality to the first (P1) "teacherly" positionality as they take over a class.

The act of positioning as symbolic self-representation (dramatization) is a discursive practice that will be extremely useful in later discussion regarding applications, where we turn to interpreting young people and their positioning in school contexts. Young people continuously try to position and reposition each other by declaratives in initial interactions and by ongoing manipulation of the storyline. The concept of positioning allows us to map how individuals are located in symbolic space—within conversations and other social interactions as they project the self they want others to process.

Positioning is discursive practice that involves interaction and contes-tation of meanings among participants in the social setting. Within any interaction between participants in a conversation, each tends to reposition the other while simultaneously positioning himself or herself (Harré & van Langenhove, 1999). Sometimes there is counterpositioning—posi-tioning self in contradistinction to the other. For example, a student who intends to position herself as academically virtuous might ask her class-mate whether he has done his homework. A response that he has not done his homework offers greater illocutionary force to the utterance, "Well, I did mine!" thus positioning the student herself as the good student in contradistinction to the one who does not do his homework. Knowledge of the person (i.e., knowing histories in persons[4]) is part of the operational ability in establishing positionality—the young girl might not have asked the question and accomplished her positioning as "the smarter of the two of us here" without a reasonable assurance of the "no" answer to her homework question to achieve this result of a superior positioning.

Many conversation initiators are apt to be angling for a position right off the bat, typically at the expense of someone else in the group. It turns out that adults and children alike are actively engaged in positioning activity in any social setting. I would argue that in a good meeting or a good class what occurred (among other things) is that most people managed to put their positionality moves on hold for some duration in each setting-holding at bay the motive for self-presentation in the interest of serving other motives (e.g., a satisfying interaction with others, solving a nagging problem, curiosity being satisfied, having fun, etc.). Other psychologists have given voice to this state when there is an ecological convergence of an individual's needs and action (activity). Csikszentmihalyi's (1991) notion of flow is an example.[5]

Narratives constitute discursive practices. I indicated in chapter 2 that a useful way to think of identity as a discursive practice is to think of it as the story people tell themselves about themselves. In chapter 3, I characterized narrativization of self as one of the discursive practices children develop through primary socialization. Even in small children narrating and self-story telling can be seen in their play, even in their solitary play. Story telling and narrativization of self is the primary form of positioning talk. This positioning talk may even be intrapersonal, as the individual revises a recent set of events in an episode more consistent with a favorable concept of self. These rewritings of personal history find their way into narratives people tell others about themselves.

The idea of narrative is important as an aspect of the discursive practices people employ. The forms, contents, and uses of narratives are what make up the discursive practices of any cultural group. In the next chapter, I analyze narratives as the discursive practices that everyone is socialized into at an early age and that are the substrate of an important school-based proficiency, namely literacy. Telling, hearing, and producing narrative are central

---

[4]This conception comes from Holland and Lave, whose work *History in Person*, fortifies the idea that our situativity is historical in multiple senses.

[5]Teachers need to encourage the "flow" of individuals by how they orchestrate the social activity—the practices of engagement in learning settings. An artful aspect of teaching might very well be how to manage an ecology of positionings students engage in.

to children's development and communicative competence (Halliday, 1976; Scollon & Scollon, 1981). What makes narrative an important practice is that its cultural forms are not equally valued in schools.

In U.S. education, there has always been, and continues to be, a widespread bias against the use of narrative as a communicative medium (Cazden & Hymes, 1978) and chapter 5 explores how this impacts cultural identities. Nonetheless, narrative figures importantly in our conceptualizing identities of achievement because it turns out that the ways in which African American (and other linguistic and ethnic minority) students are positioned as less proficient users of language are based on differences in the organization of discourse (Cazden, 1988; Scollon & Scollon, 1981). As mentioned earlier, these discourse patterns and practices are acquired by children through the process of primary socialization—socialization to a set of cultural values that become the basis of an individual's identity (Scollon & Scollon, 1981). These patterns and practices—constituting a discourse system—are acquired very early in life, and many of them are probably learned before the child speaks any words (Goodwin, 1991; Halliday, 1976). This system is acquired through a long, highly involved, interactive process of primary socialization and communication with caregivers. This system is unconscious, affects all communication, and is closely tied to an individual's identity (Scollon & Scollon, 1981).

The third key conceptualization is the notion of episode, referring to the chunk of time containing the exchanges and interactions that have social meaning. Episodes can be defined as "any sequence of happenings in which human beings engage which have some principle of unity" (Harré & Secord, 1972, p. 10). The behavior of individuals in an episode is governed in part by rules, but also in part by the positionality of individuals. That is to say, the biographical backgrounds of the people participating and the legacy of what has already been said in that episode determine, along with the rules (discursive codes), what gets said and how it gets said. As Harré and van Langenhove (1999) point out, any episode may include meanings that cannot be understood by referring only to general rules and roles. There are histories in persons (Holland & Lave, 2001) where individuals carry insights and dispositions from past experiences into the current conversations that matter in the interpretation of their performance and sense-making activity in social scenes.

Positioning theory aims to understand the dynamics of symbolic self-representation in particular social episodes. As noted earlier, there is already a substantial sociological literature aiming to understand the interactions between individuals and the social environment in which they operate based on an analysis of episodes. Goffman's work in particular has contributed much to the understanding of interactions between people acting in different roles (e.g., between teacher and student, patient and doctor, etc.). However, as we embark on social and cultural terrains that are diverse in what assumptions, forms of talk, ways of thinking, and so on, are in play in the mediation of interaction, it is important to be able to consider forms not circumscribed by traditional roles. Harré and van Langenhove (1999) provide three aspects of the mediated interactions as people symbolize themselves in social scenes. These include (a) the moral positions of participants in an episode and their rights and duties to say certain things; (b) the conversational history—the content that has preceded—of things already said, and (c) the impactfulness of the actual elocution—the power of the speech to shape aspects of the social world. Harré and van Langenhove (1999) apply these features to the interpretation of the psychic phenomena of an episode, as we see in the situated-mediated framework. These aspects of positioning theory can be taken as a conceptual and methodological framework.

Positionality and Status

The notion of positionality is similar to, but not quite the same as, what is typically meant by the term status. *Status* is an indicator of real or imagined regard of an individual within a group. It does not involve the enactment of roles and performance, as does the concept of positionality. Think of positionality as status given action based on how individuals read themselves into a social setting. Status membership in school settings is the sort of positionality determined by competence (or perceived competence) in the cultural scene or frame. Hence, positionality is partly determined by the set of competencies and personal values that are in play in a given social scene or episode. As we have discussed in chapter 3, humans have an uncanny capacity to relegate others to a status role or positionality in collective settings. We often seize the opportunity when the conversation turns to an area in which we have a particular expertise or knowledge to position ourselves as knowledgeable and worthy of elevated status in the group—if for only those few moments in the episode. This dynamic occurs despite our better selves because we all have the primary motive powered by the need for ego projection. This dynamic of self-positioning and repositioning by others recurs countless times among young people, as well as adults, who convene in their affinity or affiliation groups. Who is considered popular in an adolescent enclave, for example, is largely a matter of what individuals influence in the group in terms of their discursive ability. Who is considered the good teacher on a school faculty is a positionality ascribed by fellow teachers according to whatever the criteria for good teaching are in that given school setting. The positioning of others is therefore an important aspect of my situated-mediated identity framework that exposes how the unseemly side of human motivation enters into social settings. What I want to bring into consideration is teacher awareness of how they position students and their motivation, both conscious and unconscious. I take up this topic at length in chapter 7. I now turn to the third and final component of the identity trajectory in the framework—agency.

AGENCY

To begin this section on agency let us consider why people are motivated to assume certain positionalities and avoid others. People are motivated by, among other things, the need to feel that they belong, that they are loved and valued, that they are safe, and that they are respected. The renowned humanistic psychologist Maslow (1970) articulated these needs in the now classic formulation of the hierarchy of needs discussed earlier, usually depicted in a pyramid with the most basic needs (survival needs) at the bottom, and the most abstracted and symbolic needs (actualization) at the top. Agency entails the symbolic needs at the top of the hierarchy. Agency is a symbolization of self that is based more on what Maslow termed self-actualization, and less on self-valorization.

The theme of humanization and care is well received among audiences of urban educators who work specifically with African American children and youth. It is this theme that is at the core of what I mean by agency. Freire (1970), the Brazilian educator, articulated this idea as critical consciousness in his classic book *Pedagogy of the Oppressed*. His pedagogy is one of agency, because agency is a means for contesting all forms of subjugation and domination (Murrell, 1997). For Freire, the role of the educator is to find ways to interrupt the hegemony (e.g., racial stigma) and subordination in the classroom and society by facilitating the development of intellectual and social practices of critical thought, critical literacy, and analysis. He advocated that people's inherent ability to apprehend the oppressive dynamics of their own experience (the ability to read the world) was the basis for their critical literacy (the ability to read the word) and was agentive by exercising both as critical consciousness.

Freire believed that countering subjugation, whether in U.S. public schools or among the peasantry of Brazil, must be a process of humanization—a form of human interaction that affirms and develops key elements of becoming whole as a human being. These include critical consciousness of one's self, one's historicity, and the broader world. It also required a process of understanding power relations in the everyday, lived experiences of self and others, as well as providing the intellectual tools for changing the dynamics of those power relationships. This kind of active critical consciousness is precisely what I mean by agency. Recall that the identity in this framework is defined as one's agency in activity. Recall also that the framework focuses attention not only on the identity dynamics of learners, but also those of the adults working with them. Teachers, aides, and any other adult participants in the discursive events with learners that take place in school, whether these are conversations or instructional interactions, can have greater or lesser agency in those events. If adults have little or no agency themselves, they are unlikely to promote the development of agency among children.

Role status and positionality concepts are implicated in agency. A person who has developed agency is able to determine his or her own positionality and resist the repositioning attempts of others. If you have ever been to a meeting where someone has been volunteered to be the minutes taker by virtue of having a pen and pad at the ready, you have witnessed a positioning of one person by another. The ascribed role of minutes taker resulting from this positioning by another might be resisted by a person with a more developed sense of agency. Agency is therefore a capacity of resisting the undesired repositioning attempts of others as well as the capacity to situate one's own desired identity. I hasten to note that an agentive positionality is not merely one of resisting the repositionings of others, but rather an agentive person exercises choice. In this case, the agentive person may willingly accede to the assignment but name the frame by saying something like, "Oh, so you want to elect me as scribe merely because I came equipped! That's fine. I'll do it this time, but next time someone else can take a turn."

I have said that students developing positionality is a matter of developing greater voice and more skills in social practices for representing and expressing themselves. I have also said that the typical ways that school life is organized work against students' ability "to use language to paint a picture of" their "own reality" (Wink, 1997, p. 58) and experience. For Freire and critical theorists (e.g., Giroux, 1997, 2001), the teacher's primary task is one of rebalancing the discursive power arrangements between teacher and student in the classroom through social and intellectual practices in which "students learn the knowledge and skills necessary to live in a critical democracy" (Giroux & McLaren, 1986, p. 224). In short, the teacher facilitates the development of students' positionality to a point of agency. That is the point at which students not only recognize how situations and conditions diminish their dignity and integrity as human beings, but also exercise their awareness to counter that experience. For the critical theorist, the role of the teacher is to understand, recognize, validate, and respect students' individuality, especially in light of the ideological dimensions of their cultural location as members of subordinate groups in society. This aim is well and good, but one could argue that there are many more relationships than those that exist between the teacher and the student. I submit that the most damaging and oppressive social experiences inhere in the everyday social life of the school, not just in the student—teacher relationship. This is my jumping off point in proposing the notions of positionality and agency.

SUMMARY AND CONCLUSIONS

In this chapter I elaborated on the three developmental statuses of identity based on a social constructivist framework. These were situated identity, positionality, and agency. I argued that rather than being a static entity, selfhood is publicly manifested by a variety of discursive practices that include such things as self-narration, expressing an interest, declaring an intention, decrying the lack of fairness or justice in a situation, or forms of address. I also argued that there is no single one good identity for school achievement and proscholastic decision making such as the school kid identity proposed by Flores-Gonzáles (2002) based on her application of role-identity theory. In contrast, the discussion showed how identity is nuanced not so much by place as by practices and positionality, both of which are situationally determined by the particular contextualized social frames (Goffman would call these stagings). Particular and predictable kinds of social episodes are what structure young people's experience in schools, not an ongoing status of smart kid, school kid, street kid, oppositional kid, and so on. These identity stances, or positionalities, depend on the dynamics of the social episode, and positioning theory was applied as the theory to explain how they are determined.

5

Communities of Achievement as Culturally Configured Worlds

The formal task of schools is to promote the development of discourse competencies, word meaning, and conceptual structures in a variety of content areas. This development requires shared activity in which the concepts take on meaning by creating an interface between "schooled" concepts and those of everyday experience. The student thus develops the capacity of using academic verbal thought for the solution of practical problems of the experienced world. *This appropriation of the academic languages of school is the basic process by which a student becomes an educated person.*

—Tharp et al. (2000, p. 22, italics added)

Just as our students may develop identities of achievement, so may the social communities for learning that we create for them. Schools are places containing a variety of cultural forms in various social settings in which children interact with each other and with adults. The social settings vary in terms of physical location, social structure, and sociocultural patterns of communication. Physical locations—such as classrooms, schoolyards, hallways, cloakrooms, and lunchrooms—are the spaces in which particular types of human exchanges take place. The cultural forms are also varied as they are enacted in human exchanges. These exchanges constitute a myriad of possible cultural forms—of communicative styles, values, interests, and motivation. Human exchanges take place in activity settings—hanging out, playing a game, or working together in a learning center.

The social life in school is constituted by a variety of cultural forms that collectively can either nourish or suffocate the development of identities of achievement. There may be settings that are unsupportive of, and even destructive to, the development of children on the margins of the social scene. Moreover, many of these private social spaces are constructed by children themselves, away from the supervising eyes of adults, and can be quite inhospitable to an unfortunate recipient of censure by the immediate peer group. As we have seen in the work of Van Ausdale and Feagin (2002) and others discussed in chapter 1, the social environments children create on their own unmediated by adults can sometimes produce injurious consequences for the children of color in the group despite the best intentions of the adult teachers and caretakers. Similarly, high schools are also public spaces that may contain toxic social environments for healthy identity formation. The developmental tasks of identity formation for adolescents are made more difficult by the varied and conflicted social environments of school culture.

It matters little how much we minister to the healthy social and cultural development of individuals unless we devote equal care to the healthy social development of the peer group environment that individuals create together. The purpose of the situated-mediated identity I offer in this volume is to provide a systematic way of understanding this development as the codevelopment of individual and collective identity. The question considered in this chapter is this: How do we create socially and culturally sound collective identities of the social group such that it nurtures individual identities for all of its members? Recall that the last chapter explained the first strand of the situated-mediated identity framework constituted by the three developmental dimensions of identity—situated identity, positionality, and agency—the first column of the 3 x 3 matrix of Table 2–2 depicting the entire conceptual framework of situated-mediated identity theory. I argued that the dimensions constitute a progression of three stages of the developmental tasks adolescents grapple with as they are making sense of themselves as academic achievers, cultural beings, and worthy citizens in a multicultural democracy.

This chapter moves our explanation to the middle column of that matrix to explain the processes of this mediated identity as they operate in each of the three types of social contexts-sociocultural community, social-symbolic community (figured world), and community of practice. Using the framework I address this question: How do we create these collective identities in ways that nurture individual identities? The situated-mediated identity framework lays the theoretical groundwork for articulating how the codevelopment of identities of achievement for teachers as well as learners mediates scholastic achievement and personal development of young people. The framework allows an analysis of persons-in-context as well as consideration of the cultural and historical grounding of practices relevant to the people, school, and community where building enabled and enabling communities is desired.

We begin with the proposition that social and cultural context shapes the forms of human interaction. The social and cultural practices a given community takes on determine, at least in part, the range of roles and positions that participating members can assume. So, for example, if we want children to be respectful and caring toward each other, those behaviors need to be visible, available, and accessible to them as social forms and cultural practices of their social world in school. If we want adolescents to think deeply and critically about ethical issues and problems, then this also must be a commonly valued and enacted set of practices in school settings.

Throughout the following discussion, therefore, I pay particular attention to the cultural practices important to creating social environments that enable achievement identities through the socializing power of community. I also illustrate some of the conceptual tools and practices for a cultural reconfiguration of the social environments within schools to promote development and achievement of all children. This discussion is organized into three sections according to the three types of social context represented in the middle column of Table 2–2, which summarizes the overall situated-mediated identity framework. According to the theoretical framework, the social-cultural community, the social-symbolic community, and the community of practice constitute three degrees of the integrity and coherence of a community's meaning systems with respect to shaping identities of achievement.

SOCIAL-CULTURAL COMMUNITY

Let me introduce the concept of the social-cultural community by starting with this question: What kind of cultural community do we need to enable the development of achievers and caring human beings? When I ask this question of urban educators working in inner-city schools, their first response is typically in terms of what they see are essentials in getting control of the classroom environment. Among the first responses are things like consistent rules, school code of conduct, and clear expectations for comportment and behavior. School leadership should be explicit about setting the codes of conduct and comportment expectations, just as a society sets out laws governing the terms of the civic covenant. Laws and codes alone, however, do not make a society or a community. Although teachers create a functional classroom community by setting classroom rules, codes of conduct, and behavior expectations explicitly, these only scratch the surface of all the social forms that shape roles and conduct in a school community. Other ways this is done in schools include developing a school mission statement, credo, or creed. However, cultural communities do implicitly what institutions and society do explicitly—they communicate roles and behavior expectations through other means, especially by example, experience, and by having all of its members participating in practice. What is of interest to us here is the implicit means by which expectations, role opportunities, and practices are communicated through the meaning systems in a cultural community.

According to my framework, teachers should be working toward creating a rich cultural community of practice in classroom settings for their students that involve the common practices of civility, care, and achievement. This requires an understanding of the existing and potential symbolic and cultural resources available for children to develop these capacities and become knowledgeable, culturally aware, and critically analytic adults. However, building such communities is difficult and takes time. Creating them requires considerable attention to the social practices, the meaning systems, the enacted values, and the forms of participation available to children, youth, and adults. In other words, educators must first have a working understanding of their work environment as a social cultural community before they can determine which meaning systems and practices will best promote development of their students.

Qualities and Features of Achiever Communities

I continue this discussion with an articulation of some features of achiever communities, along with some of the conceptual tools for this work. The work requires cultural practices inquiry—the practices of deeply reading the social and cultural landscape for creating achiever communities in school settings. For adults working with other adults in the school setting, this work might include case-by-case analysis of confrontations, issues, and problems concerning racism and racialized practice in the school (Pollock, 2004). This effort might also, in rare cases, include a systematic appraisal of the discourses and ideologies of racism that may impact the way members of the school community organize schooling experience. These kinds of reflective and collective examinations of race are among those necessary tasks in which the school adults need to engage if they are to refigure the social and cultural world of achievement in a school.

Ideally, the systematic interrogation of race would be a shared effort among teachers, parents, and other professionals in a school—to collaborate and to attenuate the social forces in the social and cultural life of the school that would otherwise inhibit healthy identity formation and agency development of children. Among the cultural factors to be examined and attenuated are racism, sexism, and antidemocratic practices that always factor into the social dynamic in diverse settings. Among the social practices to be considered are impression management and meaning making, both of which are elaborated on presently.

Another dimension of a coherent, integrated community is a clear indication of the talents, practices, roles, and behaviors valued by that community. An achiever community offers multiple and varied opportunities for young people to acquire those talents, roles, and abilities through practice—the practical experience of learners plying new knowledge and skill in the company of more experienced others in a form of learning Tharp and Gallimore (1988) call assisted performance. Hence the task in creating an achiever learning community is arranging activity for the productive and purposeful collaboration of learners as engaged participants. These are the requirements for creating a community of practice (Wenger, 1998): the arrangement of the joint productive activity, the assurance that all members are engaged and participating, an acknowledgment of the relationship between the activity and identity, and most important, the children having the opportunity to grow into a rich intellectual life composed of practices of learning, cooperating, and being.

In this framework, knowledge of the content and skills in the use of knowledge get nailed down in productive action (Murrell, 2001; Tharp & Gallimore, 1991; Vygotsky, 1978). Children become what Lave and Wenger (1991) termed *legitimate peripheral participants* in the intellectual worlds defined in part by the subject matter they have yet to master. Learning achievement requires that students participate in the academic practices and hear the conceptual discourses that constitute the formal curriculum. According to the framework, learning achievement and scholastic advancement are measured in terms of learners' increasing participation in rich intellectual and social practices.

This increasing engagement and participation in the practices and discourses of school are what I have termed *secondary socialization.* Secondary socialization cannot proceed without activity—without students doing things together. They must be working and producing together for the full range of achiever practices—including those that promote the development of skill, social competence, and agency—to be acquired by all children in the setting. This is why engagement and participation of students is so critical as a pedagogical goal of teaching. Eliciting the engagement and participation of students in the classroom is the primary job of every teacher worth his or her salt. It is a necessary, although not necessarily sufficient, condition for genuine learning achievement to take place. Patterns of learning may inadvertently be created that degrade achievement and decrease productive participation of learners—such as when the destructive effects of interpersonal competition, labeling, and forms of exclusion extant in the broader social world of adults leach into the social fabric of the classroom.

Achiever communities of learning are organized as settings of productive, purposeful, and conjoint activity so that they result in the acquisition of practices. Why must the activity setting be purposeful? The major part of motivation for doing an instructional task inheres in its meaning and purpose. What student wants to do meaningless and purposeless things? Those of you who teach know well how students register this concern in the kinds of questions they sometimes ask to irritate you and push your buttons, but that are nonetheless commentaries on the meaning and purpose of what happens instructionally. Some of these include "Why do we have to learn this?" or (on entering the classroom) "Are we going to do anything today?" or "When are we ever going to have to do that in adult life?" Although these are questions that often are designed more to provoke rather than inquire, they do effectively question the manifest value of the things you ask students to do. The accomplished teacher is able to communicate the value of an instructional task or product, and to do so in terms that go beyond merely eliciting the compliance of learners. For example, the algebra teacher who is able to offer a convincing example of when the ability to solve a quadratic equation will be useful in adult life will have made this critical connection between subject matter and student identity. One particularly significant discursive practice for this is called the instructional conversation—a purposely created discursive opportunity for talk regarding the ongoing purposeful activity in the learning setting (Center for Research on Education, Diversity and Excellence, 2002). This discursive form is relevant here because of the emphasis on creating this deeper sense of meaning during instruction, and the fact that its purpose (producing understanding) is immediately manifest in its use.

Why must the conjoint activity of a caring learning community be productive? The creation of a new understanding, new skill, or other learning achievement is, ostensibly, the aim of human learning. Too often, however, the emblem of learning achievement is reduced to symbol—such as a grade or a score on an achievement test. The problem is that the value of a new knowledge or skill inheres in its use, not in its measurement. Learning of value occurs when a new skill, proficiency, or use of knowledge becomes a part of the learner's repertoire of practice—something he or she employs on a regular basis to gain new knowledge, proficiency, and skill. Learning of value is realized when it produces something—enables a set of skills for further inquiry or benefits the learner in achieving some goal. Every instructional activity should have a manifest purpose or aim from the perspective of the learner that relates to some achievement of new knowledge, skill, or curiosity satisfaction. This is the common motivation—the shared motivation of a joint goal that binds all participants (learners) in a context of purposeful doing. This makes it possible to apply the Vygotskian notion of a zone of proximal development in a setting of multiple recipients. Assisted performance is available to all learners in a setting because they can provide it to each other, in addition to that from the teacher. Providing assistance to learners in the act of learning is the essence of powerful teaching.

Activity as shared action that is productive, purposeful, and meaningful is a core concept in the situated identity framework—a notion grounded in the sociocultural theory of Vygotsky and others (e.g., Cole & Engeström, 1993; Cole, Engeström, & Vasquez, 1997; Vygotsky, 1978; Wertsch, 1985) and cultural-historical activity theory (Chaiklin et al., 1999; Leont'ev, 1978, 1981). According to this body of theory, the effort and achievement of individuals are inseparable from the kinds of activities in which they are engaged and the cultural and social environments of which they are a part. In this view, school proficiencies such as those in literacy and numeracy can be seen as cultural inventions, and specific mathematical or literacy skills can be seen as cultural tools. Thinking, according to this view, involves learning to use both symbolic cultural tools and material tools in ways that are specific to their use (Rogoff, 2003; Rogoff & Lave, 1984)—in the knowledge domain (e.g., mathematics, language arts) and the social domain (e.g., the classroom). Situated identity mediates individuals' effort and achievement in both domains simultaneously.

Application of situated identity framework means paying attention to identity positioning of both learners and teachers together, simultaneously.

So applied, it becomes an action theory for the development of learning communities. A familiar concept from sociocultural theory is the zone of proximal development, which refers to the area of student learning in conjoint activity with teachers and more accomplished peers. Thinking, reasoning, and problem solving are acquired when learners are able to engage with others in common activity requiring complex thinking and making use of the cultural tools of thought—such as in instructional conversation, mentioned earlier. Given that symbolic interactions between individuals in the cultural scene are critical to their advanced cognitive and academic development, it behooves educators to understand, in as rich detail as possible, how the learner is constructed as a learner in the myriad of zones of proximal development that constitute the actual curriculum in schools. It is equally important for educators to realize how they are constructed as teachers in specific contexts of instruction. Situated identity theory provides the interpretive framework to analyze how learners and interlocutors mutually constitute their roles and function in a teaching and learning interaction. The processes by which the positionality of teacher and learner is mutually constituted in a zone of proximal development—such as an instructional conversation—is an important dimension to understanding the school achievement of ethnic and racial minority students.

Democratic Values and Cultural Practices

Let us turn now to the quality or content of the cultural and social practices of a social cultural community. Although determining this content should rightfully be the prerogative of the community as a democratic process, I argue that democratic practices should be at the core of community development both in and outside school. It happens that, in the United States at least, democracy and democratic practices are espoused as core values in the curriculum, even while the infrastructure of U.S. democratic life is eroding (Putnam, 2001). How do students come to understand that what we teach them is valuable? How do they come to value democracy as a good idea? Good ideas are only good if they enable some human aims in practice. The vibrancy and currency of an idea depends on practice—its use as a conceptual tool to accomplish a valued, shared aim. An enabled and enabling community keeps ideas vibrant and vital through shared practice.

There is a literature on the practices of participatory or deliberative democracy (e.g., Dewey, 1933; Fung, 2004; Polletta, 2002) that is useful for considering how to build the development of civic values in school communities. I do not pursue this theory in detail here other than to say that it deserves serious consideration by adults concerned about creating vital learning communities in schools. Critical democracy and participatory democracy are important meaning systems using the democratic idea for challenging the structured inequality in organizations, institutions, and communities and promoting the highest forms of civic thought.

Schools are more than shared spaces with common activities of teaching and learning. They can be seen, if we look carefully enough, as social-cultural communities—each with its own variety of routines, rituals, customs, and practices. One cannot create a democratic classroom or school community without including democratic practices as part of the social life of the classroom. Similarly, one cannot expect social justice as a value in classrooms that are not engaged in social practices of justice and fairness. The meaning of democracy and social justice inheres in how they are enacted in the social practices and the everyday exchanges of people in a shared public space. The attention that adults devote to the democratic social and cultural practices in their schools is an indicator of the quality of such a social-cultural community as a learning environment. The set of cultural practices of that community varies in the degree to which it engenders critical-democratic awareness, character-building capacity, and scholastic skill development among all members of the community. What set of cultural practices constitute an achiever community, and how do they enable the development of all children into achievers and caring human beings?

Traditionally, this has been a core question of educational philosophy. The perspective of participatory democracy stated earlier is contained in the legacy of the work of U.S. philosopher John Dewey, but I do not pursue a philosophical extension of his work here. Rather, let me take the path that pragmatist Dewey would approve—that of concentrating on the actions and activities of a community that develop the civic and democratic capacities of the members of that community. Let us consider next the nature of the secondary socialization of democratic practices that are necessary for creating schools and classrooms as organic social entities with a social coherence, collective identity, and sense of "we-ness."

Illustrating Democracy-Oriented Cultural Practices

A community (school or classroom) has identity coherence by virtue of the degree to which it has shared systems of meaning—including symbols, core values, ideologies, images, and so on. My claim is that communities may even have multiple identities depending on who is doing what to whom for what purposes. Communities often have internal identity struggles having to do with the conflicting value systems and meaning systems among its members. Consider that, for any given conflict or dilemma, not everyone will agree on what is fair and what is just. Both examples of democratically focused school practices considered here are taken from the PBS *Frontline* documentary entitled "School Colors," which chronicles the experience of a group of students trained to do video journalism on the topic of racial and ethnic identity over the course of the school year. Let us consider two community-wide conflicts relating to democracy practices. One is the conflict between ethnic minority students' right to strident expressions of ethnic-racial pride in the special assemblies created for that purpose on the one hand, and on the other hand White students' feelings of being attacked and painted as the bad guys. The other issue concerns representation through the school newspaper. Let's look at each in turn.

The focal event in the first case is a school assembly that subsequently precipitated a number of postassembly classroom discussions about race. The assembly, sponsored by the Chicano/a Latino/a student groups on campus, seemed to have a very anti-European and anticolonial message. Here is an excerpt from one of the addresses by a young woman:

> We didn't call you over. You came to us and invaded our life without our authorization. Gave us chicken pox, measles, smallpox and flu. What is that? We never heard of it. But of course you civilized people were so compassionate and understanding that you gave us the definitions of these terms for the mere price of, oh, our women, our religion, our gold and treasure, our culture, our language, and why go on? After all, it *was* a good deal. But this was such a good deal that it just wasn't enough for your enormous egos. You had to bring African slaves down with you and force them to do the dirty work for you [the speaker pauses to cheers and applause from the audience as scene ends].

The tone of this discourse suggests a positionality that corresponds to what racial identity theorists characterize as the immersion stage of ethnic or racial identity development (e.g., Cross, 1991; Helms, 1993; Phinney, 1989). Generalized anger is one of the manifestations of individuals in this stage of identity development. In this stage the person is angry at Whites because of their role in racial oppression, and perhaps angry at himself or herself for being in the apparent role of victim. An individual in this stage also exclusively identifies with his or her own ethnic, racial, or cultural group and bases self-projection heavily from this identification. I call this *ethnicity identity assertion* (EIA) positionality, consisting of very overt demonstrations of racial pride and a demonization of the White power structure. This would seem to characterize the positionality of the speaker in the preceding excerpt.

The next scene that follows is a postassembly classroom discussion where White students express their feeling of having been targeted as the bad guys. In the scene following the assembly we see the football coach teaching what appears to be a ninth-grade health class. He began the discussion about the assembly by asking, "Overall, do you think the assembly was a success?" The first student to speak is an African American girl answering the teacher's prompt:

> Yes! I think it was a success because it caught my attention because it really talked about how the lives of the American Indians and all of those people ... the Mayans and different kinds of Indians ... how they really had a life and how the Europeans took it away from them. It is kind of the same way for African Americans. So it really caught my attention.

Not having the generalized positionality or subject position of a White American, this African American girl did not express any feeling of being victimized but rather identified with the message of historical victimization and oppression. Moreover, it is quite possible her remarks come from an EIA positionality because she identifies with the Native Americans' victimization from the subject position of a Black person. This contrasted with the comments of White students, who began expressing their sense of being attacked, as indicated in these remarks by a White male in the class:

> There were people going on and they didn't really pick a subject. Then they start beating the White person ... the White man because like a, like a figure, a symbol, of something ... a symbol of oppression and I don't think that's necessarily fair. Maybe people in power in Europe or kings and queens maybe or maybe the traders were bad and exploited people. But I don't think the majority of White people were bad. And I don't think that the majority of White immigrants should be blamed for something that some people did. I mean, did the majority of people own slaves in the United States? Was it really the majority that did that? Maybe some people and they were wrong but don't think everyone should be labeled for that.

In this discourse that ranges from immigrants to kings and queens to slave traders, we see an articulation and defense of Whiteness. The excerpt suggests that this White student identifies with being White. Following this, the teacher conducting the discussion emitted a speech act that established solidarity with the White students by saying:

Berkeley High historically has sort of ... and I am certainly not in agreement with this ... has a history of bashing White people, the Caucasian people in these assemblies. I am very proud of who I am, proud to be Samoan and a Polynesian. But I felt ... my heart kind of ached for White people.

The other conflict concerns the representation and membership on the school newspaper, the *Jacket*. On one hand is an organization of ethnic minority students, concerned with their lack of representation on the school paper, that ultimately petitioned to have a special page of the paper set aside for them each issue. On the other hand are mostly White and mainstream staff members that feel that this proposal is an infringement of their authority to determine policy of the paper as members of the staff. A young man who appears to be leading the staff meeting described the resolution that was made with the student organization as a matter of a new policy approach:

One thing that we have started now is that we have been talking to *La Raza Unida* in light of some of the things that have happened with the last issue where the page with the articles that were important to them got omitted and one good thing that has come out of the conversation is that they have agreed to do a page in the *Jacket* for every issue in which they would write articles covering things from their per- spective and maybe have some stuff in Spanish to bring in more readership and ... represent the student body more so they are, in fact doing a page for this coming issue and hopefully [interruption by a girl's voice interjecting the question "For *this* coming issue"?]. Yes for this coming issue ... if we could get more student groups to ... uh ... contribute to the paper and get more people involved so that we can be a better newspaper. So we are trying to do that.

One young woman staff member expressed the concern that many in the room visibly shared:

I wanted to know like, who made the decision that we're going to have this page every single time? I was wondering did they make it or did we make it and whether it is their right to have it ... because it should be like, what we want to do. And I'm not denying that we should have the right for us to have the page but I don't think anybody on staff was asked, "Do we want to do this?"

The young man leader at the meeting (somewhat defensively) responded with:

Our purpose as a paper is to represent Berkeley High School and to get everyone to feel that the student newspaper is the *student* newspaper. And I think, especially in light of how past efforts [at better representation] have not worked at all that this is the most promising way I have seen in a long time. And since it is working I don't see why we should get bogged down in questions of policy.

Even though, on the surface, the issue breaks down as one of the integrity of staff membership versus representation of other groups, we know that much more is going on in terms of the racial and political positionalities of students and staff. It is these "goings on" that it is our responsibility to understand and mediate. The student leading the meeting was especially eloquent in expressing democratic values regarding the role and function of the newspaper—favoring representation over membership—by drawing on themes of social justice and the greater good of representation of underrepresented people over people's need to restrict the membership of the newspaper staff. An instance of the democratic cultural practices I have been arguing for would have been for some adult to acknowledge the democratic values expressed by the young man, as well as his courage to articulate it in the face of opposition from his peers.

From these two vignettes we see that there are at least two issues of collective identity that particularly plague diverse learning communities like Berkeley High School that could potentially subvert the socialization of democratic practices. One of these is the conflict of core values and the meaning systems in play in public schools that derive from the fact that many of the adults in the building tacitly (and sometimes explicitly) hold to an assumption of white privilege and Black inferiority (Loury, 2002; Steele, 1997, 2004; Tatum, 1997). For reasons I discussed in chapter 1, people typically are not as ready to recognize and acknowledge the messages of inferiority and threats to self-integrity that are ongoing and ubiquitous for children of color (especially Black children and youth) as they are to address the discomfort of Whites at the expression and self-assertion of ethnic and racial pride. The documentary suggested that, at least at that time in 1994, the high school was a community not quite ready to read these "over the top" assemblies as legitimate expressions of the critical identity work in which young people of different ethnic and racial groups must engage.

I argue that the reason for the school's underpreparedness is the assumption of White privilege and Black inferiority as two meaning systems tacitly operating for White people below the surface of their awareness. In my framework these are the positionalities of GAWP and GRS, respectively, as described in chapter 4. More will be said later about how a community combats this implicit assumption. First, let me state the other identity issue of urban schools is the diffusion of meaning. The documentary suggests the potential of a school community where the leadership struggles to make explicit all of the values and meaning systems (especially GAWP positionality, GRS positionality, and EIA positionality) that are in play in the various settings in the shared public life of the community. For example, it is one thing to permit free, open, and public expression of ethnic pride in the form of assemblies with ethnic-pride themes, but it becomes a challenge when every ethnic group represented in the school begins to petition for the same opportunity. The school did not yet have the means to decide the balance points between this pressure from ethnic minority groups and the impact on the relationships among its mostly White members.

I argue that this problem in the vignette from Berkeley High is common and widespread among public schools in the United States and that the problem is one of collective identity. A community that has no clear sense of identity (e.g., We are a democratic, multicultural, and multiethnic school) leads to a lack of purpose, instructional focus, and capacity to build community. The absence of these aspects of collective identity—shared purpose, intentional focus, and dedication to building a just and caring community—are particularly detrimental to the educational fortunes of African American children and other children of color in urban school contexts laboring within pedagogies of poverty. The tacit assumption of White privilege and Black inferiority is a serious detriment for building an enabling community, but the diffusion of meaning can compound the problem because school communities with no manifestly or deliberatively shared value system (e.g., a commitment to social justice) are much less likely to scrutinize their unexamined racialized practices, assumptions of privilege, and ideologies of exclusion. Without a critical perspective on race, for example, a school community is just as likely to adopt a commonsense or color-blind approach to complex racially and culturally defined conflict—one that merely reproduces and reinforces popular cultural values and assumptions of U.S. consumer culture. This is the same popular culture that permits (some would say reinforces) assumptions of White male privilege and superiority, racism, sexism, and other forms of symbolic violence.

My concern with urban schools in this analysis is that they too often are settings lacking a collective meaning and purpose owing to features of extraordinary stress experienced by urban schools, such as teacher turnover and fewer resources (e.g., Haberman, 1991; Murrell, 1998; Noguera, 2003; Payne & Kaba, 2001). When communities of practice (whether of learners, teachers, or insurance claims adjustors) lose or fail to develop shared meaning, lose focus, and lose momentum, the process can be seen as a measure of a process of identity diffusion for the organization. The collective identity counterparts to the individual's existential question, "Who am I?" are the questions, "What do we stand for? What are we about? What are we doing this for?" In both the individual and the organizational case, inability to answer these questions spells trouble for the social integrity of the group. Resolving conflicts in collective values of the group requires a collective process of sense making of the type that Freire (1970) termed conscientization. In developing the situated-mediated identity framework I draw on the critical sense-making practices articulated by Freire and the democratic engagement practices of Dewey. These particular kinds of cultural practices of critical democratic inquiry—both inherited and invented—leading to civic consciousness and critical awareness are considered next.

Sense Making as a Cultural Practice

Sense making is an essential cultural practice for both individuals and collectives, particularly when there are unexamined, conflicting, and degrading assumptions and ideologies. I consider sense making a democratic cultural practice in that it entails being clear about what values, ideologies, and positionalities are in play when a community attempts to work through a problem or dilemma. Here I claim sense making as a collective practice in the tradition of critical theory, critical race theory, and epistemology of participatory democracy. One of the reasons why educational innovations in urban schools are not sustainable and transportable to other contexts has to do with the sense-making features of human interaction that determine identity—both of the collective, and of the individuals in the collective (as well as the total constellation of interplays between the individual and collective identity). Instructional innovations fail whenever they overlook the rights, responsibilities, and roles of the community attempting to make sense of "the new." Shared meaning systems are the glue to a social-symbolic community. Most people are generally unaware of the differences in meaning and value systems operating among those with whom they interact in the social environments in which they work—such as schools. Somewhat understandably, they are unaware of their assumed White privilege, for example, and rarely think about how their individual positionalities play out in their actions and interactions, nor are they likely to realize how they are implicated in the persistence of racial privilege in the community as a whole. Most people assume that the same ideals, standards, constraints, and opportunities that exist for them also exist for inner-city families who send their children to school—except that maybe they imagine maybe a few less resources (e.g., fewer books in the home) and a few more constraints.

Do not misunderstand me here regarding the assumption of White privilege and racial superiority. I am not referring here to overt acts of racism such as people walking around spewing racial epithets or telling racist jokes. I am talking here about the everyday biases and cultural myopia that make deep understanding of the issues inaccessible. These are the invisible stances of GAWP positionality and GRS positionality that are enacted in the subtleties of interaction. The cultural practice of sense making is designed to uncover these embedded biases, cultural myopia, and positionalities. Let me provide some examples of the cultural practices of sense making based on the modeling of this practice that I do in my work with teachers in professional development settings, assembled for the specific purpose of developing this deeper understanding. In examining this case, I am also illustrating one of the achievement practices among educators.

The case material that I use in my modeling of sense making was based on an actual event. It is about a millionaire who made the class of second graders in one of the low-performing schools in Cambridge, Massachusetts, an amazing offer—a college education conditional only on their successful completion of high school. In 1991, in front of the 69 second-graders in the auditorium, he tossed each child a football. He told them that their end of the deal was to work hard in school to make it through to high school graduation; if they did that, he would pay for their entire college tuition. The time of this writing was the year that this class would have been graduating from college if they all went through Grades 3 through 12 in the typical time, and finished college in 4 years. The case material was a newspaper article documenting the results (Sacchetti & Jan, 2005).

Of the 69 children, 12 did not attempt college and 16 tried but dropped out. Of the remaining 47 students, 16 completed college or technical school and 25 are still in college. The interesting twist of this case study is not so much the disappointing numbers of students from the second-grade class to actually finish college with the gift of the full tuition. What was interesting about this case is the extent to which people seemed to express surprise at the somewhat disappointing numbers, as if virtually every second grader receiving the offer would be all set and college degrees would virtually be a "done deal" for them. For instance, one teacher who actually taught at the school expressed this naiveté about the importance of social-cultural context by stating, "It's unbelievable with all the help and support these kids were given, that they just couldn't get it together a little more."

The use of this case to examine schools and classrooms and social-cultural communities illustrates the application of sense making to explore the new cultural racism I alluded to in chapter 1. It is not that these educators were speaking or even thinking about the children of color in derogatory terms. Rather, this racism is a matter of limited perspective from culturally mainstream White socialization experience. For example, I think most people from culturally mainstream U.S. backgrounds would assume that the promise of a full-ride college scholarship made to inner-city second graders, if they would but complete high school, should pretty much guarantee access to college and a good life. The mistaken assumption, of course, is that the opportunities for realizing this achievement are basically the same for inner-city youth as for middle- and upper-middle-class children.

Multicultural educator James Banks once termed this kind of cultural naiveté cultural encapsulation. This kind of naiveté speaks directly to the absence of the necessary cultural knowledge for building identities and communities of achievement. It also points to the need for a variety of sense-making practices. The scenario regarding the promise of a full-ride college scholarship, which actually happened, offers an interesting case study regarding this lack of perspective. Interestingly, when I present this article as a case study to audiences of inner-city teachers from large Midwestern school districts at professional development events on educating the Black child, very few of the African American teachers but virtually all of the White teachers shared this naiveté. It is as if the Black teachers, owing to a shared positionality, already understood why some of the cohort struggled and came up short. They revealed an understanding of what the lives and experiences of inner-city children might have been like and how that might have prevented them from achieving graduation. In a sense, they "got it" regarding the social and cultural contexts of urban life and urban schooling. Presenting this case to the audience of White and Black inner-city teachers exposed the points on which the two groups differed in values and meaning systems. Examining these differences was, and always is, a good thing. It is part of the necessary work of building and creating a figured world and a community of practice, which are discussed in the next two sections of this chapter, respectively. However, it is also just the beginning of the work toward building communities of achievement.

White racial and class privilege is one of the U.S. cultural values inscribing the fault line between the African American teachers and the White teachers. It persists as an unexamined, tacit cultural value among White people and is expressed in how they position themselves vis-à-vis people of color. White privilege and class privilege certainly should be the focus of the sense-making educators as they attempt to build communities of achievement. The energy and animation among the mixed group of African American and White teachers is always further elevated when I share a personal anecdote illustrating these phenomena.

The first time I used this case material, I told the audience of educators about a recent experience in the coffee shop, when an individual in front of me struck up a conversation with a person he knew immediately behind me. After a few moments, the fellow in front invited the fellow behind me to come up to his spot in line, as he was about to order so that "they could order at the same time and save time." This was the enactment of privilege. The second fellow came up in front of me, noting my stiff reaction out of the corner of his eye. The first fellow continued chatting, but before I could say anything in protest, the young fellow returned to his place in line behind me before the server took the order. To his credit, he did not partake in this assumption of the positionality of White privilege. He repositioned himself (or perhaps I repositioned him by my nonverbal communication of disapproval) from the GAWP positionality he first adopted by accepting the offer to skip in line.

When people do things that provide themselves a benefit at the expense of others, those others who are disadvantaged typically are not present the way I was present in the assumption of the privileged positionality the young man had in the queue in the coffee shop. The idea that the relative privilege of being first in line could be extended to another person of his choosing is a graphic example of the assumed privilege that many of the African American teachers readily recognize in their White colleagues. Describing my episode opened the sense-making dialogue among African American and White teachers concerning privilege. Sharing this coffee-shop episode always animates the discussion about the assumption of privilege by White people because it illustrates how it operates in everyday encounters. Virtually every African American educator who spoke had similar episodes of their own to share, relating to their experience both in and out of school.

One other thing worth pointing out about the episode is that it afforded the opportunity to talk about cultural competence—specifically, the ability to read people in situations. Between these two young White men, one had a much greater degree of cultural competence. The fact that they both acted on their assumption of White privilege was mitigated by the one with the greater cultural awareness, who realized the social inappropriateness of his act. The second young man, by reading my reaction, was able to reflect on the positionality of privilege he was assuming, and subsequently repositioned himself by not taking advantage and returning to the end of the line. This is an example of the awareness called for regarding the social-cultural component of my framework.

To summarize, we need to have a working understanding of the notion of social-cultural community in promoting identities of achievement in diverse school settings. What social-cultural community refers to is the integrity of the relationships among members of the community based on a shared system of values, beliefs, and meanings. It is important to recognize this semiotic quality of communities when we attempt to create them in schools and classrooms. It is also important to realize that not all of the manifest values and meaning systems of a community are shared by all, and that there may be, consequently, some detrimental impact on the minority members of that community. The detriment should be recognized, and relationships renegotiated.

Several traditions of research and scholarship within education specifically address this detriment and sense making of the meaning systems in play—including critical race theory (e.g., the work of Bell, Collins); feminist critical theory (e.g., Lorde, 1984; hooks, 1989); social reproduction theory exemplified by the work of Bourdieu, Bowles, and Gintis (Bowles & Gintis, 1976); and critical pedagogy exemplified in the work of Freire (1970), McLaren, and Giroux (Giroux, 1997, 2001; Giroux & McLaren, 1986; McLaren, 1994).[1] The point is that, whether we recognize them as such or not, schools and classrooms are social-cultural communities that derive much of their identity and coherence from shared values, ideals, and meanings. Hence, in every classroom and every school, there is a coherent, albeit inexplicit, set of values, ideologies, and practices that are in operation.

---

[1]Scholars from the previously mentioned traditions have examined from their perspectives the subtle yet potent ways in which the cultural values, practices, and ideology of the dominant culture holds sway in the organization of social life in schools, classrooms, and schoolyards. The range of educational writers from a number of traditions—including social reproduction theory, critical race theory, and critical pedagogy-all have acknowledged that the mainstream cultural values, ideologies, and worldviews that are embedded in school experience place children from ethnically, racially, and culturally diverse backgrounds at a disadvantage. For example, social reproduction theory holds that the mainstream ideologies actually lead schools to create different prerogatives for working-class children, based on foregrounding values of obedience, punctuality, and neatness over values of such as critical thinking. More recent scholarly work has specifically focused on the shared values of racial privilege and assumption of racial inferiority that are played out in the racialized discourse practices in schools.

To conclude this section, I return now to the question of what kind of cultural community will enable the development of achievers and caring human beings. It is clear the preliminary answer to the question of what kind of community is one in which the adults possesses the cultural competence to recognize and eliminate practices that reinforce social toxins of racism and exclusion, racialized discourse, and other expressions of White superiority and Black inferiority. Such a cultural community would, as a minimum requirement, contain adults who understand the importance of attending to the meanings and values communicated to children in the social fabric of the school community. Finally, it would be one where adults, in the tradition of Dewey, both create and socialize democratic practices. It might also include the infusion of the particular forms of sense making that have been socialized by one's particular cultural group and are passed down as a form of cultural knowledge for building social cohesion. For example, the African American cultural values of literacy for freedom and the counternarrative to inferiority is a means of transforming the shared values of a school (Perry, 2004). For schools to promote growth of achievement and development, therefore, there must be shared practices that interrogate the shared meaning systems and shared values that shape all human activity in that community. Moreover, there must be an understanding of how the meaning systems and values not shared by everyone connected with the school community are negotiated. That is the subject of focus of the next section—the social-symbolic community or figured world.

SOCIAL-SYMBOLIC COMMUNITY (FIGURED WORLD)

It is difficult to make the distinction between what I have termed the social cultural community and the social-symbolic community. The distinction has a great deal to do with imagination and the shared symbolic constructions of individuals. In the figured world there is a high degree of shared meaning created with a high degree of intersubjectivity among members of a group regarding a set of shared imagined social and symbolic material. Often, affinity groups of students—a clique, a posse, or a crew—are bound together by a shared imagery of self-definition.

A social-symbolic community (or figured world) is a term used to represent a community with a tighter integrity of shared meaning systems than the previous category, and with a greater responsiveness to the type of people we want our young people to become. It certainly has to recognize a greater range of student positionalities than the simplistic good student–bad student dichotomy that is, unfortunately, how most of our educational innovations currently view the character and identity options for young people. The key question for this section is this: By what means can we draw on appropriate and rich cultural material for the creation of a symbolically and semiotically rich teaching and learning environment? This question begs another: What are the meaning systems, symbols, and representations we have to deal with?

The formal study of such questions is the focus of scholarly traditions mentioned previously—critical theory and critical race theory, for example. Although these are questions pursued by scholars, there is no reason why these questions could not be the focus of deliberative work of cultural practices inquiry in the service of community building—whether those school communities are grade-level teams, houses, pods, mods, or whatever. To build a new common culture, a third space so to speak, it is necessary to know the cultural material that is present and available. The consideration of cultural material does not have to be so open ended, because you and your colleagues have children in front of you for whom you have (or should have) some vision of how you would like to see them unfolding. By cultural material, I mean the patterns of relationships, styles of discourse, and other forms of interaction that encompass both the cultural identities aspect and the situated activities of people in an enclave. We are used to thinking about cultural material in terms of what defines us socially and culturally—representations that exist both as the personal symbols and signs that we "put out there" and also in terms of proficiencies (competencies). However, it is important to recognize that we are defined by symbols—categories of membership such as male, African American, and academic—as well as our use of symbols in the form of shared discursive practices. Throughout this volume I have argued the importance of both ego-defining and knowledge-enabling cultural material in the definition of self. This is the cultural material that needs to be built in the new cultural community. The capacity to solve a quadratic equation or to summarize a paragraph is no less important than the cultural material we want to make explicit for young participants. It is through participation that young people learn and achieve in school.

Figured Worlds and Communities of Achievement

The notion of the figured world is a metaphor for a symbolic community with a recognizable coherence and integrity. The term *figured world* refers to a symbolic-cultural community in which the relationships among identity, ability, and developing competence become tighter for the individuals and more clearly understood by members of the group. By figured world, I mean a socially and culturally constructed reality of interpretation in which particular characters and actors are recognized, certain acts are assigned significance, and particular outcomes are valued over others.

A good example of a figured world is the conceptual world of children involved in play. Figured worlds of play are conceptual in the sense that individuals are able to transport themselves beyond the immediate surroundings into a shared context of meaning. A large cardboard box becomes a spaceship, a railroad car, a refrigerator, or whatever the current game or mode of play shared by children at play happens to be. The important point about this idea of a figured world is that the meaning system both shapes and is shaped by the interactional context of human activity in play—but this setting scaffolds a number of significant human communicative and cognitive proficiencies. The social worlds in schools can be constructed along those lines. Once the integrity and coherence of the symbolic and cultural material of a community are understood by its members, it is in a better position to develop and improve on its shared practices. This is what is meant by a community of practice.

Activity Setting, Activity Venue, and Cultural Practices

The most important concept in acting on a cultural read of identity and performance dynamics is the notion of an activity setting as the unit of analysis. Activity settings (Leont'ev, 1981) are arrangements, including discourse patterns that are enacted within such arrangements, that help socialize learners to become better participants in the ongoing activity. I use the term *activity venue* in this framework to denote the description of a setting, its participants, participants' common goals, and the nature of both individual and collective doings. Activity venue will connote the combination of activity setting and the cultural scene as one single unit of analysis. It is similar to Leont'ev's (1981) and Tharp and Gallimore's (1991) notion of the activity setting, but also incorporates the cognitive content elements of knowledge structures (Galambos, Abelson, & Black, 1986) including their notion of *script* and Goffman's (1959) notion of *frame*, and cultural content present in Geertz's (1973) notion of cultural scene. These elements allow in the framework the presence of both structure and open-endedness: the structure of expected interactions and the open-endedness of alternative and creative interaction. This element of an activity venue is best described as a script with multiple improvisational opportunities for participants.

Activity venues can be proposed as thematic activity settings. For example, the Berkeley High School community might benefit from school-wide activity venues with a "renewing democratic leadership" theme or even an "ethnic identity in America" theme. As stated in chapter 2, this is an application of the situative identity framework to the organization of school life that takes full advantage of the situated cognitive approach to learning, drawing on cultural psychology and cultural-historical-activity theory.[2] Recall also from chapter 2 that the framework views learning, as well as identity development, as socially mediated processes. On this account, learning is not merely the internalization of knowledge or information, but is regarded as changes in the quality of the learners' participation in cultural practices of a given social community. Cultural practices acquired through primary socialization are historically inherited as ways of doing things that are reinforced through institutions, such as the family, the church, the school, the workplace, and other social networks (Brofenbrenner, 1979). The acquisition of these practices is socially mediated and developed through interaction with more capable others such as adult caregivers and older siblings (Vygotsky, 1978). Cultural practices acquired through secondary socialization are also socially mediated and negotiated through interpersonal relationships among individuals in pairs and in groups (Lave & Wenger, 1991; Rogoff, 2004).

Cultural practices emanating from secondary socialization in this framework are not merely traditions passed down, but proficiencies of individuals built up and supported by the collective proficiency of the collective or social group. These are the practices of disciplinary communities, some of which can be situated within ethnic and linguistic communities. There have been some attempts by educational researchers to incorporate cultural practices from cultural, ethnic, and linguistic traditions that have historical legacies for the children attending school into academic disciplines. For example, there is some design work on math curriculum at the primary level that nurtures funds of knowledge of Latino children (Fuson, Smith, & Lo Cicero, 1997; González, Moll, & Amanti, 2005) and for African American children (Moses, Kamii, Swap, & Howard, 1989). There is work on

---

[2]For an example of the approach applied to an African American literacy-learning context see Lee's (2003) cultural modeling framework.

connecting cultural community modes of reasoning to the practices of scientific reasoning (Moll & Greenberg, 1990) for Mexican American learners.

Cultural models and cultural schemata are ways researchers talk about and represent socially constructed ways of knowing. These terms are useful ways for us to refer to organizations or communities with cultural repositories of knowledge that are the substrate of particular abilities or proficiencies. Because our cultural knowledge is organized in ways that allow the structure to be recognized and anticipated by learners, it makes sense to incorporate school subject matter knowledge according to cultural knowledge. New fields of inquiry have emerged, such as ethnomathematics (Ascher, 1991), to systematically study the relationships between the way people in different cultures conceptualize mathematics and the formal school-based and discipline-based conceptions for the purpose of increasing their participation in academic discourse. When we begin considering the practices in domains of knowledge, we can then regard the learning community as a community of practice.

COMMUNITY OF PRACTICE

As we have seen in the previous discussion of social-cultural communities and symbolic cultural communities, communities of learners are bound together by more than shared practices and activities. People in a community of learners are bound together by joint enterprises, a shared repertoire of skills, and a common stake in something (like learning achievement outcomes for the students). *Community of practice* is a term coined by Lave and Wenger (1991) that captures this idea, focusing on how practices, repertoires of skills, and joint aims come together to determine the success of the organization, the development of the individual, and, as is our interest, individual identity.

The concept of community of practice is a conceptual tool for identifying the settings and communities with the particular set of proficiencies and aims we are interested in developing in young people. For example, earlier I invoked the idea that deliberative democratic practices should be incorporated as a set of cultural practices by public schools that value developing civic values and sensibilities among their students. In short, I suggested that every school should strive to be a community of practice with regard to participatory democracy. The adults in the building may have an understanding about what democracy is, what democracy should be, or even what a critical democracy looks like, but knowing something and practicing something are quite different things. If democracy and social justice are to be features of the learning community (for both children and adults), then there must be practices of democracy and social justice that are a part of the cultural life of the community. The practice of critical democracy has to be socialized by doing and deliberative reflection on that doing. The work of creating a critical democratic social environment that empowers and develops children is work that is at least as much about the culturing practices of adults in the school as it as about culturing practices for the pupils.

Earlier, I offered "doing" deliberative or participatory democracy as one example of the set of social and intellectual practices that can be made cultural practices in school communities as a way of addressing issues of equity, diversity, race, and identity. In the introductory chapter, I alluded to a whole myriad of much more specific social issues and conflicts that young people are pretty much left on their own to figure out and figure into their own self-construction. I have argued that the cultural reconfiguration of school environments, therefore, has to recognize and deal with all of the problematic aspects of racism, genderism, and other social issues in society to re-create the necessary new common culture in the school (cf. Feldman & Matjasko, 2005; T. Perry, 2004). This is an extremely complex task, but there are resources, such as the Center for Research on Education, Diversity, and Excellence, which have done some interesting work articulating standards for formulating the type of figured world using the sociocultural perspective I have been arguing for throughout the previous chapters.[3]

Both behavior problems and achievement performance problems should be understood as dynamics to be resolved within the social relationships among the child, the teacher, and other children in the classroom setting. Every child has a particular positionality—an identity embedded in the social context of the instructional setting. The practice surrounding successful pedagogical engagement with a child identified as having instructional need is difficult to ascertain, but there are always practices that exist as a legacy of how that community has dealt with similar problems in the past. The skilled practice in engaging a child instructionally often is informed by tacit knowledge (Polanyi, 1958, 1967), which refers

---

[3]Some of this work is applied in a recent book by Tharp et al. (2000). In the second chapter of their book, they illustrate this in a vignette comparison of two teachers: Ms. Lee and Ms. Young. Ms. Young is presented as a teacher who has organized her classroom with careful consideration to the social and cultural constitution of community. She is presented as a teacher who formulates a vision of instructional activity that has a balance of values, interests, abilities, and relationships in an ecology of participation and engagement among her students.

to both the ability to do things without being able to explain them completely and the inability to learn to do them from a canonical understanding of the task (e.g., by direct instruction). If we were to apply cultural practices inquiry to build a community of learners in a school, we would examine closely the community's usual way of doing things, particularly aspects of tacit knowledge, which are part of the information of codified practice culturally embedded in the community memory of practitioners. It is the common experience of practice, and the shared symbolic world in that the ranges of interactions teachers have with children is a shared domain of information. The common experience of practice in this shared domain of information is what would make meaningful the missing points of tacit knowledge that would make it explicit. The tacit knowledge underlying the proficiency of an expert practitioner is never completely available to others, nor does it become completely meaningful to others without the experience in which the knowledge was applied as action becomes available. Again, this is where narratives become important.

SUMMARY AND CONCLUSIONS

The key idea in all three of the types of context—social-cultural community, social-symbolic community, and community of practice—is that human performance and identity are codetermined by "inside the person" and "outside the person" capacity of the human network surrounding the individual. Regardless of the nature of the activity, be it an everyday task of cooking an omelet or conducting a chemistry experiment, people's performance depends in large part on the circumstances that are routine in their community and on the cultural practices they are used to (Rogoff, 2003). Proficiency in the practices at hand determines the success of the individual in a cultural scene. Moreover, according to the community of practice notion, a mutually constitutive relationship exists between people and their cultural communities. We thus conceive of people and the cultural communities as mutually creating each other (Bruner, 1990; Cole, 1990; Lave & Wenger, 1991; Rogoff, 2003; Wertsch, 1998).

6

Acquisition of Cultural Practices of Achiever Identities as Learners

Take a walk down any hallway in any middle school or high school in America. The single most common put-down today is, "That's so gay." It is deployed constantly, casually, unconsciously. Boys hear it if they dare to try out for school band or orchestra; if they are shy or small, or physically weak and unathletic; if they are smart, wear glasses, or work hard in school ... And they often hear it not as an assessment of their present or future sexual orientation but as a commentary on their masculinity.

—Kimmel (2004, p. 77)

Students produce forms of culture, as well as race, and new cultural practices that facilitate their everyday social relations.

—Yon (2000, p. 44)

The previous two chapters examined the first two columns of Table 2–2 summarizing the situated-mediated identity framework. Chapter 4 sought to explain the operation of the three dimensions of mediated identity depicted in the first column—situated identity, positionality, and agency. They constitute three aspects of critical developmental tasks young people face as they struggle to make sense of themselves as academic achievers, cultural beings, and worthy human beings. Chapter 5 focused on the middle column of the matrix, distinguishing the three types of social context—social cultural community, social-symbolic community (or figured world), and community of practice—associated with the development tasks of identity formation. In this chapter I explain the connection of the third column of the matrix consisting of primary socialization, secondary socialization, and improvisational self-determination, to focus specifically on those cultural practices young people appropriate as the tools for defining, projecting, and improvising self in school settings and the role these play in achievement motivation.

As stated in the epigraph from the work of Yon (2000), young people do in fact create forms of culture, race, and cultural practice. I contend they do this largely through their acts of identity—their improvisations of self as they experience the variety of shifting, changing, and demanding social scenes in school environments. As I argued in chapters 2 and 3, humans are strongly motivated by the need to realize a social identity in ways that meet their belongingness and self-esteem needs (Maslow, 1970), especially in social settings where some form of performance is expected. Schools offer a variety of social settings, many of which demand performance and comportment of students the moment they walk through the school doors. Performing and interacting in ways that meet the social demands and in ways that the individual feels safe and belongingness to the group becomes a socially situated set of human needs. Meeting these needs—which Maslow termed deficiency needs when they dominate an individual's primary motive structure—is a powerful motivation among those who are feeling less than capable and insignificant. Out of this framework comes a notion of human motivation that is not based solely on individual needs and wants. Traditionally theory posits human motivation as based on internalized needs pushing outward so that they seek expression in the form of goal-directed behavior. However, the total story of human motivation is not just one of a push from within; it also involves a pull from without.

According to my situated-mediated identity framework, the motivation of school achievement is based on higher order symbolic and social needs, needs that are constructed and developed in the contexts of ongoing interaction in specific social settings (Maslow, 1970). The motivation constituting the pull from without is the individual's need to participate and make meaning in the broader social world. This is the locus of our work with young people and the focus of the situated identity framework. The symbolic needs of human beings are, in fact, socially and culturally constructed—socialized in the course of growing up in social and intellectual life. Human beings are motivated by goals that are both ephemeral and lasting, material and symbolic, but always based in human activity. Now, the efforts of students in school settings to achieve at the higher levels of meaning, interest, and self-development are sometimes thwarted by school environments that do not allow any pursuits higher than the "I'm special" generalized projection of ego.

The drive learners have to situate an identity in a school setting, assume positionality, and exercise agency constitutes a major portion of the motivational energy that both teachers and learners expend in the social interactions of school. As we have seen, human beings vary in their capacity to read themselves into social settings, depending on their prior socialization. However, this is a capacity that can always be developed in ways that elevate both achievement (for the student) and teaching ability (for the teacher) provided the conditions are right. Creating conditions that elicit cultural practices of inquiry, democratic engagement, affirmation, community building, and so on is a good place to start. It is the goal of successful work with diverse student populations. In this chapter, we consider which of these cultural practices are vital to school achievement and need our attention in the academic socialization of young people.

CULTURAL PRACTICES OF ACHIEVEMENT

Situated identity theory (and cultural practices inquiry) is the framework I have presented in this volume to provide a working theory of this change in individuals in a school setting. To this point I have been advocating a form of analysis—doing "cultural reads" of individuals-in-settings—based on cultural practices and understanding school performance and school achievement of students engaged in activity. I have argued throughout this volume that the formation of identities and the acquisition of proficiency are the core processes of learning achievement. It is a systematic understanding of how cultural activities in school settings can be scripted, sculpted, and organized to promote the acquisition of the knowledge practices that constitute learning achievement. Whether mediated by processes of primary or secondary socialization, learners simultaneously and concurrently construct content-based knowledge at the same time they seek to realize identity goals as they participate in the social and cultural activities constituting learning experiences in classrooms. The identity goals determine how the individuals seek to define themselves (situated identity) and how they inscribe themselves (positionality) in the social scene of the activity setting of learning (be it a lab, group work activity, etc.). The unit of analysis for student learning and development consists of persons-in-situations, including cultural practices of the particular site of social and instructional interaction. To fully account for achievement requires an understanding of both cognitive capability and social capability operating together—and the nexus of both sets of ability is situated in identity and the way in which identity mediates motivation.

Primary socialization, secondary socialization, and improvisational self-determination are examined in turn.

PRIMARY SOCIALIZATION AND IDENTITY

To begin our discussion of primary socialization let us consider some of the cognitive capabilities that are shaped by both experience and by culture and how they mediate achievement motivation. Some of these cognitive abilities constitute the cultural capital and cultural strengths educational writers talk about, as being acquired prior to children's arrival in school. Other cognitive capabilities are absolutely shaped and socialized by how we organize school life, especially as they build on and extend earlier ability. As we move from primary socialization to secondary socialization, we will have an increasing interest in the role social identity plays in academic activity and the many forms of social interaction in school settings. There is an array of identity designations students can take on in the school context and how they are created and negotiated. Our interest in this discussion of primary socialization is in early cognitive capabilities, and the early experiences of children's cognitive and social development that are foundations of achievement orientation and agency.

Some of the cognitive capabilities required for achiever identity are only made possible by democratic, caring, and critically conscious early learning environments. The discussion of these follows in a later section. Improvisational-self determination is the outcome resulting from agency in the framework. This is the practice shared by agentive students and teachers who adapt in situations according to a critical consciousness and critical literacy as they assume a positionality appropriate for full participation in a multicultural democracy.

To restate the central thesis of this volume, the processes by which young people situate themselves as learners and as individuals in the social settings of school and beyond determine their interest, engagement, participation, and ultimately their successful academic performance. Families—parents, brothers and sisters, and kin—are important first contexts in which individuals are socialized in ways of being, as well as in the operational capacities for adult life. What social routines and cultural practices in early family life promote identities of achievement, and which detract from it? As we have seen in the discussion of culturally congruent and culturally responsive teaching, the best answer to this question is that it depends—it depends on how well the social-cultural context of school matches the social-cultural context of early socialization.

An important task for educators is to understand how the cultural practices socialized prior to school enable achievement positionalities in children when they arrive at school. There is a body of educational literature on cultural incongruity that documents ways that children from ethnically, linguistically, and racially diverse backgrounds bring cultural practices to school that place them at a learning disadvantage because they do not match the cultural patterns of school (e.g., Heath, 1983).

As we have seen from the development of the mediated identity framework presented thus far in the previous chapters, identity expression is a key factor in how individuals participate in any human enterprise, and this includes participating in school. How an individual situates and positions himself or herself in any of the settings in school will also reveal the individual's culturally shaped discursive practices and communicative abilities which figure importantly in school success. Whether it is in building a sense of belonging or positioning oneself as capable in a setting involving performance—in the playroom, classroom, or schoolyard—an individual's situated identity is the crux of the social motivation and ultimate achievement motivation. Because of this, it is important to consider the cultural practices that socialize the cognitive capacities that mediate identity expression.

Primary Socialization of Cultural Cognition

An important tenet of mediated identity theory is the idea that complex academic proficiencies are found in cognitive abilities socialized in early human interaction prior to school age. Let us turn now to what some of these cognitive abilities might be and draw the connection between academic skills and cultural practices. In this discussion I draw liberally from research in cognitive science, human development, and cognitive learning (Anderson, Greeno, & Reder, 2000; Anderson, Reder, & Simon, 1996, 1997). In the early stages of my academic career I was profoundly intrigued by an edited book entitled *Children's Thinking: What Develops?* (Siegler, 1978). It began my career-long interest in this question: What, indeed, develops as children acquire greater proficiencies and cognitive skills? The research traditions of that time were based in individual psychology, particularly the paradigms of neo-Piagetian theory and the emerging information processing approach in cognitive psychology, so that answers of that time rarely considered the role of human activity. Later, with the growing interest in the work of Vygotsky and others in the sociocultural tradition, inquiry into the question of what develops was richly informed by other paradigmatic lenses from those in the disciplines of cultural psychology, anthropology, semiotics, and sociology who are interested in the ontogenetic development of human knowledge (Corsaro, 1996). From our present perspective of cognitive development mediated through situated identity, the question now becomes, If we allow that cognitive development is not exclusively an inside-out process, but is also a concurrent, collateral process of the outside in as posited by Vygotsky (1978) and sociocultural theory, what cognitive skills or abilities can we track from primary socialization (early acquisition from among parents and family) to secondary socialization (later acquisition from school adults and wider society)?

One group of researchers that has explored the origins of cultural cognition (Tomasello, Carpenter, Call, Behne, & Moll, 2005) argued that these primal human cognitive skills include the capacity to read intentions and the capacity to share intentionality. They examine evidence that these two cognitive proficiencies are unique to the human species, and proposed "that human beings, and only human beings, are biologically adapted for participating in collaborative activities involving shared goals and socially coordinated action plans (joint intentions)" (Tomasello et al., 2005, p. 676). They conclude that what is unique about human cognition is the capacity to participate with others in conjoint, purposeful activity with shared intentions. They write:

> Participation in such activities requires not only especially powerful forms of intention reading and cultural learning, but also a unique motivation to share psychological states with others and unique forms of cognitive representation for doing so. The result of participating in these activities is species-unique forms of cultural cognition and evolution, enabling everything from the creation and use of linguistic symbols to the construction of social norms and individual beliefs to the establishment of social institutions … the developmental outcome is children's ability to construct dialogic cognitive representations, which enable them to participate in earnest in the collectivity that is human cognition.

Whether we agree with these researchers that intention reading, cultural learning, and shared intentionality are uniquely and biologically specific to the human species, we can certainly consider them to be among the candidates for culturally and socially determined human proficiencies that play a role in human interaction that are shaped by the human interaction of primary socialization of learners by their parents before they even begin school. There are many communicative practices in which these abilities—reading intentions, cultural learning (reading patterns of intention), and shared intentionality—take form in the language socialization of children in ways that have implications for their later interaction in school. The field of sociolinguistics provides a wealth of research on this relationship. Sociolinguistics examines, among other things, the discursive practices that define gender, social stratification, and stylized speech patterns to understand the variations and differences in culture and the social world.

The point I wish to make here is that these cognitive abilities—reading intentions, cultural learning (reading patterns of intention), and shared intentionality—are not fundamentally different as children move from exclusively home life interaction to school life interaction. They are expressed in all of the forms of human interaction we seek to document in our cultural reads that take place in and around school settings and largely make up the general capacity of sense making that takes place in discourse. It is my claim that these three innately human sense-making capacities are distributed by the early socialization practices of one's cultural and familial group, and this distribution has implications for how individuals represent self and perform in school settings. Directing our cultural practices inquiry to forms of discourse is important because discourse is the medium through which young people are socialized into the cultural community.

For example, the cognitive abilities of reading intentions, cultural learning (reading patterns of intention), and shared intentionality are more prominent in the socialized communicative forms of African Americans than in Whites. Black communications (BC) is a linguistic style that both formulates and informs cultural identities of African Americans and other users of BC. Use of BC is an act of shared social identity and heritage linking its interlocutors to the socially constructed and historically transmitted patterns of meaning that define what it means to be African American (Bloome, Champion, Katz, Morton, & Muldrow, 2001; Smitherman, 1986). When a speakers use BC they evoke a metadiscourse of discernable significations, connotations, and denotations that transcends the oratory and signals of standard communication. For those learners whose daily experience of school requires a reliance on mainstream, standardized speech acts, the purposeful invocation of BC can be a powerful statement of identity.

The Skills of Cultural Cognition in Literacy

Cultural practices acquired in primary socialization provide children the rudiments of sense making in a variety of forms including making inferences, deductions, and interpreting symbolic material—the foundation of literate proficiency in schools. These are also the rudiments for more advanced forms of sense making, including those that are the basis of academic skills in literacy and numeracy. The knowledgeable reader of sociolinguistics will already recognize some of these connections, such as that between intention reading and signification, because most of the practices are communicative or discursive practices. Some would argue that the discursive practices of the individual are what situate that individual's identity (e.g., Saxe, 1991). Gumperz and Cook-Gumperz (1982) wrote:

> To understand issues of identity and how they affect and are affected by social, political, and ethnic divisions, we need to gain insights into the communicative processes by which they arise. (Gumperz & Cook-Gumperz, 1982, p. 1)

The point is that discursive activity situates identity, and is always the means by which positionalities are assumed by individuals in a given setting.

The ability to read intentions, to quickly learn and appropriate the new cultural signage in play, and to recognize the multiple layered meanings in discourse may be more highly developed in the primary socialization of some communities as compared with others. The language socialization in African American cultural communities involves cultural practices constituting a kind of social-literacy intelligence that children acquire before they even begin school (see Vernon-Feagans, 1996). These cultural practices include narrativization of self, reading intentions, sharing intentionality, and signifying. There is a growing literature in cultural educational psychology demonstrating that, taken together, these practices constitute a form of social intelligence and communicative competence that African American children and youth often have in greater abundance than their middle-class White counterparts (Bloome et al., 2001; Meier, 1998, 1999; Morgan, 1993; 2002; Murrell, 1993; Nobles, 1991; Smitherman, 1986; Wilson, 1978). According to my situated-mediated identity theory, the cultural practices inquiry that teachers of African American children engage is the study of BC, literature, and art as the foundations for enriching the social and cultural world of their schools and classrooms.

Cultural practices inquiry for any cultural group should ask this question: What are the cognitive proficiencies children bring that are central in learning performances in school settings? There are several key cultural cognitive skills important to learning interaction all children bring. There are others that are particular to ethnic-cultural groups. For example,

African American children are socialized with a greater degree of subtlety and richness of forms of communication (e.g., multivoicedness)—particularly the ability to read intentions—than are their White mainstream counterparts and even their White culturally mainstream teachers (who often misinterpret the intentions of those culturally different from themselves). These are often not recognized by their teachers.

The uniqueness of human cognition is the ability to participate with others collaborative activities with shared aims, goals, and especially intentions. In other words, human cognition is distinguished by shared intentionality. Participation in conjoint, purposeful activity with shared intentions requires important and relatively underresearched cognitive capacities of meaning making (e.g., reading intentions) and cultural learning. In particular, the capacity to read the intentions of others together with our need to create intersubjectivity—our innate motivation to share psychological states and common meaning with others—is the basis of a good deal of human cultural cognition. Participation in conjoint activity using these three capacities enables a wide variety of uniquely human abilities ranging from the creation and use of linguistic symbols to the establishment of social norms, the social construction of identity, and the establishment of social institutions. Intentionality, and the capacity to read intentions, is perhaps the key piece in cultural cognition (Harré & Gillet, 1994; Harré & van Langenhove, 1999; Tomasello et al., 2005).

Tomasello et al. (2005) offered an explanatory account of how humans come to (a) understand intentional action, and (b) participate in activities involving shared intentionality, and how these two skills interweave during normal human ontogeny. According to Tomasello et al., children's skills of shared intentionality develop gradually during the first 14 months of life as two ontogenetic pathways intertwine: (a) the general development of understanding (shared by all primates) of others as animate, goal-directed, and intentional agents; and (b) a uniquely human motivation to share emotions, experience, and activities with other persons. The developmental outcome is children's ability to construct dialogic cognitive representations, which enable them to participate in earnest in the collectivity that is human cognitive life.

Human beings are unique in their ability to discern what others perceive, intend, desire, know, and believe. Reading intentions is the foundational skill for all this discernment because it provides the interpretive frame for exactly what someone is doing in the first place. For example, a physical movement may be seen alternatively as giving an object, sharing it, loaning it, disposing of it, returning it, trading it, selling it, and on and on—depending on the goals and intentions of the actor (Tomasello, 2004). The important implication is that children are much more sophisticated than adults realize in reading the subtleties of communication, such as the use of sarcasm, indirection, and other forms of figurative speech.

Narrative

No discussion of the cultural-cognitive ability that is socialized prior to school would be complete without mention of narrative. Narrative and narrativization of experience is a prime instance of a Level 1 proficiency that is very much keyed into one's situated identity in a social group, positionality, and agency. This is the set of discursive practices that everyone takes up because it is socialized at an early age and is ultimately important to scholastic proficiency. Telling, hearing, and producing narrative is central to children's development and communicative competence (Halliday, 1976; Scollon & Scollon, 1981). A good deal of what educators read as cultural learning styles is the discourse patterns and practices acquired by children through a process of socialization—socialization to a set of cultural values that become the basis of an individual's identity (Scollon & Scollon, 1981). These patterns and practices—constituting a discourse system—are acquired very early in life, and much of it is probably learned before the child speaks any words (Halliday, 1976; Scollon, 1976). This system is acquired through a long, highly involved, interactive process of primary socialization and communication with caregivers. This system is unconscious, affects all communication, and is closely tied to an individual's identity (Scollon & Scollon, 1981).

What makes this key is that, in U.S. education, there has always been, and continues to be a widespread bias against the use of narrative as a communicative medium (Cazden & Hymes, 1978). The ways in which African American students are positioned as less proficient users of language are based on differences in the organization of discourse (Cazden, 1988; Scollon & Scollon, 1981) is a problem of the racial stigma that influence how students of color are positioned in schools. For example, African American English constitutes a discourse system that is rich in many qualities of the skilled use of language. Yet the variety of English variously termed African American English, African American Vernacular English, and Ebonics, is stigmatized in school curriculum. For African American children in U.S. schools, the African American discourse system is critical to literacy learning. Although there are many aspects of discourse, I only focus on those few for which I draw direct linkages between identity and cognitive performance in school tasks: (a) presentation of self (Goffman, 1959, 1974) and (b) sense making.

To end this section on primary socialization, I want to draw a connection to social competence. I turn again to Erikson's theory of psychosocial development and the concept of ego identity, Harré and van Langenhove's positioning theory, Goffman's concept of framing, and Rogoff's notion of development as increasing participation in a wider social community. In the conceptual framework I have laid out thus far, I posited that academic achievement is a matter of acquiring cultural practices in a manner not unlike the way in which young people learn manners and appropriate social behavior. Learning of this sort is more a matter of acquisition of skill and proficiency—learning in the Vygotskian sense. School learning involves acquiring practices through socializing human discursive activity and interaction, not merely through internalizing information.

SECONDARY SOCIALIZATION

We turn now to aspects of human ability in the domain I call secondary socialization. Among these are discursive practices for interacting with others. Recall from the previous chapters that positioning theory provides a formal system for explaining the positioning that individuals do in interactional settings—both self-positioning and positioning of others—in a social context. I now turn to the question: Why do they do it? Why are people motivated to project particular symbolic representations of themselves to others? In other words, what makes people so invested in positioning themselves in a social setting? In mediated identity theory, two forms of human motivation are of particular importance—impression management and sense making. These are examined in turn.

Impression Management as Discursive Activity

Erikson's theory of psychosocial development characterizes the dynamic interplay between the social cultural world in which a child grows up and the set of developmental tasks or challenges the child faces at particular stages of life. The internalized drive for maintaining ego integrity is therefore organized in a personality pattern that has been established (typically by the end of adolescence) as a developmental trajectory en route to a relatively stable, integrated, and coherent adult identity. The main thesis of mediated identity theory is that the basic pattern may be expressed in a multitude of ways, mediated by social context. The prime example of this type of mediation is called *impression management.*

Consider the way two people might prepare themselves for a job interview. Regardless of whether one has a personality that is self-assured and outgoing and the other person is shy and reserved, both operate to create and maintain an impression of competence and capability when situated in the context of the job interview with the personnel director. Regardless of the status or integrity of the ego identity of each of these people, both will, in this setting, seek to create, project, and maintain an image of themselves (as capable and competent to do the job) they want others (principally the person in a position to hire them) to consume. This is positioning of the first order—the intentional projecting of an image of self for others to consume pursuant toward a particular goal (e.g., getting a job or being accepted by the group). There is also a more sophisticated second order positioning, a topic I return to presently.

Impression management among children in school presents potential challenges. One challenge is the variety of cultural scenes. In elementary school, there are varieties of groupings in the schoolyard, in-class settings, independent small-group work, and so on. In high school and middle school, there is greater variety of groupings in the interstices of time between, before, after, and even during instructional time. The additional complicating feature about impression management for children and youth going to school has to do with their positioning with respect to scholastic performance. It is virtually impossible for learners to avoid the generic, first-order positioning of good student versus average student versus bad student.

Because the rewards or the reinforcement for this first-order type of positioning are rather apparent (e.g., positive regard from the teacher for young children), it is not hard to explain the motivation for this type of positioning. All other factors being equal, most learners strive to manage an impression of themselves as being the good student. However, all other factors are not equal, which is the basic truth about the social-cultural context of any social setting. For example, the quintessentially American cultural values of competition and rugged individualism constitute a meaning system in public schools that prevents all the children in an elementary classroom adopting the generalized positionality as the good student. The values of individualism and competition constitute a meaning system that defines the good student in contradistinction to the not-so-good student. Hence, regardless of the teacher's intent to affirm every child to the same degree, the structure of all the other aspects of classroom experience such as ability groups, reading groups, and other indicators of relative ability are symbolic indicators of their worth.

Teachers interpret their students' behavior and performance as first-order positionings all of the time. People like attention, and in a cultural inquiry we seek to determine, in our cultural read, how the reinforcement of attention mediates positioning behavior with respect to identities within academic skill domains—such as an identity as a poet, historian, or mathematician. We also want to explain the seemingly inexplicable choices adolescents sometimes make in school contexts. In a cultural inquiry into achievement identity, we should seek to become aware of the instances in which aims of learners are not always apparent. In a cultural practices inquiry into achievement identity we seek to be aware of the human motivation of impression management based on the complexities inherent in the social setting as well as the complexities of racial identity in a racist society. For example, an African American child might simultaneously be motivated to assume a good student positionality in some intellectual task and at the same time hold back to avoid the risk of racial stigma if he or she should happen to not do well on the task.

Finally, in a cultural practices inquiry into achievement identity we seek to identify cultural resources in the social construction of resiliency, especially as it is predicated on the meaning young people make of themselves in activity and especially given contradictory messages, the democracy-distorting values of "sort-and-select" competition and individualism, and racial privilege that suffuse the adult world and U.S. popular culture. Humans are prone to using whatever symbolic material, or cultural signage is available in a social setting. The most common example of this is the notion of *role model*, an available adult symbolizing both person and activity for the learner.

The need for self-expression and self-projection are very important in social emotion development because we know that young people are powerfully motivated to "be somebody"—if they cannot find legitimate means of being recognized, they may find ways that are troublesome. Unless you are a parent, school teacher, child care worker, or someone in a position to interact on a regular basis with children, it is easy to forget how important social being and identity are to them. Everything about their world revolves around relational being—who is their friend, who is not their friend, who can play with whom, and so on. It is this intense social interest that is significant in figuring the material and symbolic worlds of children. Even if we do not know a learner's immediate interest, we can at least ensure a social field where they can actively and openly explore possibilities and the positive values we offer.

When I have spoken about figuring a symbolic world—creating an enabling social environment for identity development—it is important to recognize that it is not at all a "start from scratch" enterprise. The entire landscape of what a particular child wants, is interested in, and desires is already drawn. That social landscape, unfortunately, complicates the available range of social tools, inscribed as it is by race and other forms of implicit privilege. These must be well understood by the adults before they can create a new common culture that enables and supports strong development.

Goffman's work provides foundational social psychology that looks at the process of impression management as an individual enters a new social scene. Why do people invest so heavily in creating an image of themselves? Recall that in chapter 2 I showed that a major part of this answer is based in what we already know about human motivation. Maslow's (1970) hierarchy of needs places being and belongingness needs just above survival needs. Humans have a basic need to express "I am, I'm here, and I matter." The major type of ego investment draws on the work of Goffman (1959), who credits an unpublished paper by Tom Burns of the University of Edinburgh. The argument is that in all interaction a basic underlying theme is the desire of each participant to guide and control the responses made by others present. Humans in social settings seek to manage the impression that others have of them.

In my situated-mediated identity theory, as is the case in Goffman's work, an individual's desire to influence impressions of others is not merely a response to discursive reactions of that collective audience, but rather the attempt to inscribe a symbolic representation of one's own choosing. So more than simply evoking desired or favorable regard from the group, what I am formulating is a way to account for how individuals inscribe themselves as a symbolic field of self. Goffman (1959) wrote:

> Sometimes the individual will act in a thoroughly calculating manner, expressing himself in a given way solely in order to give the kind of impression to others that is likely to evoke from them a specific response he is concerned to obtain. Sometimes the individual will be calculating in his activity but be relatively unaware that this is the case. Sometimes he will intentionally and consciously express himself in a particular way, but chiefly because the tradition of his group or

social status require this kind of expression and not because of any particular
response other than vague acceptance or approval) that is likely to be evoked from
those impressed by the expression. (p. 6)

Using cultural practices inquiry, we should seek to determine, by doing a
cultural read of an individual learner, the occasions in which that learner
intentionally and yet unconsciously creates an impression, as the result of
the improvisation of self-representation based on audience, the available
symbolic material, and other factors in the setting. What we need to
account for is the nexus of the individual expression given off and the
collective (audience in the setting) group's impression taken up. It is this
broader area of individual acting and group perceiving that is critical to
my theory of situated-mediated identity. Goffman (1959) writes:

When we allow that the individual projects a definition of the situation when he
appears before others, we must also see that others, however passive their role may
seem to be, will themselves effectively project a definition of the situation by virtue
of their response to the individual and by virtue of any lines of action they initiate
to him. (p. 9)

In other words, the impression created is a product of what the individual
projects, as well as how the collective responds to that projection. This is
exactly the idea of positionality in the situated-mediated identity theory.
Now, however, the challenge is to go deeper in the dynamics of interaction to the reasons why certain self-images are selected and presented over
others. Another important part of the dynamics of interaction concerns
how the individual appropriates or rejects the definitional claims of the
group. This also has to be a working part of the explanation of human
motivation according to situated identity theory. For example, an African
American student in an all-White setting may project an impression that
contests the definitional claims of Black inferiority (Perry, 2004).

Once an individual projects an identity, it is not just the response of the
group that determines the positionality of the individual. For example,
when an African American student seems to be overly forceful in his or
her argumentation in a classroom of all White students, the other students'
perception that the individual is too pushy and loud does not solely determine a positionality as oppositional or sassy or a man of words, but is just
as much determined by what happens in activity—what all participants
end up doing in the course of the image negotiation. Building on Goffman's
framework that foregrounds the group's responses to the individual, I argue

that the activity, especially the shared activity in some manifest purpose of the group, has a larger role in defining the individual in the situation than the group's repositioning of the individual. By virtue of the fact that individuals typically become members of a group by doing more than by declaration or by assignment or merely showing up, I think that the activity setting is the appropriate unit of analysis. In cultural inquiry we seek to discover the "definitional disruptions" (Goffman, 1959, p. 13) that occur in interactions of the instructional activity setting that encompasses more of the learner's self-expression than his or her initial entry into a social scene. According to Goffman (1959):

> Given the fact that the individual effectively projects a definition of the situation when he enters the presence of others, we can assume that events may occur within the interaction, which contradict, discredit, or otherwise throw doubt upon this projection. (p. 12)

Making Sense of Self

In the last chapter, I briefly discussed sense making in the collective sense in relation to how a group of people interprets their condition and their collective action. I raised the notion of collective identity in seeking to achieve participatory democratic aims (cf. Weick, 1979; Wenger, 1998). Impression management is a centrally important form of sense making in a collective sense as well, as collective identity serves as a backdrop or canvas for individual self-expression. Earlier in this chapter, I detailed cultural-cognitive capacities socialized in early life: narrativization of self, reading intentions, sharing intentionality and signifying. Each of these is a component of the generalized sense making. Each may be deployed by the individual managing an impression of self in a social scene. What I want to consider next for promoting identities of achievement among learners is how this generalized sense making can be focused on making sense of self in social context. Let us consider now a particular form of sense making that is the secondary socialization of school practices—referred to in the educational literature as *critical literacy*.

To begin the discussion of cultural practices that constitute important academic proficiencies we note the centrality of the notion of literacy and critical literacy as practices situated in everyday activity (Rogoff & Lave, 1984; Scribner & Cole, 1986). Literacy is central for two reasons. First, there has been perhaps no time in our history when literacy proficiency has been more critical to the well-being and life success of young people.

Second, there has perhaps never been a time when the literacy proficiencies of an increasingly racially, linguistically, and culturally diverse student population have been so poorly recognized by public schools. In schools across the country, especially in urban settings, students whose language, practices, and experiences diverge from the modal expectations of academic literacy struggle to develop academic literacy and its uses necessary to be successful in school.

It is important to recognize that there is an important connection between a young person's literacy capacity or skill, his or her positionality in the learning setting, and his or her participation in that setting. It has been my experience that the teachers who are most successful in eliciting participation and engagement of students have made available aspects of popular culture that mediate and increase students' interest and, more important, their expectation that what they are involved in is interesting and matters to their lives. I have said that children and youth are active appropriators and consumers of the cultural material around them, and are capable of appreciating and appropriating that material in their social interaction. You might recall from the earlier discussion of the Van Ausdale and Feagin (2002) study in chapter 1, children as young as 3 and 4 years old are already users, active appropriators if you will, of the surrounding cultural material in the form of discursive practices of exclusion and control. Popular culture is a rich pallet on which they select and use the material for creation—especially the creation and re-creating of self in settings where they are expected to display achievement in various forms of literacy proficiency in school.

Urban educators such as Morrell, Lee, and Mahiri argued for, as well as demonstrated, this connectivity of context in working on developing young people's literacy achievement in their work (Lee, 1993; Mahiri, 1998; Morrell, 2004). This body of work is important for several reasons. First, it situates students' learning and development in the cultural practices of literacy in which they actually engage. Authentic activity is the core element of my theoretical framework. Second, this body of work advocates the transition from the informal discursive practices socialized in the ethnic cultural communities children come from to the formal discursive practices of school that constitute academic literacy. The third important feature that distinguishes this body of work is that it is based in the activities—both formal and informal, in school and outside of school—that are culturally accessible and socially available through which young people employ (perhaps without knowing it) and develop academic literacy skills such as interpretation and composition. Morrell (2004), in particular, applies this pedagogy grounded in practice by extending the intellectual field of interest to popular culture—engaging secondary literacy instruction by illustrating instructional practices that draw on youth popular cultural literacies as scaffolds into more formal academic literacy acquisition. Despite this kind of work in literacy, there is still a dearth of research on the ways in which popular cultural literacies are exploding traditional definitions of being, and becoming, literate. Popular cultural forms that students exhibit in and around school clearly involve literacy proficiency, but are scarcely recognized as doing so and rarely incorporated into instructional practice.

The functional linkages between individuals' identity—their sense of well-being and concept of self—and their proficiency and skill development in school settings has been of primary interest in education and human welfare, and across social science disciplines. Within psychology alone, the concepts of resiliency, self-esteem, self-concept, and self-efficacy as well as attribution theory, social learning theory (Bandura, 1986), and supplemental educational theory (Gordon, Bridglall, and Meroe, 2005) constitute a considerable proportion of the educational literature focused on learning achievement and motivation.

IMPROVISATIONAL SELF-DETERMINATION

It is here that I want to call back to mind the notions of agency and positionality. One important distinction between the two terms is the moral dimension of social position that the individual implicitly demands from the group. Goffman (1959) writes:

> Society is organized on the principle that any individual who possesses certain social characteristics has a moral right to expect that others will value and treat him in an appropriate way.

> In consequence, when an individual projects a definition of the situation and thereby makes an implicit or explicit claim to be a person of a particular kind, he automatically exerts a moral demand upon the others obliging them to value and treat him in the manner that persons of his kind have a right to expect. (p. 13)

Goffman's work is again useful here, not just because he theorized the process of impression management as an individual enters a new social scene, but also because it offers a foundation for the activity that is a prime motive in adolescent social behavior—*dramatives*. Young people have affirmative identity when they are doing things they like and are good at.

> To summarize, I assume that when an individual appears before others he will have many motives for trying to control the impression they receive of the situation.
>
> The specific content of any activity presented by the individual participant, or the role it plays in interdependent activities of an on-going social system, will not be at issue; I shall be concerned only with the participant's dramaturgical problems of presenting the activity before others. (Goffman, 1959, p. 15)

In contrast, I assume that the attempt to control the impression individuals receive in a situation is the primary motivation in social behavior, personal decision making, and action. It is the driving core of the motive structure. Moreover, as we have a few more theoretical and conceptual tools than were available in 1959 (i.e., activity theory), our cultural practices inquiry will look to uncover both the content of the activity (as this is important to relating the framework to achievement performance) and the individual's techniques and strategies for impression management.

The nature of the ego investment of adult practitioners is also critically important to successful urban practice, because there is no greater barrier to human connection and successful work than the investments adults have in being better than others. This is especially damaging when they unintentionally but very clearly communicate this in interactions with young people. When I work with adults and young people, and the young people explain what they hate about the relationship, it is often about being judged. The young people list being judged as their top complaint. Yet, rarely are there explicit statements of judgment that come from the adults. It is in the fabric of the communication over time—in positionality and nonverbal communication. Young people will, in fact, go to considerable extremes to avoid being judged. Many parents of adolescents can attest to this in moments when they discover the unusually elaborate efforts adolescents have taken to avoid the discovery of a relatively minor infraction.

Improvisational Self-Determination

Based on what we know about the psychosocial dynamics of identity and agency in school settings thus far, my framework suggests that the developmental task of young people is to achieve the capacity for improvisational self-determination. Improvisation is defined as the skill or creative process of creating and performing something without any script or text to follow, without preparation, and without prior strategizing. Improvisational self-determination is, therefore, the exercise of agency as a creative process. Creative potential will, given the right circumstances, always find creative expression in the definition of identity. A good recent example of improvisational self-determination is documented in the film *Rize,* which chronicles a dance movement that rises out of South Central Los Angeles with roots in clowning and street youth culture. The dance forms are revolutionary artistic expressions born from oppression of Black youth in urban California.[1]

The central principle here is that focused creative activity, what Csikszentmihalyi (1991) called *flow,* mediates not only identity, but also the improvisation of the new cultural forms and self in the same process. Young people taking up these forms and taking them to new frontiers of art and self-expression are engaging in improvisational self-determination, the highest form of agency in my situative identity framework. The implication for practice for the accomplished urban teacher would be to create space for this creativity and allow for a wider expression of roles and positionalities than are typically available in classroom organization, such as note taker and timekeeper in collaborative activity. The accomplished urban teacher encourages improvisational agency in children and youth.

Improvisational-self determination is most often based in things that learners already do extremely well, but typically are not the abilities permitted in school settings. When self-esteem is challenged as it often is in school when children are asked to do things they are not good at, students often imagine themselves doing the things they are good at. Everyone imagines himself or herself doing what he or she is good at during moments of low efficacy. Most often, these are activities. The implication for educational practice is to look to create opportunities for improvisational self-determination. For example, DG, a 6-foot-tall middle school student of mine, often imagined himself playing basketball during class because he did poorly on almost every academic task asked of him. However, if we could incorporate a sense of efficacy in the academic task, it would be possible for students to actively work on developing an identity of achievement.

Let me illustrate this idea regarding the power of activity in mediating identity and positionality with a personal experience early in my career as an urban teacher. It is a variation of a narrative that describes the experience

---

[1]Tommy Johnson (Tommy the Clown), who first created the style as a response to the 1992 Rodney King riots, named it clowning. Others in the movement developed other forms called krumping. The movement is revolutionary in that young people are using dance as an alternative to gang activity and hustling. They form troupes, paint their faces, and have meets to compete or merely hone their dance skills.

of many new teachers—that moment when you realize that a particular student, who is your nemesis in class, is in fact a much different person outside of that context. That student for me was DG, a 6-foot, 4-inch eighth grader during my first year of teaching middle school social studies in the Midwest. In class, DG was terrible, taking every opportunity to disrupt the class to the point that I was convinced that the young man hated me. It was not until I had to supervise lunch hour recreation time on the basketball court that I realized two things. The first was that he was quite a basketball player; the second was that he did not, in fact, hate me. I discovered this the first time I had to supervise recreational time in the gymnasium where he was playing a pick-up game of basketball. My discovery occurred when DG, on seeing me, left the game momentarily to come over to me with a big smile to ask me how I was doing and if I would like to play later. This was my first graphic lesson about the situativity of identity and positioning. In what was clearly his element (playing basketball), DG was transformed (at least, in my eyes at the time) from a mean, wisecracking, and menacing future thug to a friendly, engaging, sweet kid. Although significant, this was not my most important discovery of the situativity of student identity. Much more important than this was realizing the power of conjoint activity in an endeavor where the young person is proficient.

The experience of seeing DG play and then accepting his invitation to play the next game was a powerful one for me as an educator and psychologist. It was not just the discovery that a student I was convinced hated me when we were in class actually did not, nor was it merely a matter of seeing DG's delight at being able to show me that he was good at something. It went much further than that. It was rather the nature of identity in activity—in a context where the young person has skills. It was about how this positionality of being in the position to offer me an invitation into his domain mediated an amazing new relationship with my student. All of a sudden, I saw in DG qualities of leadership, generosity, and generativity, which became increasingly more apparent in the course of playing the game. When I did take up on playing in the next pick-up game, DG made sure to choose me for his team. Over the course of the game, we found ourselves looking to each other for passes and assists, much more than we did the other players. There was a level of on-court communication with DG in this first time that I typically only experienced with friends with whom I played frequently and over time.

The activity of playing the game of basketball mediated a new relationship between teacher and student, a new identity in the learner as capable and generous, and a new identity in the teacher. That is, as a consequence of this experience, I became much more able to look beyond the disruptive behaviors of my students like DG because I was better able to see how these behaviors were an extension of how the immediate instructional context in my "Justice and You" classroom mediated a negative positionality.

This episode with DG and basketball is more than an illustration of value of him feeling more himself, nor was it merely a matter of the experience of greater competence and efficacy. Playing basketball with my troublesome student at his invitation created the opportunity for him to improvise a new positionality with me. It is important to note that I also improvised my positionality as a teacher. The outcome was a newfound relationship that manifested in the activity of basketball by how we become connected as players. A new bond was established that was based in the activity, but more important, it emerged as a new role that better fit who he was and what he was able to do.

It was a powerful lesson for me. It resulted in my completely restructuring my class format to become totally and entirely activity based, organized so that each student could assume an agentive positionality. Instead of continuing the semester with my format of lecturing on the court system, we embarked on a project of producing a video dramatizing a court case. Students had to research how the system worked, develop a storyline for the dramatic enactment, write the script, stage the taping, and so on. This was a powerful learning experience for me as well, as I discovered that, in opening up the field of activity, individuals in my class (many of whom were held back a grade or two) improvised participatory roles in our joint enterprise that included the legitimate use of academic skills—in writing, researching, editing, composing, and performing. Ever since, this experience has become my living metaphor for accomplished practice in urban settings. Our tasks as teachers are to create these conditions of possibility. Note, however, that it is not simply a role ascription, but a role assumption. DG found agency in a role (basketball player) and positionality (a pick-up game that included his social studies teacher) that transformed his academic experience and my teaching experience. The agency was acting on terms that included generosity and generativity. It is a matter of finding those proficiencies in the cultural and lived experiences of your students.

Extant Proficiency and Repositioning

For African American youngsters brought up in the cultural tradition of loving language (Smitherman, 1986), language play is a prime medium for this improvisation. Even as the teacher tries to position the student as not so good, that student may counter this positioning with verbal adroitness and improvise an identity of capability. I observed this many times in observational work I have done in public schools over the years. To illustrate this battle for positioning in my work with teachers and teacher candidates, one of the resources I use is an excerpt from the commercial film *Boyz N the Hood* directed by John Singleton.

Tre Styles, the main character in the film, illustrates a typical African American male student possessing the cultural legacy of being a man of words—a person who values and is proficient in verbal dexterity in a social scene. The opening scenes of the movie provide a graphic portrayal of the battle of positionality carried out in virtually every classroom at some point, and most frequently between White female teachers and African American boys. The scene dramatizes this basic contested positioning between White teachers and African American children, given the racialized and troubled schooling landscape discussed in chapter 1. The dynamic would seem to be an unavoidable fact of life in school interaction, but could still be better understood in the course of improving instructional practice. Toward that end, let us look at an illustrative episode in detail, our last example of improvisational self-determination.

Boyz N the Hood opens with Tre, an African American young man, walking to elementary school in East Los Angeles with his friends. The critical episode occurs moments later when he and his friends are in the classroom. It is clear that the filmmaker intended to depict the problematic relationship between Black boys and White women teachers (as have some educational scholars[2]) as well as the way African American children's verbal adroitness is used to improvise their positionality. What takes place is not merely an instance of impression management, but an agentive improvisation of self as capable and knowledgeable. The critical episode opens with the camera panning across the student drawings mounted on the wall depicting gang shootings, funerals, and civilian surveillance by a Los Angeles Police Department helicopter while the teacher is droning on about the first Thanksgiving. The critical episode is provided in the following dialogue:

---

[2]Such as Spencer Holland, Jawanza Kunjufu, and Asa Hilliard.

Teacher: So that's how the settlers survived that long hard winter that took so many of their lives … by eating all those special foods that were given to them like turkey and the … umm … squash … and all the foods we think of as our traditional holiday meal. And that's why we celebrate Thanksgiving in order to commemorate the peace between the Indians … excuse me … the Native Americans, and the early English settlers who were called … class?

Class
(in unison): The Pilgrims.

Teacher: That's right. The Pilgrims. Very good.

Tre: The penguins!

Teacher: Who said that?

Class: [All point to Tre Styles]

Teacher: Mr. Styles!

Tre: [Calmly, nonchalantly while coloring.] That's me.

Teacher: How is it that you always have something funny to say?

Tre: Because I'm a comedian.

Teacher: Would you like to come up and teach the class?

Tre: Yeah. I can do that.

Teacher: Very well. Come up and instruct us. And what will be the basis of your lecture?

Tre: What?

Teacher: What are you going to talk about?

Tre: I'mma tell ya if you let me talk, shoot! Okay. Alright. Does anybody now what the name of this place is?

Girl: That's Africa. I know that.

Tre: That's right. That's Africa. But did you know that this is the place where the body of the first man was found? My daddy says that makes it the place where all people originated from. That means everyone is originally from Africa. Everybody. All y'all. Everybody.

At each turn of the interchange the teacher (for better or worse) discursively attempts to position Tre as the bad student. However, each attempt gives Tre an opening to improvise a positionality as clever user of language—a man of words—discursively controlling the situation. This includes responding to the teacher's speech act ("Would you like to come up and teach the class?") that was intended as an inhibition but only served as another opening—another invitation to improvise his identity as being "large and in charge." The perlocutionary intent was to dissuade Tre from further talking, but the illocutionary outcome was to afford Tre a stage to assume the positionality as a capable man of words.

The rules of this language game between teacher and student are not that different from any of the other forms of ritualized play (e.g., playing the dozens): It is the audience response that is the indicator of proficiency. For one, Tre is simply resisting an attempt by someone to position him as a chump. Second, this can become a contest of words and cleverness. Third, the audience response determines the "winner" of such verbal jousts. It is the class's laughter at Tre's initial utterance of "penguin" as a word play on "Pilgrim" that led the teacher to view this utterance as misbehavior that had to be sanctioned.

Many times students in a classroom setting are countering the under-the-surface microaggressions by the teacher and other students through an improvisation using the discursive material available at that moment in the social scene. Those who use the film and vignette as a resource will see that the teacher's attempt to punish the student ultimately succeeds, as she allows another student to challenge his "teacher" positionality to the point of it erupting into a fight that results in Tre being suspended.

I have seen a few teachers who have been able to successfully engage with African American students in this type of word play, but only on terms that were culturally authentic and understood by everyone in the class as just that—word play—in the same way as dozens of other forms of ritualized insult. This is rare, however, because on these occasions, the positionality of student and teacher have to be (and be understood by everyone to be) on an equal par for the duration of the exchange, and everyone has to understand that it is not truly a contestation of power for control of the classroom, but rather a form of relationship building.

SUMMARY AND CONCLUSIONS

This chapter provided a more detailed explanation of the three processes of primary socialization, secondary socialization, and improvisational self-determination to focus specifically on those cultural practices young people appropriate as the tools for defining, projecting, and improvising self in school settings and the role these play in achievement motivation. These are necessary to understand as part of the urban educator's cultural read of individuals-in-activity.

7

The Cultural Practices of Achiever Identities of Teachers

> In schools, we learn *how* to be, as well as *what* to be. We learn how to value, to be fair or hateful, to be generous or argumentative or curt, and we learn all that from teachers as surely as we learn from them the list of "the pretty kings of France."
>
> —Tharp et al. (2000, p. 43)

In chapter 6, it was argued that the achievement motivation of learners is constituted, in part, by a drive for competence in a social group in whatever activity earns the individual cache as a capable performer and a good person in that social group. The social groups consist of students in school, the performance competence is academic proficiency, and the drive for competence can be reflected in the individual striving for personal objectives. These objectives may be as lofty as learning to critically interpret prose or as pedestrian as getting good grades. The aim of many educational programs aimed at building the academic self-efficacy of children and youth who occupy the downside of the achievement gap is to socialize them into seeing school success as a worthwhile way to define oneself that can be achieved with effort. It is the determination to become a proficient participant in social life or a social activity, whether that activity is telling stories on the front porch on a hot summer night, leading a literature circle, or determining the composition of a water sample. Our challenge is to create conditions in which students seek to become proficient participants in the academic life of the school.

I have made the case for refiguring school life so that young people can access formal school proficiencies and academic discourses as easily and naturally as they do in the less formal settings of family, friends, and kin.

On the basis of the framework thus far, I can make this same argument for teachers. That is, the motivation for teachers to be effective is based on the demonstrable quality of instructional activity with, and by, their students.

The focus in this chapter is the application of cultural practices inquiry in the elevation of student self-efficacy in conjunction with, and as a function of, teacher self-efficacy. In this chapter, I thus illustrate the proposition that teachers' motive structure in a learning interaction is determined by how they situate themselves (as learners and teachers) and how they position themselves as agents (of their own learning as well as their students' learning), and by how these motive structures are mutually constituted and jointly constructed. I attempt to articulate the cultural practices appropriated by adults who deliberately assume achiever identities who subsequently are able to create achiever communities of learners. I do this from the standpoint of a teacher persona that assumes responsibility for the trajectory of identity development (in conjunction with the academic success) of the students. According to my theory, this trajectory starts with social identification (situated identity), moves to agentive self-awareness and representation (positionality), and culminates with agency. I address the teachers' awareness of their own achievement identity in codevelopment with those of the students with whom they work. In short, I apply the method of cultural practices inquiry.

THE METHOD OF CULTURAL INQUIRY
INTO TEACHING PRACTICE

When we look at instructional practice using the method of cultural inquiry, there are a number of interests. First, we are interested in the symbolic and relational composition of the activity settings in which the learning takes place, especially the aims of students and instructional aims of teachers as they are grounded in authentic academic proficiencies. Second, in a cultural inquiry into teaching practice we are interested in the interaction of the motive structures of teachers with those of students, especially in the symbolic interaction of impression management taking place between teachers and students in discursive activity in the classroom. For teaching practice in urban schools and diverse contexts, it is important to know the points at which motive structures impact achievement motivation, such as the occasions of impression management and the ways they sometimes operate at cross-purposes to achievement. On this account, we have noted earlier, but not yet explained, how impression management and drive to be seen as competent can operate at cross-purposes for African American learners and other learners of color. In this discussion, we also examine the contribution of teachers' impression management to successful learning outcomes as they interact with their learners.

Third, in doing cultural inquiry into achievement we are interested in the basic motive structure inherent in the learners' need to make meaning, to make sense of one's experience of the curriculum and the relationships to others in the school. Exploring this interest will entail a brief discussion of the nature of learning achievement in a zone of proximal development. Fourth, when we engage in cultural inquiry we are interested in interpreting human motivation as patterns of impression management involving both learners and teachers together, as well as conjoint meaning making. On this account we ask what kind of interactive social chemistry among learners and adults promotes the drive to proficiency, and how we create this chemistry given the complexities inherent in school environments given the complex dynamics of race, identity, and meaning in a racist society. Understanding these patterns, we develop the cultural practices for building achievement identities and achievement communities. Finally, we are interested in the social construction of *resiliency*, especially as it is predicated on the meaning young people make of themselves in activity and especially given contradictory messages, distorted values, and assumed racial privilege that suffuse the adult world and popular culture.

In short, the task in this chapter is to piece the different components of the framework together as a conceptual framework to provide the interpretative tool for processing school settings as cultural scenes. The positioning of self and the repositioning of the self by others is an important theme of my situated-mediated identity framework explained in chapter 3 that we now return to in regard to the positionality and agency of teachers and other adults. Let us turn next to the cultural competence concerning teacher awareness of how they position students and their motivation.

Cultural Competence for Cultural Inquiry Into Achievement Identities

Before defining cultural competency, let me suggest that the practice of a culturally competent teacher must exhibit five discursive features (Murrell, 2001, 2002): (a) engagement and participation of every learner, (b) promoting achievement identity and agency of every student, (c) building community integrity and cohesion among learners in the instructional setting, (d) eliciting critical and discursive inquiry as learning practices (habits of mind) from all learners, and (e) encouraging improvisational self-determination, each learner's capacity for intellectual agency. When these five features characterize a teacher's practice, the teacher is most apt to be exhibiting a positionality that promotes identities of achievement among students.

These five features constitute my own rendering of the types of practices that create socially, scholastically, and culturally rich learning environments for learners from diverse backgrounds, but there are others sharing common themes. For example the Center for Research on Education, Diversity & Excellence (2002) has published an even more specific set of teaching standards for teaching to diversity. Both are frameworks designed to account for teacher cultural capacity for successful interactional dynamics needed to create rich learning environments in diverse settings.

My claim is that what stands in the way of teachers' ability to exhibit culturally responsive practice, whether or not they apply these standards of culturally responsive teaching, is the lack of awareness of their own positionality in the processes of teaching and learning. To further develop this claim, let us first elaborate the meaning of culturally relevant pedagogy and cultural competence. Advocates of culturally relevant pedagogy (e.g., Gay, 2000; Irvine, 2002, 2003; Ladson-Billings, 1994) speak of cultural competence as the defining feature of a teacher who can teach and reach all children in racially, linguistically, and ethnically diverse school settings. Although vitally important, this literature unfortunately does not offer a single clear articulation of what cultural competence consists of as a set of abilities or practices. Rather, cultural competency is distinguished by a set of behaviors and operations a culturally competent teacher does (e.g., Ladson-Billings, 1994). As a teacher educator who has attempted to use this framework to develop cultural competence I have always encountered the frustration of preservice and practicing teachers who, when they appropriate those behaviors and operations, still find that they are not culturally competent.

The issue in developing cultural competence among teachers as a set of practices (as opposed to a laundry list of qualities) is that we have not gone far enough in specifying the core practices of cultural competence. Despite the fact that there are teaching performance standards articulating this competence such as those mentioned earlier (CREDE, 2002; Murrell, 2001; National Board for Professional Teaching Standards, 2002), the degree of reflective self-awareness required for greater cultural competence is difficult to come by. The method of cultural practices inquiry is my attempt to specify the sense-making practices of the culturally capable practitioner.

Cultural Competence as Being a Cultural Learner

Cultural competence is formally defined as a set of congruent behaviors, attitudes, and policies that come together in a system, agency, or among professionals and enables that system, agency, or those professionals to work effectively in cross-cultural situations (Cross et al., 1989; Isaacs & Benjamin, 1991; Leigh, 1998). As it is operationally defined in professional practice, cultural competence is the integration and transformation of knowledge about individuals and groups of people into specific standards, policies, practices, and attitudes used in appropriate cultural settings to increase the quality of services, thereby producing better outcomes (Davis, 1997, referring to health outcomes). In short, being culturally competent means having the capacity to function effectively in a variety of cultural contexts and settings unlike those of one's primary socialization.

Taking this definition into account, my claim is that what cultural competence means in the situated identity framework is the ability of a person to be a cultural learner. This ability in a teacher would permit him or her to recognize just how each student is striving to enter into the social life of the classroom by drawing on all that goes into defining the student as a cultural being. The root of this ability is to accurately read intentions—a capacity that all human beings innately have, although they differ in their level of proficiency in real situations of human interactions. However, the ability is also developed by an individual's openness and deliberate attempts to know the varied ways of reading the world.

At the very beginning stages of this development, some of the skills or abilities are obvious, such as attenuating one's racial biases or assumptions of inferiority about cultural, ethnic, and racial groups different than one's own. This beginning level of ability would also include the capacity to think of culture not as a static category, but as an organization of human systems, meanings, language, and perspective. In this beginning level, ability, cultural, and racial groupings are not seen as static categories or stereotypes. This basic level of cultural competency or cultural proficiency is what many first courses in diversity or multicultural education in teacher preparation programs target for the high percentage of young, White, mainly female and suburban, culturally encapsulated preservice students. It has been my experience that most teachers in training rarely move beyond this beginning level of cultural competence, even after their first few years of teaching. It is a proficiency that is difficult, if not impossible, to teach. Yet it is arguably the most important determining factor to their effectiveness in diverse settings.

Without the situated mediated identity framework or something like it, the best we can do as teacher educators is to create the opportunities for preservice teachers to develop this competency through hard work, guided practice, and deep self-reflection. It has been my experience that the most significant increment of beginning teachers' ability to teach—especially those in settings populated by students with backgrounds different from theirs—is the development of cultural competence by becoming a cultural learner. A teacher demonstrates cultural competency as a cultural learner when he or she attends to the cultural and social requirements of an effective learning activity setting as much as he or she attends to the pedagogical and content requirements.

This sort of cultural competency is not likely to be seen in a single episode of teaching (e.g., in a single videotaped lesson or classroom observation), but is certainly determined by the environment created by the teacher and the long-term evidence of achievement success among the children of color in the setting. Cultural competence is seen in the teacher's practice over time, not necessarily in the in-the-moment demonstration of knowledge about a particular cultural or ethnic group the teacher reveals in his or her portfolio entries. Whether one is or is not culturally competent is not determined by what he or she knows about a given cultural or ethnic group, but by whether he or she can effect positive educational outcomes for members of the group. The demonstration of cultural competence by being a cultural learner might be regarded as a form of social intelligence that includes an ability to accurately read the intentions of others, recognize the nuances of complex human interactions, and improvise in one's communication based on rapid, in-the-moment reappraisals of children's changing needs, significations, and intentions.

The Cache of Culturally Diverse Urban Students

It has been the cruel irony of my work in urban schools over the past two decades that, as a group, African American children have richer and more variegated forms of this kind of social intelligence than do their White teachers. This difference merits a closer look. Let us begin by looking next at the psychological dimensions of social competence and cultural competence, and then look at the implications for achievement motivation. A good illustration is a critical episode from the *Frontlines* presentation entitled "School Colors." In this episode Geoffrey Marihia, an African American senior male, is intentionally representing his street kid persona in his manner of dress, discourse, and personal style during a meeting with the assistant principal regarding an altercation with a teacher. He simultaneously demonstrates his school kid persona in his Perry Mason-like precision in making the case for his defense. Here is a transcript of that interaction:

Student: So now I'm suspended, and I'm sitting here and I'm supposed to tell you what happened. It's simple. I walked up, I saw a girl that I knew about to get into a fight. Here comes you talking about all this stuff at once that I can't hear that all equals out to I'm not supposed to be here when I know that I've already made the decision that I'm going to calm her down, make sure that she doesn't get into any trouble, especially in a fight. Finally you put your hands on me. That was the first ... that was the first mistake you had. Second, you not only put your hands on me, but you put your hands on me in a way that was threatening, that should have been dealt with in another manner, but because I was in school, and under—quote, unquote—school rules, I'm not supposed to do something so I had to put down my own values, which is if a man touches me, me and that man are going to have it out in whatever way I feel is necessary.

VP: If a student threatens a faculty member, then it is a suspension.

Student: I did not threaten him. There is nothing that you can say to me or show me to say that I threatened him.

VP: I mean, "I'm going to fuck you up," what ...

Student: Hey! P-H-U-K in my language. A'ight? "If you touch me again" is a warning. Go to your English class, he'll tell you that "if you touch me again" before "I'll fuck you up," it becomes a warning. "I'll fuck you up" is a threat.

[a few moments pause]

VP: You wanna say something, Dave?

Teacher: Yeah, um, quite a bit. I think there's a number of things that are already becoming much clearer to me and that, uh, I'm glad you had the opportunity to say what you did because the first thing I'm seeing is that you have some very strong values and you believe in them and you're willing to act on them. For you, if somebody is, uh, touching you in a way that's not appropriate for you, it's appropriate to give the, what I will call a threat. We also have some very strong values here at Berkeley High, and some of them seem to be in conflict with your values. I don't want to have to walk through the hallways here feeling that there are a number of students, or even just one, who might, um, you know, go off on me if I touch them the wrong way.

Student: Well, I don't want to have to walk through the school knowing that a teacher can put his hands on me in any manner that will start a fight in the street if I did not know that man and know that I can't do anything about it. That's bullshit. How can a person put their hands on you and you can't do shit about it?

Teacher: Um, you could have asked who were ... who am I and what am I doing there, and I would have quickly answered.

Student: There was no way in that time period to ask either of you, of the two men ...

Teacher: If that were true for you, do you think it could have been true for me?

VP: The rules are laid out there. We'll talk about it, and I'm not going to do anything arbitrary, but I am letting you know that, that you will receive a suspension if it comes to a point in some place where it looks like that you have stepped over and threatened somebody when there was not a, when, when there was a situation that could have been avoided. We can learn from this.

Student: It's your opinion that it was a threat, it's my opinion that it was a warning, but your opinion outweighs my opinion.

Teacher: And that I agree with, yes. Well, unfortunately, the administration does make that decision.

VP: Alright, well, thank you, Jeff. Good luck.

            [Student leaves.]

VP: Thanks, Dave.

Teacher: Yeah. There was one or two moments when he was a little bit quiet when I thought maybe something sank in there.

The meaning systems that conflicted in the case study from "School Colors" just discussed can form the basis of deliberative work toward a vision of the caring and development-oriented community. Before that can happen, however, that community has to be envisioned. I have found a useful way of thinking about community at this global level with the notion of a figured world. A figured world is a meaning system. Suppose the world of Berkeley High (where this episode took place) was deliberatively refigured as a multicultural democracy. How would we then interpret the series of utterances in the critical episode?

Let us examine the episode at length using the method of cultural inquiry, because of all that it reveals about the dynamics of positionality and the cultural practices relevant to the social bonds between White adults and the African American youth. It is a useful excerpt to illustrate the cultural values in play, the conflicts in the values and social practices, and how these conflicts are based in subtle ways on race. The content of the analysis is the report of the recurrent patterns of interaction in professional development workshop settings where I am presenting to mixed groups of veteran urban school teachers, who work primarily with African American students in cities including Boston, Milwaukee, Chicago, Cleveland, Cincinnati, and Minneapolis.

In this analysis I am sharing with you the content of conversations that take place in these group settings that have African American and White teachers. I purposely use the excerpt from the documentary of Berkeley High School that appeared in the 1991 episode of the PBS program *Frontlines,* "School Colors," to encourage urban educators to appropriate it as a conceptual tool. The critical episode appears about midway through the 90-minute video. Because of its effectiveness in eliciting the key issues of identity, race, power, and achievement in a contemporary urban high school, I use this excerpt for virtually every workshop and professional development event devoted to creating communities of achievement in urban schools. I have used the excerpt a number of times and have been refining my approach to leading a discussion and analysis among veteran Black and White veteran teachers to better exploit the patterns that always emerge.

First, let me describe the patterns that typically emerge in the discussions. When I ask for an open-ended general reaction to the episode, such as asking, "What in this scene struck you as most important or significant?" White teachers invariably comment first regarding the students' behavior with a critique about his mannerisms, his dress, and his comportment—noting in particular that he was dressed inappropriately, used inappropriate language, and did not behave in a proper manner. On further probing, these teachers would rather have seen the student come into the meeting more contrite (not combative). African American teachers by contrast, notice the self-representation of the student but key more on the two White adults, noting a number of insufficiencies about how they handled the situation.

Another difference between the two groups was that very few White teachers saw that the young man was actually successful in making his case. Virtually all of the African American teachers not only noticed that

Geoffrey was far more verbally proficient in the argument by logically besting the two adults, but also that he did most of the talking—in fact more than the two adults combined. Virtually all of the African American teachers indicated that the young man made a reasonable case for his actions and for not being suspended, although about half of this group indicated that they personally were not swayed by the argument and would have still suspended the student. Virtually all of the White teachers discounted the argument, and indeed, on early probing scarcely seemed aware of the line of argument and the important elements. These included questioning the appropriateness of teachers physically restraining students they do not know and in situations they do not understand, Geoffrey's claim that he was trying to prevent a friend of his from getting into a fight, and the distinction between a threat and a warning.

Another difference between the two groups in the initial prompt to discussing the episode is that Black teachers recognized the cultural practice of being a man of words, appreciating the fact that Geoffrey was more verbally adroit in the interaction with the two adults. It is only after a period of discussion and multiple viewings of the episode that the White teachers are actually able to perceive this reality. The ability to compel people with words is a cultural value to African Americans. The cultural positionality in the tradition of the Black preacher and the public orator, the man of words positionality is assumed by this young man, perhaps even as a result of benefiting from a strong African American studies experience (Berkeley High at that time mounted the first African American studies program in a high school). This positionality was particularly apparent in contrast to the two adults—neither of whom was there to reason through what had happened, but apparently only to establish the facts of the wrongdoing.

White teachers were very much distracted by the student's appearance, showing little recognition of the fact that this was a purposefully constructed appearance by the student. The hoody, dark glasses, and the earphones are all part of an image the student constructs. This street kid positionality provides a clear example of self-representation and projecting the street kid persona by means of attire and posture. A substantially greater number of the Black teachers recognized this as a form of positioning—as a strategy. In contrast, there was no indication from the White teacher comments that suggested recognition of the possibility that the student deliberately dressed and spoke as he did. In short, the African American teachers more readily read the student's presentation as a stance, as positionality. This constitutes a greater cultural capability than the White teachers in interpreting the content of the exchange, because by getting more quickly to the meaning they have more options for generating teachable moment outcomes for the episode.

Another difference is in the interpretation of *frame* depicted in this episode. Was it a hearing to determine the facts of the scene of the altercation between the teacher and the student, or was it simply a fortified occasion (two men and one student) to notify the student, who is to be suspended from school? Black teachers were much more likely to note the indeterminacy of the meeting purpose and outcome, whereas White teachers were far more apt to regard the end as a resolution, which they took to be telling the student that the administration is the ultimate authority. So the perceptual frames differed across race as to whether the setting was an official notification of suspension or a fact-finding hearing. African American participants pointed out and articulated the apparent patent disregard for both the case the young man made and the apparent disregard for anything he said, as was explicitly marked by the teacher's final comment.

Cultural learners attend to the framing of the critical episode. If the framing for this speech event was that of a hearing, then the argumentation made by the student should have been taken into account, which apparently it was not. Cultural learners raise this question: If the purpose of the three-way meeting were to sort out what happened, would it not have been appropriate to consider the teacher's role in the altercation? No mention was made of that. If, on the other hand, the framing in play during the critical episode was that of a notification of a suspension, that should have been made clear. The final statement of the vice principal was a perfect statement of indeterminacy: "I am letting you know that, that you will receive a suspension if it comes to a point in some place where it looks like that you have stepped over and threatened somebody … ." African American teachers, by a ratio of two-to-one, remark on this indeterminacy, asking questions like these: If *what* comes to a point? If *what* looks like …? So is the student suspended or not?

It took the student to name the frame to provide the determinative frame that the adults did not, stating, "It's your opinion that it was a threat, it's my opinion that it was a warning, but your opinion outweighs my opinion." With this speech act Geoffrey exposes the real intent of the adults and the frame as notification of a suspension. He also exposes that the adults did not intend to address the ethics of the situation, including the fact that it was precipitated by Geoffrey's commitment to a friend, and a teacher's ill-advised, inappropriate (if not illegal) action of restraint. White teachers and Black teachers alike acknowledge in the segment of our analysis on practices the inappropriateness of teachers placing their hands on students. In a true hearing, democratic in practice, the wrongdoing of the teacher should have been considered.

In summing up the exercise on cultural learning applied to interpreting this critical episode, I note how the repositioning the teacher did of the student as the "bad other" is a good illustration of the new racism. The teacher was "othering" Geoffrey in terms of his street values by suggesting that they were different than school values, which was a false dichotomy. In fact, not only is it a matter of public law that adults may not manhandle a student, but it is ingenuous to suggest that students give up their right to defend themselves.

We noted a positionality of authority by both adults, but from different motive structures. The teacher was asserting his right to power, apparently to be able to place restrictive force on a student without just cause and without fear of reprisal, something that prison guards might covet, but that is neither legal nor appropriate in an environment where the care and development of other people's children is the main responsibility. The student, in his positionality as a man of words, articulated the counterposition that he did not wish to be in an environment in which teachers could claim that authority "how can a person put hands on you and you can't do shit about it?" A closer inspection of this claim made by the teacher in the post-hoc discussion of the excerpt with teachers surfaced the insight regarding the teacher's presumption that this was purely a street value. Young African American teachers most frequently note this, and wonder whether this teacher really could have been socialized in a context where you would let an adult put their hands on you in a restrictive way.

Note that in the final line of the episode the stance of gaining new information or new understanding on the part of the adults was transparently fake, one that the student called them on by naming the frame and exposing the real purpose of the conference. The student exhibited the African American discursive tradition of naming—of "making it plain." The attempt to reposition the student as having different values than those of the school was equally feckless and incompetent, especially in light of the fact the student expressed higher order values (ensuring that a friend did not get into a fight) than the teacher's mere desire to exert his authority. Note also how the positioning influenced the interpretations of the issues and symbols. When Geoffrey is positioned as the oppositional street kid, the only allowable interpretation of his speech act during the altercation is that of a threat. Although Geoffrey adroitly distinguished between a threat and a warning in the interaction with the two adults, the teacher was unswerving in his intent on positing the more violent *threat* interpretation.

Finally, I note that this microcosm of the school was set up to teach the student. Ultimately, the groups note that what was socialized in this frame is little more than the administration's ultimate authority to punish wrongdoing, despite evidence or any mitigating circumstances. This is an example of the absence of ethical, moral, and intellectual authority to go along with the authority of power.

Summary Practice Implications of Positionality and Achiever Identity

Let me conclude with a succinct statement of the practice implications of the framework—the notion of positionality, the context of the sociosymbolic community, and the processes of secondary socialization—as it applies to creating achiever identities.

Practice Implication 1. People seek to position themselves as capable—as worthy, valuable, likable, interesting, and so on. In everyday language, people want to be positioned in a positive light. Very few people seek to inscribe a public identity as dislikable, unworthy, worthless, contemptible, boring, and so on. This fact is the engine of motivation in much of human social interaction. This is particularly true in urban school environments where a higher proportion of young people will value verve and energy in their social life and their relationships as compared to culturally mainstream, affluent, suburban settings. Here I am not just referring to the instrumental roles one gives to students in setting up, for example, a cooperative learning group with note taker or timekeeper roles. Rather, I refer to positionalities, roles determined both by what students do and the self they are representing in the setting.

The offer of appealing roles could simply be a matter of the teacher recognizing and accepting, for example, students' ability to b-box, rap, krump, or some other hip-hop performance form in school space. In other words, an aspect of learner participation and engagement, and subsequent school success, is framed by this question: Is there anything here I can identify with? Here, the action phrase *identify with* might alternatively refer to teachers, curriculum content, classmates, learning activity, and virtually any and every form of symbolic material or activity individuals use to situate themselves. As discussed in chapter 1 in the discussion of U.S. culture and the crisis of meaning, too often the implicit answer to the question if there is anything they identify with for many students is "No." The crisis of meaning surfaces in the classroom setting when there is little that students can identify as meaningful to their existence.

The major implication is that every teacher in every classroom should strive to create an identity-affirming social environment in every school setting—both the settings they have immediate control over (e.g., classroom) and those they need to shape and structure (e.g., the relationships, the learning stations, code of conduct in the schoolyard). I have offered five dimensions of creating this identity-affirming community in both kinds of activity settings. These five dimensions are depicted in Figure 7–1 as discursive practices: (a) participation and engagement, (b) situated identity, (c) community integrity, (d) critical-reflective consciousness (resulting from a sense-making positionality), and (e) improvisational self-determination (resulting from agency). The first three of these practices speak most to the quality of social-cultural and social-symbolic community, as it relates most to the developmental task of situating identity of individuals. Recall the phrase from the theme song of the once popular television sitcom *Cheers*—as it applies to the disposition the good urban educator is creating for his or her students—"You want to go where everybody knows your name."

A teacher seeking to create a positive learning climate should, therefore, not just be looking to create opportunities for learners to take on positive roles in the social makeup of the classroom, but looking as well to enrich relationships between the individual and the collective. Part of this effort, as indicated by the practices of community integrity, is helping students realize their stake in a creating their "beloved community" to borrow Martin Luther King's term. At the same time, the teacher should be vigilant of the negatively constructed roles that are bound to occur in the day-to-day interactions of young people, including those disabling positionalities they may take up themselves.

Practice Implication 2. Human beings draw on socialized cognitive abilities readily available to them in the immediate social environment to position themselves as capable (e.g., verbal adroitness of African American youth), likable, interesting, and so on. They also draw on socialized cognitive abilities and cultural content available to them. This content may be used for positive positioning or negative positioning. We know that themes of

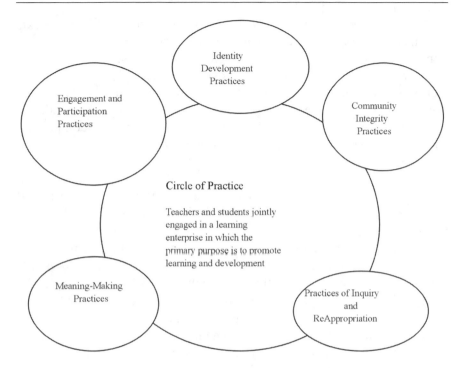

FIGURE 7–1 Essential practies in a community of educational practice.

racial stigma are part of the cultural material. As we saw in the research of Van Ausdale and Feagin (2002), even preschool children can be quite adept at drawing on the cultural signage of racial privilege in their daily interactions with their peers of color in discursive use of power to get what they want.

Students may also be negatively positioned by the teacher with respect to performance proficiency and behavior. This negative positioning can be significantly reduced by the urban educator skilled at culturally reading situations in which children and youth are engaged in instructional activity requiring proficiency. Here, the vigilance in the cultural read includes learners' relationship to peers and to the proficiency or skill being required. We want the setting to mediate achievement by eliciting effort optimism—a belief in learners that their participation, engagement, and effort will pay off. The terms of "payoff" need to be multiple—in terms of heightened sense of self-efficacy, in terms of self-regard, and in terms of enablement for doing other things for which the current accomplishment is a prerequisite.

A second aspect of this positioning as it applies to schooling contexts is whether or not the social environment offers appealing roles or the opportunity for improvising new ones. Much of what we learn is through observation and activity. The knowledge associated with a given proficiency is often tacit knowledge (Polanyi, 1967), and acquired through its use with more experienced others. Achievement identity is best mediated in a context where the desired proficiencies—be they in composing, calculating, researching, or whatever—actually constitute the fabric of instructional activity.

Practice Implication 3. There are a number of culturally constituted socialized cognitive abilities among African American children that are neither recognized nor capitalized on in the design of instructional environments. I have made this argument with illustrations extensively elsewhere (Murrell, 2001) as has the work of Boykin and colleagues (Boykin & Bailey, 2000; Boykin et al., 2004) and Nobles (1985). For example, the work of Boykin and his colleagues has identified African cultural features that could qualify as culturally constituted socialized abilities—spirituality, harmony, verve, movement, affect, communalism, expressive individualism, and orality—that can be successfully reapplied in constituting learning environments in schools (e.g., Boykin & Bailey, 2000; Boykin et al., 2004). The practice implication for urban educators is to do their homework regarding the cultural features of Black life if their students are Americans of African descent, and similarly for each of the cultural and ethnic groups represented in the school community.

Practice Implication 4. There are a number of culturally mainstream school practices that are inimical to the development of the socialized cognitive abilities brought by young people who have been socialized in African American cultural frames. In some cases, these socialized cognitive abilities may be thwarted by practices of control and compliance (e.g., the tedium of morning circle rituals). In other cases, there are preschool literacy abilities clearly the result of socialization in the African American cultural community that are simply not recognized (Meier, in press) but would constitute cultural capital, giving them an advantage over the White, culturally mainstream peers (Meier, in press). Again, the implication for urban educators is to do their homework regarding the conditions that are advantageous for access. Effective instruction in this regard would entail social practices that encourage positioning practices leading to greater productive participation and engagement in the social life of the instructional activity settings. Positioning practices should be determined that (a) ensure participation and engagement in the social life of the instructional activity settings, (b) create legitimate and positive identity locations with the social field of the instructional activity settings, (c) strive to maintain an ecology of roles and positionalities among learners, and (d) reduces all forms of symbolic violence leveled against individuals in the social space.

Positioning of individuals is always determined against a backdrop of normed practices and the subject positions (roles) of the other participants in the social space of an activity setting. This backdrop may be analyzed both in terms of the social context of the setting with a given network of relationships (e.g., classroom sociogram) and as the immediate discursive context of the episode of activity in question.

Finally, comportment cannot be your only or even your primary aim as the urban teacher seeking to organize the social life of the instructional activity settings in the classroom. It should always be secondary to what I call higher order instructional aims. For example, as a teacher you want students to follow the classroom rules you constructed with your students and you want your instructional activities to have what Phillips (1972) called participation structures. Of the two, however, the second is a higher priority as an instructional aim. Positionality as engaged, motivated, and participatory learning requires a well-designed instructional environment that pays attention to both the cognitive skill demands and the social-interactional demands (e.g., Tharp et al., 2000). A well-designed instructional environment necessarily involves intentionality, and intentionality is a requirement for the acquisition of reasoning, expertise, and intentional learning (Bereiter & Scardamalia, 1989, 1993).

Epilogue

So what do we make of all of this? How do we apply situated-mediated identity theory, with its cultural practices inquiry, to positive school change? As I write this epilogue, I am engaged in the reconstitution of an urban elementary school. The application of the framework in the ongoing work with the faculty, the parent leadership group, and the central office administration offered the perfect opportunity to crystallize a summary of how the theory in general, and cultural practices inquiry in particular, operates in positive school change—especially in contexts troubled by issues of underachievement, racial divisiveness, and student disengagement. The value of the situated-mediated identity theory is its interpretation of human interactions and meaning systems in school settings without having to account for each person's racial identity, White identity, ethnic identity, and so on, in the process.

If we were content to use only the contemporary theory of ego psychology for interpreting individual motives in identity and achievement, and subsequent school behavior, there might still be ways to handle the contextual situativity of human interaction, although it would not be in terms of the broader social and cultural context.[1] Of course, we have not been content with the contemporary theory and have instead brought forth a sociocultural-historical analysis, and incorporated this new understanding of adolescent identity in our considerations of race, class, and gender in school success, especially in the schooling and identity

---

[1]For example, there was a few years ago an interesting framework called transactional analysis by Berne (1964) that actually provided an interactional interpretation of human interaction based on an ego identity conception of positionality of individuals according to how they received and expressed meanings in one of three states: the child (id), parent (superego), or adult (ego; Berne, 1996). However, as we are not just content with interpreting interactional dynamics based on ego psychology, this volume has extended our purview to identities of achievement, how they get socialized and situated in school contexts in ways that either promote or inhibit successful academic development and personal integrity.

processes of children of color (e.g., Evans-Winters, 2005; Flores-Gonzáles, 2002; Lopez, 2002; Murrell, 1999).

Although this volume presents a new psychology of identity, I intentionally grounded the exposition in background knowledge that many educators already have. This was done as a matter of making the framework immediately accessible to those working directly with children and youth in school settings. This background knowledge includes the educational psychology, human development theory, and learning theory most educators acquire in their teacher preparation. The additional theoretical constructs in cultural psychology, semiotics, sociology, and anthropology helped me articulate the situated-mediated identity theory as a sociocultural framework and as a conceptual tool for change. Although it is a system for explaining the immediate face-to-face interactions of teachers with students, it also shows how interpersonal dynamics are only part of the whole picture of the complex issues of identity, race, culture, ethnicity, and achievement in multicultural urban schools.

The whole picture is summarized in Table 2–1, where the three identity statuses (situated identity, positionality, and agency) were explained in references to the social-cultural processes (primary socialization, secondary socialization, and improvisational self-determination) according to the three types of social-cultural contexts (social cultural community, social-symbolic community, and community of practice). Situated-mediated identity theory is the blueprint to help educators actualize achievement identities for students and teachers conjointly. It is imperative that teahers realize that the effort they put into their own *identity work*—understanding their shifting positionality in accordance with a variety of cultural settings, ethnic groupings of students, and situations—determines how successful they will be in promoting academic identity development among all of their students. It is just as critical to this work as what they do to promote positive student identity because they must develop together in the creation of the cultural space for learning. Teachers, educators, and other adults are responsible for the quality of social life for children and are the primary users of cultural practices inquiry as a conceptual tool. Teachers have much more responsibility for exhibiting agency in the understanding and inquiry of individuals in context. Remember, identity is our agency in activity: Who we are is a matter of what we choose to do and how we choose to invest in that doing.

This volume thus urges that we expect a particular kind of agency from teachers and others who work with children and youth, especially those of color, in school settings that are complicated by matters of race, ethnicity, and identity. It urges you to become agents of the socialization of our young people and to invest in whatever cultural, social, and intellectual practices will help them be successful in working through the concurrent and intermingled developmental tasks of achieving academically and forming identity. The thesis is that the processes by which young people situate themselves as learners, and as individuals, in the social settings of school and beyond determine their interest, engagement, participation, and ultimately their successful academic performance. Hence the process of positive whole-school change for a troubled urban school is a matter of targeting and changing its cultural practices.

I end this volume with a brief description of the four critical areas of cultural practices inquiry that are important for positive whole-school change. The first of these concerns the development of adult identities of achievement. As I have argued throughout this volume, facing the challenges of underachievement are not unilateral interventions we adults do for or to young people. As we are part of the social-cultural context of learning and development, we have to attend to our own situated identity, positionality, and agency as part of the work of building enabling learning communities. How else can we be agents of development and self-understanding in settings where students are struggling to find themselves, make meaning, and find agency in their own learning and development? How can we expect young people to do what we do not do ourselves? Adults working with young people contribute to their social identification, but only if they are clear about themselves and engaged in a process of social identification of their own.

Positioning is the concept in situated-mediated theory I used to analyze the setting-by-setting analysis of this identification of self and others. To recap, situated social identification not only goes on simultaneously with academic learning as argued compellingly by Wortham (2006), but the situated social identification of both students and teachers in specific learning settings are mutually constitutive. For example, the normally easy-going teacher may adopt an authoritarian positionality if one or more students project a positionality that seems to overtly challenge the authority of the teacher. The academic identity (social identity in academic settings) of participants (teachers and students alike) is mediated by the nature, quality, and dynamics of interactions among those participants in a given setting. It is particularly mediated by the consumption of symbols and the interpretation of signs. So for instance, student behavior that creates a high frequency of interruptions that is *taken* as a sign of challenge by the teacher may be *given* as sign of interest and desire to participate on the part of the student. The importance of exposing the mutual misreads of one another's positioning is not just a matter of ensuring clear and unproblematic communication across racial or cultural groups (e.g., Kochman, 1983). Additionally, the significance inheres in the fact that a student's misread and negative positioning can become institutionalized over the course of the school year in ways that permanently marginalize that student both with respect to his or her classmates and, most important, with respect to academic learning itself (e.g., Wortham, 2006).

In chapter 3 I illustrated the integration of the theory's working parts of this agency. I refer back to the cultural practices inquiry represented in Tables 3–1 and 3–2 and depicted in Figure 3–1. The tables show a total of six positionings: one table depicts three levels of positioning based on a deficiency need motive structure (e.g., I'm special and you're not), and the other depicts the three levels based on actualizing motive structure (e.g., I'm special and so are you). The syntax of cultural practices inquiry depicted in Figure 3–1 indicates the two aspects of human activity to key on: (a) symbolizing self (either oneself or others), and (b) reading (either oneself or others) into a situated social scene. This turned out to be the most powerful framework in working through the disagreements among teachers and administrators in the reconstitution meetings, where race, seniority, and administrative authority is an interesting and complex brew of people's positioning in discourse about the direction the school should take. Many, but not all, of the racially charged disagreements involved the GAWP and GRSP.

Recall the GAWP and the GRSP, where the former is the socialized tacit assumption of having steps up on those who are not White in the United States and the latter is the negative repositioning of Black people. In chapter 6 we saw how this differentiated White and African American teachers in their analytical responses to the critical episode "School Colors." What White teachers responded to before noticing anything else about the situation (in which the young African American student came before the vice principal and the teacher involved in the dispute) was the dress of the student and his demeanor. They just could not get past how he looked in his hoody, the dark glasses, the earphones, and what they described as a bad attitude.

In their initial comments, the White teachers operated with an optic that did not permit them to recognize a positionality of agency, but rather merely oppositionality and bad attitude. What most revealed the operation of a GAWP positionality was the argument about appearance in the form

"What if this were a job interview?" The fact that this ambiguous activity setting was nothing like the job interview setting did not matter. The White teachers read the symbols of the street kid and the eventual use of profanity as the basis for immediate forfeiture of any honest and fair hearing (which, of course, it was not in the first place). What would account for teachers equating the positionality in this setting to a job interview, given the stark difference between one of winning acceptance on one hand, and exerting the agency of making one's defensive case on the other hand? It is the assumption of the GAWP and the judgment that this Black kid simply was not acting right. What we should be thinking about is how to recognize the qualities and abilities exhibited by the young man, independent of the decision to suspend him, and look to these qualities as a basis of building a better community. This eventually began to happen when teachers began to interpret all three participants, their roles, their responsibilities, and how they were reading themselves into the script of a disciplinary hearing.

The White teachers, in their initial reactions, also did not recognize the verbal ability of the student, which, in this episode at least, is clearly superior to that of the adults. The initial optic of the White teachers also did not allow them to recognize, for instance, that of the three speakers the student (Geoffrey Marihia) was the only one who addressed the issues at hand and produced a cogent argument for his position. The adults in the setting did not. Geoffrey Marihia in fact did most of the talking, and did not introduce profanity until the teacher suggested that he had the right to put his hands on any student in the school in any manner he chose without there being any recourse by the student.

The second critical area on which to focus our cultural practices inquiry is on symbol consumption of images and signage that communicate ideas and ideology. Symbol consumption is a special case of how images influence human behavior—the instance in which individuals seem to be making a choice but often do so without really interpreting what the symbols mean. For example, consider the young person who dons a Charlie Manson t-shirt without really knowing who the person was, what he did, and why he had any sort of notoriety. One of the qualities that differentiate critical from uncritical thinkers is how deeply they interpret the signs and symbols. The less critical thinker responds to and consumes symbols in ways arbitrary to the meanings intended by those who produce the images. The more critical thinker tries to read beyond the immediate or apparent signification, to the historical, social, and cultural production of the image. Young people are bound to respond to, react to, and even appropriate symbols in ways that are arbitrary to the original and intended meaning. Doing a deep and critical read of meanings is something that is learned, but only if adults value and participate in this cultural practice. That is what we should be doing with cultural practices inquiry to shape school culture.

It is the use of symbolic material with little interpretation of its deeper meaning in a historical, cultural, or political context that needs to be addressed in every learning community. Many young people and too many adults take in symbolic material (e.g., use for self-representation) in undigested form, unexamined in terms of what the material might signify in the wider social world. Cultural practices inquiry in schools should therefore be a project of critical awareness, of *conscientization* to use Freire's term. People who consume symbols without appreciating or recognizing their deeper meaning would benefit from practices of critical literacy applied to images and messages from the popular media, advertising, and the wider world. Now consider once again Geoffrey Marihia, who more than likely deliberately chose symbols he knows represent to the adults in Berkeley High the street kid persona. However, what these features of self-representation mean for a young person coming into identity, especially in the context of the struggles of the school community, must be much more intelligently and carefully interpreted by adults. At the very least, cultural practices such as improvisation, multiperspective taking, and signifying exhibited by the student in this scene and in others throughout the video should be recognized by teachers, as they are important foundations for advanced academic skills in literary interpretation, empirical investigation, and text analysis.

The third critical area for cultural practices inquiry has to do with the practices embodied in academic learning. This area involves closely examining practices designed to produce certain outcomes like learning to read and write. Rather than looking to find inadequacies in the children, or in the teachers, as we traditionally have done, we should look to the adequacies of the teaching and learning practices. Academic activities that go on in classrooms should increase the academic operational capacity of learners in particular subject matter areas. Reading, text analysis, and computation are examples of activities done by individual learners that are regularly appraised according to the appropriate level of operational capacity. The purpose of cultural practices theory is to create the combination of cultural-social practices with those operational capacities required for achievement in the setting.

By academic activities I mean those operations students engage as part of some instructional process, through which they learn new content and are afforded opportunities to internalize new knowledge. Academic activities can refer to microlevel and in-the-moment operations such as summarizing a passage, adding two two-digit numbers, or balancing an oxidation-reduction equation. Academic activities may also refer to macrolevel, multiskilled, and long-term operational capacity such as composing a persuasive essay, writing a book review, or conducting a componential analysis on a chemical solution. The point here, however, is that the academic operational capacities expected in the curriculum should be part and parcel of the cultural and social practices in classrooms and schools. Examples of this in literacy learning that is intensely social, cultural, political, and identity affirming were given earlier (e.g., Mahiri, 1998; Morrell, 2004).

In current practice, too little attention is paid to the context that develops either level of academic operational capacities, particularly the aspects that mediate a positive social identification in students of diverse backgrounds. This must change. With situated identity theory we have the means to create learning environments in academic settings to fully develop integrated operational capacities that are academic and scholastic, as well as social and cultural. Applying cultural practices inquiry in the design of instruction and the organization of classroom life is more complex than merely making curriculum decisions, but need not be overwhelmingly difficult when teachers bear in mind that academic development and scholastic achievement are best understood as a process of increasing participation in richly academic and intellectual social environments. Doing this work is never simply a matter of a teacher making a decision about curriculum. It is also about simultaneously applying cultural practices inquiry as summarized by Figure 3–1. The truism that schools are a microcosm of society means that ideologies of racial privilege and stigma, sexism, and other forms of exclusion are part of the larger backdrop of critical reading and decision making, as well as the larger social context in which children are socialized.

The fourth critical area is actually a composite of the prior three; it is the inquiry for creating a figured world of achievement. The application of cultural practices inquiry requires researching, recognizing, and including those symbolic resources of culture to be figured into the school learning community. In this figured world, the principal cultural value of development and critical self-awareness among all participants (students, teachers, parents, staff, administrators) in a shared dedication to excellence, and a commitment to establish a social world we all wish to live in. On this account, cultural practices inquiry would aim to locate the necessary symbolic resources for configuring a symbolic world of achievement and development.

There are two ways the idea of symbolic resources of culture are important to this work. One is the recognition that culture—such as African American culture—provides symbolic resources for the developmental tasks of identity integration and scholastic success. The other way symbolic resources of culture are important to this work is the notion of appropriating, say, for example, symbolic resources in African American culture into the new common culture created in a classroom learning community to more specifically and emphatically support the development of African American children (Murrell, 1993, 2002; T. Perry, 2003).

I shared in this volume a few critical episodes and attempted to show how the different levels of meaning shaped the immediate social scene. Figure 3–1 offers the syntax for interpreting how you and others are symbolizing self (positioning self) and reading self into the situated social scene (exhibiting agency) in the activities of learning, conversation, and social interaction. In doing this work I would urge the use of the PBS *Frontline* video "School Colors" as a beginning resource to examine how all levels of the social context-the microsystems, mesosystems, and macrosystems of meaning-come together to determine social settings. What makes it so valuable for exploring the contrast between African American and White cultural worlds is that the school presents a case where the Africanist cultural values are experienced in a very direct way by a significant number of African American students. This is due to the fact that Berkeley High was, at the time of the first airing of the video in 1994, the only high school to have an African American Studies department in which a large proportion of the school's African American population was active.

Hopefully this volume has provided a preliminary framework for this important work.

References

Alton-Lee, A. G., Nuthall, G. A., & Patrick, J. (1993). Reframing classroom research: A lesson from the private world of children. *Harvard Educational Review, 63,* 50–84.

Anderson, J. R. (1993). Problem solving and learning. *American Psychologist, 48,* 35–44.

Anderson, J. R., Greeno, J. G., & Reder, L. M. (2000). Perspectives on learning, thinking, and activity. *Educational Researcher, 29*(4), 11–13.

Anderson, J. R., Reder, L. M., & Simon, H. A. (1996). Situated learning and education. *Educational Researcher, 25*(4), 5–11.

Anderson, J. R., Reder, L. M., & Simon, H. A. (1997). Situative versus cognitive perspectives: Form versus substance. *Educational Researcher, 26*(1), 18–21.

Anyon, J. (2005). *Radical possibilities: Public policy, urban education, and a new social movement.* New York: Routledge.

Aronson, J., & Good, C. (2002). The development and consequences of stereotype vulnerability in adolescents. In *Academic motivation of adolescents.* Institute for Policy Research, Northwestern University.

Ascher, M. (1991). *Ethnomathematics: A multicultural view of mathematical ideas.* Pacific Grove, CA: Brooks/Cole.

Austin, J. L. (1961). Ifs and cans. In J. O. Urmson & G. J. Warnock (Eds.), *Philosophical papers of J. L. Austin.* London: Oxford University Press.

Bakhtin, M. (1981). Discourse in the novel. In M. Holquist (Ed.) & C. Emerson & M. Holquist (Trans.), *The dialogic imagination* (pp. 259–422). Austin: University of Texas Press (Original work published 1935)

Bakhtin, M. M. (1999). The problem of speech genres. In A. Jaworski & N. Coupland (Eds.), *The discursive reader* (pp. 121–132). London: Routledge.

Bandura, A. (1986). *Social foundations of thought and action: A social cognitive theory.* Englewood Cliffs, NJ: Prentice-Hall.

Bandura, A. (1997). *Self-efficacy: The exercise of control.* New York: Freeman.

Banks, J. A., & Banks, C. A. (Eds.). (2004). *Handbook of research on multicultural education.* New York: Macmillan.

Bauman, Z. (1996). From pilgrim to tourist—Or a short history of identity. In S. Hall & P. du Guy (Eds.), *Questions of cultural identity* (pp. 18–36). London: Sage.

Beach, K. (1995). Activity as a mediator of sociocultural change and individual development: The case of school—work transition in Nepal. *Mind, Culture, and Activity, 2,* 285–302.

Bereiter, C., & Scardamalia, M. (1989). Intentional learning as a goal of instruction. In L. B. Resnick (Ed.), *Knowing, learning, and instruction: Essays in honor of Robert Glaser.* Hillsdale, NJ: Lawrence Erlbaum Associates, Inc.

Bereiter, C., & Scardamalia, M. (1993). *Surpassing ourselves: Inquiry into the nature and implications of expertise.* Chicago: Open Court.

Berne, E. (1964). *The games people play: The psychology of human relationships.* New York: Grove.

Berne, E. (1996). *The games people play: The basic handbook of transactional analysis.* New York: Ballantine Books.

Bloome, D., Champion, T., Katz, L., Morton, M. B., & Muldrow, R. (2001). Spoken and written narrative development: African American preschoolers as story-tellers and storymakers. In J. L. Harris, A. G. Kamhi, & K. E. Pollock (Eds.), *Literacy in African American communities* (pp. 45–76). Mahwah, NJ: Lawrence Erlbaum Associates, Inc.

Blumer, H. (1969). *Symbolic interactionism: Perspectives and methods.* Englewood Cliffs, NJ: Prentice-Hall.

Bourdieu, P. (1977). *Outline of a theory of practice* (R. Nice, Trans.). Cambridge, UK: Cambridge University Press.

Bourdieu, P., & Passeron, J-C. (1977). *Reproduction in education, society, and culture.* Beverly Hills, CA: Sage.

Bowles, H., & Gintis, S. (1976). *Schooling in capitalist America: Educational reform and the contradictions of American life.* New York: Basic Books.

Boykin, A. W., & Bailey, C. (2000). *The role of cultural factors in school relevant cognitive functioning: Synthesis of findings on cultural contexts, cultural orientations and individual differences* (Rep. No. 42). Washington, DC, & Baltimore: Howard University & Johns Hopkins University, Center for Research on the Education of Students Placed at Risk (CRESPAR).

Boykin, A. W., Coleman, S. T., Lilja, A. J., & Tyler, K. M. (2004). *Building on children's cultural assets in simulated classroom performance environments research vistas in the communal learning paradigm* (Rep. No. 68). Baltimore: Johns Hopkins University, Center for Research on the Education of Students Placed at Risk (CRESPAR).

Brislin, R. (1993). *Understanding culture's influence on behavior.* Fort Worth, TX: Harcourt Brace.

Bronfenbrenner, U. (1979). *The ecology of human development: Experiment by nature and design.* Cambridge, MA: Harvard University Press.

Bronfenbrenner, U. (1986). Ecology of family as a context for human development: Research perspectives. *Developmental Psychology, 22,* 723–742.

Brown, J. S., Collins, A., & Duguid, P. (1989). Situated cognition and the culture of learning. *Educational Research, 18*(1), 32–42.

Brown, M. K., Carnoy, M., Currie, E., Duster, T., Oppenheimer, D. B., Shultz, M. M., et al. (2003). *White-washing race: The myth of a color-blind society.* Berkeley: University of California Press.

Bruner, J. (1990). *Acts of meaning: Four lectures on mind and culture.* Cambridge, MA: Harvard University Press.

Bruner, J. (1996). *The culture of education.* Cambridge, MA: Harvard University Press.

Burke, K. (1937). *Attitudes toward history.* Berkeley: University of California Press.

Bush, M. E. L. (2004). *Breaking the code of good intentions: Everyday forms of whiteness.* New York: Rowman & Littlefield.

Callero, P. L. (1985). Role-identity salience. *Social Psychology Quarterly, 48*(3), 83–92.

Canada, G. (1998). *Reaching up for manhood: Transforming the lives of boys in America.* Boston: Beacon.

Carbaugh, D. (1996). *Situating selves: The communication of social identities in American scenes.* Albany: State University of New York Press.

Carter, P. L. (2005). *Keepin' it real: School success beyond Black and White.* New York: Oxford University Press.

Cazden, C. B. (1988). *Classroom discourse: The language of teaching and learning.* Portsmouth, NH: Heineman.

Cazden, C., & Hymes, D. (1978). Narrative thinking and storytelling rights: A folklorist's clue to a critique of education. *Folklore, 22*(1–2), 21–35.

Center for Research on Education, Diversity and Excellence. (2002). *The five standards for effective pedagogy.* Retrieved September 2, 2002, from http://www.crede.org/standards/standards.html

Chaiklin, S., Hedegaard, M., & Jensen, U. J. (Eds.). (1999). *Activity theory and social practice.* Aarhus University Press.

Cole, M. (1996). *Cultural psychology.* Cambridge, MA: Belknap.

Cole, M., & Engeström, Y. (1993). A cultural-historical approach to distributed cognition. In G. Salomon (Ed.), *Distributed cognitions: Psychology and educational considerations* (pp. 1–46). Cambridge, UK: Cambridge University Press.

Cole, M., & Engeström, Y., & Vasquez, O. (Eds.). (1997). *Mind, culture, and activity.* Cambridge, UK: Cambridge University Press.

Collins, P. H. (2000). *Black feminist thought: Knowledge, consciousness, and the politics of empowerment.* New York: Routledge.

Collins, P. H. (2005). *Black sexual politics: African Americans, gender and the new racism.* New York: Routledge.

Comer, J. P. (1998). *Waiting for a miracle: Why schools can't solve our problems—And how we can.* New York: Plume.

Connolly, P. (1998). *Racism, gender identities and young children.* London: Routledge.

Connolly, P., & Healy, J. (2004a). Symbolic violence and the neighborhood: The educational aspirations of 7–8 year old working class girls. *British Journal of Sociology, 55,* 511–529.

Connolly, P., & Healy, J. (2004b). Symbolic violence, locality and social class: The educational and career aspirations of 10–11 year old boys in Belfast. *Pedagogy, Culture and Society, 12*(1), 15–33.

Corsaro, W. (1996). Transitions in early childhood: The promise of comparative, longitudinal ethnography. In R. Jessor, A. Colby, & R. Shweder (Eds.), *Ethnography and human development: Context and meaning in social inquiry.* Chicago: University of Chicago Press.

Côté, J. E., & Levine, C. G. (2002). *Identity formation, agency and culture.* Mahwah, NJ: Lawrence Erlbaum Associates, Inc.

Couclelis, H. (1995). Bridging cognition and knowledge. In R. F. Goodman & W. R. Fisher (Eds.), *Rethinking knowledge: Reflections across the disciplines.* Albany: State University of New York Press.

Coulter, J. (1981). *The social construction of the mind.* London: Macmillan.

Crenshaw, K. (1997). Colorblind dreams and racial nightmares: Reconfiguring racism in the post-civil rights era. In T. Morisson & C. B. Lacour (Eds.), *Birth of a Nation'hood* (pp. 97–168). New York: Pantheon.

Cross, T. L., Bazron, B. J., Dennis, K. W., & Isaacs, M. R. (1989). *Towards a culturally competent system of care: A monograph on effective services for minority children who are severely emotionally disturbed.* Washington, DC: CASSP Technical Assistance Center, Georgetown University Child Development Center.

Cross, W. E. (1991). *Shades of black: Diversity in African-American identity.* Philadelphia: Temple University Press.

Csikszentmihalyi, M. (1991). *Flow: The psychology of optimal experience.* New York: Harper Perennial.

Cunningham, M., & Meunier, L. N. (2004). The influence of peer experiences on bravado attitudes among African American males. In N. Way & J. Y. Chu (Eds.), *Adolescent boys: Exploring diverse cultures of boyhood* (pp. 219–234). New York: NYU Press.

Davies, B., & Harré, R. (1999). Positioning and personhood. In R. Harré & L. van Langenhove (Eds.), *Positioning theory* (pp. 32–51). Thousand Oaks, CA: Sage.

Davis, K. (1997). *Exploring the intersection between cultural competency and managed behavioral health care policy: Implications for state and county mental health agencies.* Alexandria, VA: National Technical Assistance Center for State Mental Health Planning.

Delpit, L. (1988). The silenced dialogue: Power and pedagogy in educating other people's children. *Harvard Educational Review, 58,* 280–296.

Dewey, J. (1933). *How we think: A restatement of the relation of reflective thinking to the educative process.* Boston: Henry Holt.

Doane, A. W., & Bonilla-Silva, E. (Eds.). (2003). *White out: The continuing significance of racism.* New York: Routledge.

DuBois, W. E. B. (1989). *The souls of Black folk.* New York: Bantam Books. (Original work published 1903)

Education Trust. (2002). *Dispelling the myth revisited: Preliminary findings from a nationwide analysis of high-flying schools.* Washington, DC: Author.

Engeström, Y. (1987). *Learning by expanding: An activity-theoretical approach to developmental research.* Helsinki, Finland: Orienta-Konsultit.

Engeström, Y. (2001). Expansive learning at work: Toward an activity theoretical reconceptualization. *Journal of Education and Work, 14,* 133–156.

Erickson, F. (2004). *Talk and social theory: Ecologies of speaking and listening in everyday life.* Cambridge, UK: Polity.

Erikson, E. H. (1963). *Childhood and society* (2nd ed.). New York: Norton.

Erikson, E. H. (1968). *Identity, youth, and crisis.* New York: Norton.

Erikson, E. H. (1980). *Identity and the life cycle* (2nd ed.). New York: Norton.

Evans-Winters, V. E. (2005). *Teaching Black girls: Resiliency in urban classrooms.* New York: Peter Lang.

Feagin, J. R. (2000). *Racist America: Roots, current realities, and future reparations.* New York: Routledge.

Feldman, A. F., & Matjasko, J. L. (2005). The role of school-based extracurricular activities in adolescent development: A comprehensive review and future directions. *Review of Educational Research, 75,* 159–210.

Flores-Gonzáles, N. (2002). *School kids/street kids: Identity development in Latino students.* New York: Teachers College Press.

Fordham, S. (1988). Racelessness as a factors in Black students' success: Pragmatic strategy or pyrrhic victory. *Harvard Educational Review, 58,* 29–84.

Fordham, S. (1996). *Blacked out: Dilemmas of race, identity, and success at Capital High.* Chicago: University of Chicago Press.

Fordham, S., & Ogbu, J. U. (1986). Black students' school success: Coping with the burden of "acting white." *The Urban Review, 18,* 176–206.

Foster, M. (1989). It's cooking now: A performance analysis of the speech events of a Black teacher in an urban community college. *Language and Society, 18,* 1–29.

Freire, P. (1970). *Pedagogy of the oppressed.* New York: Continuum.

French, S. E., Seidman, E., Allen, L., & Aber, J. L. (2000). Racial/ethnic identity, congruence with the social context, and the transition to high school. *Journal of Adolescent Research, 15,* 587–602.

Freud, A. (1959). *The psychoanalytical treatment of children: Technical lectures and essays* (Reprinted). New York: International University Press.

Fung, A. (2004). *Empowered participation: Reinventing urban democracy.* Princeton, NJ: Princeton University Press.

Fuson, K. C., Smith, S. T., & Lo Cicero, A. (1997). Supporting Latino first graders' ten-structured thinking in urban classrooms. *Journal for Research in Mathematics Education, 28*(2), 738–766.

Galambos, J. A., Abelson, R. P., & Black, J. B. (Eds.). (1986). *Knowledge structures.* Mahwah, NJ: Lawrence Erlbaum Associates, Inc.

Garbarino, J. (1999). *Lost boys: Why our sons turn violent and how we can save them.* New York: The Free Press.

Gay, G. (2000). *Culturally responsive teaching: Theory, research and practice.* New York: Teachers College Press.

Gee, J. P. (2001). Identity as an analytic lens for research in education. *Review of Research in Education, 25,* 99–125.

Geertz, C. (1973). *The interpretation of cultures.* New York: Basic Books.

Gibson, M. A., Bejínez, L. F., Hidalgo, N., & Rolón, C. (2004). *Belonging and school participation: Lessons from a migrant student club.* In M. A. Gibson, P. C. Gándara, & J. P. Koyama (Eds.), *School connections: U.S. Mexican youth, peers and school achievement.* New York: Teachers College Press.

Gilligan, C. (1992). *Meeting at the crossroads: Women's psychology and girls development.* Cambridge, MA: Harvard University Press.

Gilligan, C. (1993). *In a different voice.* Cambridge, MA: Harvard University Press. (Original work published 1982)

Giroux, H. A. (1997). *Pedagogy and the politics of hope: Theory, culture, and schooling. A critical reader.* Boulder, CO: Westview.

Giroux, H. (2001). *Theory and resistance in education: Towards a pedagogy for the opposition.* Westport, CT: Bergin & Garvey.

Giroux, H. A., & McLaren, P. (1986). Teacher education and the politics of engagement: The case for democratic schooling. *Harvard Educational Review, 56,* 213–238.

Goffman, E. (1959). *The presentation of self in everyday life.* New York: Doubleday.

Goffman, E. (1963). *Stigma: Notes on the management of spoiled identity.* New York: Simon & Schuster.

Goffman, E. (1967). *Interaction ritual.* New York: Anchor.

Goffman, E. (1968). *Stigma.* Englewood Cliffs, NJ: Prentice-Hall.

Goffman, E. (1974). *Frame analysis.* Cambridge, MA: Harvard University Press.

Goffman, E. (1981). *Forms of talk.* Philadelphia: University of Pennsylvania Press.

González, N. (1999). What will we do when culture does not exist anymore? *Anthropology and Education Quarterly, 30,* 431–435.

González, N., Moll, L. C., & Amanti, C. (Eds.). (2005). *Funds of knowledge: Theorizing practices in households, communities, and classrooms.* Mawah, NJ: Lawrence Erlbaum Associates.

Goodenough, W. H. (1971). *Culture, language and society.* Reading, MA: Addison-Wesley.

Goodwin, M. (1991). *He—said, she—said: Talk as social organization among Black children.* Bloomington: Indiana University Press.

Gordon, E., Bridglall, B. L., & Meroe, A. S. (2005). *Supplementary education: The hidden curriculum of academic achievement.* New York: Rowman & Littlefield.

Gumperz, J. J., & Cook-Gumperz, J. (1982). Introduction: Language and the communication of social identity. In J. J. Gumperz (Ed.), *Language and social identity.* New York: Oxford University.

Haberman, M. (1991). Pedagogy of poverty versus good teaching. *Phi Delta Kappan, 73,* 290–294.

Hall, G. S. (1904). *Adolescence: Its psychology and its relations to physiology, anthropology, sex, crime, religion and education* (Vol. 2). Boston: Adamant Media.

Hall, S. (1980). Encoding and decoding. In S. Hall, D. Hobson, A. Lowe, & P. Willis (Eds.), *Culture, media, language* (pp. 122–138). London: Hutchinson.

Hall, S. (1996). Who needs "identity"? In S. Hall & P. du Guy (Eds.), *Questions of cultural identity* (pp. 1–18). London: Sage.

Hall, S. (1997). *Representation: Cultural representations and signifying practice.* London: Sage.

Hall, S., & du Gay, P. (Eds.). (1996). *Questions of cultural identity.* London: Sage.

Halliday, M. A. K. (1978). Meaning and the construction of reality in early childhood. In H. L. Pick, Jr., & E. Saltzman (Eds.), *Modes of perceiving and processing information* (pp. 67–96). Hillsdale, NJ: Lawrence Erlbaum Associates, Inc.

Harré, R., & Gillet, G. R. (1994). *The discursive mind.* Thousand Oaks, CA: Sage.

Harré, R., & Secord, P. F. (1972). *The explanation of social behaviour.* Oxford, UK: Blackwell.

Harré, R., & van Langenhove, L. (Eds.). (1999). *Positioning theory: Moral contexts of intentional action.* Oxford, UK: Blackwell.

Heath, S. B. (1983). *Ways with words: Language, life and work in communities and classrooms.* Cambridge, UK: Cambridge University Press.

Helms, J. E. (1993). *Black and White racial identity: Theory, research, and practice.* Westport, CT: Greenwood.

Hilliard, A. (2004). No mystery: Closing the achievement gap between Africans and excellence. In T. Perry, C. Steele, & A. G. Hilliard, III (Eds.), *Young, gifted, and Black: Promoting high achievement among African American students* (pp. 131–167). Boston: Beacon.

Hoffman, D. M. (1998). A therapeutic moment? Identity, self, and culture in the anthropology of education. *Anthropology and Education Quarterly, 29,* 324–346.

Hogg, M. A., Terry, D. J., & White, K. M. (1995). A tale of two theories: A critical comparison of identity theory with social identity theory. *Social Psychology Quarterly, 58,* 255–269.

Holland, D., & Lave, J. (Eds.). (2001). *History in person: Enduring struggles, contentious practice, intimate identities.* Santa Fe, NM: School of American Research Press.

Holland, D., Lachicotte, W., Jr., Skinner, D., & Cain, C. (1998). *Identity and agency in cultural worlds.* Cambridge, MA: Harvard University Press.

Holland, S. H. (1996). PROJECT 2000: An educational mentoring and academic support model for inner-city African American boys. *Journal of Negro Education, 65,* 315–321.

Hollins, E. (Ed.). (1996). *Transforming curriculum for a racial diverse society.* Mahwah, NJ: Lawrence Erlbaum Associates, Inc.

Holloway, W. (1984). Gender difference in the production of subjectivity. In J. Henriques, W. Holloway, C. Urwin, L. Venn, & V. Walkerdine (Eds.), *Changing the subject: Psychology, social regulation and subjectivity* (pp. 222–236). London: Methuen.

hooks, b. (1989). *Talking back: Thinking feminist, thinking Black.* Boston: South End.

Howard, J. (1990). *Getting smart: The social construction of intelligence.* Boston: The Efficacy Institute.

Hunter, G. A., & Davis, J. E. (1992). Constructing gender: An exploration of Afro-American men's conceptualization of manhood. *Gender & Society, 6,* 464–479.

Hunter, G. A., & Davis, J. E. (1994). Hidden voices of Black men: The meaning, structure, and complexity of manhood. *Journal of Black Studies, 25,* 20–40.

Hymes, D. (1972). On communicative competence. In J. B. Pride and J. Holmes (Eds.), *Sociolinguistics* (pp. 269–293). Harmondsworth: Penguin.

Ignatiev, N. (1996). *How the Irish became white.* Boston: Routledge.

Irvine, J. (1990). *Black students and school failure.* Westport, CT: Greenwood Press.

Irvine, J. J. (Ed.). (2002). *In search of wholeness: African American teachers and their culturally specific classroom practices.* New York: Palgrave.

Irvine, J. J. (2003). *Educating teachers for diversity: Seeing with a cultural eye.* New York: Teachers College Press.

Isaacs, M. R., & Benjamin, M. P. (1991). *Toward a culturally responsive system of care (Vol. II): Programs that use culturally competent principles.* Washington, DC: Georgetown University Child Development Center, CASSP Technical Assistance Center.

Kimmel, M. S. (1994). Masculinity and homophobia: Fear, shame and silence in the construction of gender identity. In H. Brod & M. Kaufman (Eds.), *The theorizing of masculinities* (pp. 119–141). Newbury Park, CA: Sage.

Kimmel, M. S. (1997). Masculinity as homophobia: Fear, shame, and silence in the construction of gender identity. In M. Gergen & S. Davis (Eds.), *Towards a new psychology of gender* (pp. 223–242). New York: Routledge.

Kimmel, M. S. (2004). "I'm not insane; I'm angry": Adolescent masculinity, homophobia, and violence. In M. Sadowski (Ed.), *Adolescents at school: Perspectives on youth, identity, and education.* Cambridge, MA: Harvard University Press.

Kimmel, M., & Messner, M. (1992). *Men's lives* (2nd ed.). New York: Macmillan.

Kochman, T. (1983). *Black and white styles in conflict.* Chicago: University of Chicago Press.

Kozol, J. (1991). *Savage inequalities: Children in America's schools.* New York: Crown.

Kozol, J. (2005). *The shame of the nation: The restoration of apartheid schooling in America.* New York: Crown.

Kunjufu, J. (1985). *Countering the conspiracy to destroy Black boys.* Chicago: African American Images.

Ladson-Billings, G. (1994). *Dreamkeepers.* San Francisco: Jossey-Bass.

Lave, J. (1988). *Cognition in practice.* Cambridge, UK: Cambridge University Press.

Lave, J. (1991). Situated learning in communities of practice. In L. B. Resnick, J. M. Levine, & S. D. Teasley (Eds.), *Perspectives on socially shared cognition* (pp. 63–82). Washington, DC: American Psychological Association.

Lave, J. (1997). The culture of acquisition and the practice of understanding. In D. Kirshner & J. A. Whitson (Eds.), *Situated cognition: Social, semiotic, and psychological perspectives* (pp. 17–36). Hillsdale, NJ: Lawrence Erlbaum Associates, Inc.

Lave, J., & Wenger, E. (1991). *Situated learning: Legitimate peripheral participation.* Cambridge, UK: Cambridge University Press.

Lee, C. D. (1993). *Signifying as a scaffold for literary interpretation: The pedagogical implications of an African American discourse genre* (NCTE Research Rep.). Urbana, IL: National Council of Teachers of English.

Leigh, J. W. (1998). *Communicating for cultural competence.* Prospect Heights, IL: Waveland.

Lemke, J. L. (1997). Cognition, context, and learning: A social semiotic perspective. In D. Kirschner & J. A. Whitson (Eds.), *Situated cognition: Social, semiotic and psychological perspectives* (pp. 37–55). Mahwah NJ: Lawrence Erlbaum Associates, Inc.

Lemke, J. L. (2000). Across the scales of time: Artifacts, activities, and meanings in ecosocial systems. *Mind, Culture, and Activity, 7,* 273–290.

Leont'ev, A. N. (1978). *Activity, consciousness, personality.* Englewood Cliffs, NJ: Prentice-Hall.

Leont'ev, A. N. (1981). The problem of activity in psychology. In J. V. Wertsch (Ed.), *The concept of activity in Soviet psychology* (pp. 37–71). Armonk, NY: Sharpe.

Lewis, A. E. (2003). *Race in the schoolyard: Negotiating the color line in classrooms and communities.* New Brunswick, NJ: Rutgers University Press.

Lopez, N. (2002). *Hopeful girls, troubled boys: Race and gender disparity in urban education.* New York: Routledge.

Lorde, A. (1984). *Sister outsider: Essays and speeches.* Freedom, CA: Crossing Press.

Loury, G. C. (2002). *The anatomy of racial inequality.* Cambridge, MA: Harvard University Press.

MacLeod, J. (1995). *Ain't no making it: Aspirations and attainment in a low-income neighborhood.* Boulder, CO: Westview.

Mahiri, J. (1998). *Shooting for excellence: African American youth culture in new century schools.* Urbana, IL: National Council of Teachers of English.

Majors, R., & Billson, J. M. (1993). *Cool pose: The dilemmas of Black manhood in America.* New York: Touchstone.

Marcia, J. E. (1994). The empirical study of ego identity. In H. Bsoma, T. Graafsma, H. Grotebanc, & D. LcLivita (Eds.), *Identity and development.* Newbury Park, CA: Sage.

Marks, S. R. (1977). Multiple roles and role strain: Some notes on human energy, time and commitment. *American Sociological Review, 42,* 921–936.

Marks, S. R., & MacDermid, S. M. (1996). Multiple roles and the self: A theory of role balance. *Journal of Marriage and the Family, 58,* 417–432.

Markus, H., & Nurius, P. (1987). Possible selves: The interface between motivation and the self-concept. In K. Yardley & T. Honess (Eds.), *Self and identity: Psychological perspectives* (pp. 157–172). Chichester, UK: Wiley.

Maslow, A. (1970). *Motivation and personality* (2nd ed.). New York: Harper & Row.

Maslow, A., & Lowery, R. (Eds.). (1998). *Toward a psychology of being* (3rd ed.). New York: Wiley & Sons

McCall, G. J., & Simmons, J. L. (1978). *Identities and interactions: An examination of human associations in everyday life.* New York: The Free Press.

McLaren, P. (1994). *Life in schools: An introduction to critical pedagogy in the foundations of education* (2nd ed.). Toronto: Irwin.

McLaren, P. (2003). Critical pedagogy: A look at the major concepts. In A. Darder, M. Baltodano, & R. D. Torres (Eds.), *The critical pedagogy reader* (pp. 69–99). New York: Routledge Falmer.

Mead, G. H. (1934). *Mind, self, and society.* Chicago: University of Chicago Press.

Mehan, H., Hubbard, L., & Villenuava, I. (1994). Forming academic identities: Accommodation without assimilation among involuntary minorities. *Anthropology & Education Quarterly, 25,* 91–117.

Meier, T. (1998). Teaching teachers about Black communications. In T. Perry & L. Delpit (Eds.), *The real Ebonics debate: Power, language and the education of African-American children* (pp. 117–125). Boston: Beacon.

Meier, T. (1999). The case for Ebonics as part of exemplary teacher preparation. In C. T. Adger, D. Christian, & O. Taylor (Eds.), *Making the connection: Language and academic achievement among African American students* (pp. 97–114). McHenry, IL: Delta Systems.

Meier, T. (in press). *Black communications and learning to read: Building upon children's linguistic and cultural strengths.* Mahwah, NJ: Lawrence Erlbaum.

Moll, L. C., & Greenberg, J. (1990). Creating zones of possibilities: Combining social contexts for instruction. In L. C. Moll (Ed.), *Vygotsky and education* (pp. 319–348). Cambridge, UK: Cambridge University Press.

Morgan, M. (1993). The Africanness of counterlanguage among Afro-Americans. In S. S. Mufwene (Ed.), *Africanisms in Afro-American language varieties* (pp. 423–435). Athens: University of Georgia Press.

Morgan, M. (2002). *Language, discourse, and power in African American culture.* New York: Cambridge University Press.

Morrell, E. (2004). *Becoming critical researchers: Literacy and empowerment for urban youth.* New York: Peter Lang.

Morrell, E. (2004). *Linking literacy to popular culture: Finding connections for lifelong learning.* Norwood, MA: Christopher Gordon.

Moses, M. S. (2002). *Embracing race: Why we need race-conscious education policy.* New York: Teachers College Press.

Moses, R. P., Kamii, M., Swap, S. M., & Howard, J. (1989). The algebra project: Organizing in the spirit of Ella. *Harvard Educational Review, 59,* 423–443.

Murrell, P. C., Jr. (1991). Cultural politics in teacher education: What's missing in the preparation of African-American teachers? In M. Foster (Ed.), *Readings on equal education,* (Vol. 11, pp. 205–225).

Murrell, P. C., Jr. (1993). Afrocentric immersion: Academic and personal development of African American males in public schools. In T. Perry & J. Fraser (Eds.), *Freedom's plow: Schools as multiracial, multiethnic democracies* (pp. 231–260). New York: Routledge.

Murrell, P. (1994). In search of responsive teaching for African American males: An investigation of students' experiences of middle school mathematics curriculum. *Journal of Negro Education, 63,* 556–569.

Murrell, P. C., Jr. (1997). Digging again the family wells: A Freirean literacy framework as emancipatory pedagogy for African American children. In P. Freire, J. Fraser, D. Macedo, T. McKinnon, & W. Stokes (Eds.), *Mentoring the mentor: A critical dialog with Paulo Freire* (pp. 19–58). New York: State University of New York Press.

Murrell, P. C., Jr. (1998). *Like stone soup: The problem of the professional development school in the renewal of urban schools.* Washington, DC: The American Association of Colleges for Teacher Education (AACTE).

Murrell, P. C., Jr. (1999). Class and race in negotiating identity. In A. Garrod, J. Ward, T. L. Robinson, & R. Kilkenny (Eds.), *Souls looking back: Life stories of growing up Black* (pp. 3–14). New York: Routledge.

Murrell, P. C., Jr. (2002). *African-centered pedagogy: Developing schools of achievement for African American children.* New York: SUNY Press.

Murrell, P. C., Jr. (2006). *Mediated identity, agency, and oppositionality: A sociocultural activity theory account of Black achievement and educational attainment.* Presentation. American Educational Research Association annual meeting, April, 2007.

Murrell, P. C., Jr., & Borunda, M. (1998). The cultural and community politics of educational equity: Toward a new framework of professional development schools. In N. J. Lauter (Ed.), *Professional development schools: Confronting realities* (pp. 65–86). New York: National Center for Restructuring Education, Schools and Teaching (NCREST).

Nakkula, M. (2003). Identity and possibility: Adolescent development and the potential of schools. In M. Sadowski (Ed.), *Adolescents at school: Perspectives on youth, identity and education* (pp. 7–18). Cambridge, MA: Harvard University Press.

Nasir, N. S., & Saxe, G. B. (2003). Ethnic and academic identities: A cultural practice perspective on emerging tensions and their management in the lives of minority students. *Educational Researcher, 32,* 14–18.

National Board for Professional Teaching Standards. (2002). Retrieved September 2, 2002, from http://www.nbpts.org/.

Newman, F. M., & Oliver, D. W. (1967). Education and community. *Harvard Educational Review, 37,* 61–106.

Nobles, W. (1985). *Africanity and the Black family: The development of a theoretical model.* Oakland, CA: Black Family Institute Publishers.

Nobles, W. W. (1991). African philosophy: Foundations of Black psychology. In R. L. Jones (Ed.), *Black psychology* (pp. 47–64). Berkeley, CA: Cobb & Henry.

Noguera, P. (2003). *City schools and the American dream: Reclaiming the promise of public education.* New York: Teachers College Press.

Ogbu, J. U. (1981). Origins of human competence: A cultural ecological perspective. *Child Development, 52,* 413–429.

Ogbu, J. U. (1983). Minority status and schooling in plural societies. *Comparative Education Review, 27,* 168–190.

Ogbu, J. U. (1988). Black education: A cultural-ecological perspective. In H. P. McAdoo (Ed.), *Black families* (pp. 169–186). Beverly Hills, CA: Sage.

Ogbu, J. U. (1992). Understanding cultural diversity and learning. *Educational Researcher, 21*(8), 5–14.

Ogbu, J. U., & Davis, A. (2003). *Black American students in an affluent suburb: A student of academic disengagement.* Mahwah, NJ: Lawrence Erlbaum Associates, Inc.

Olneck, M. R. (1990). The recurring dream: Symbolism and ideology in intercultural and multicultural education. *American Journal of Education, 98*(2), 147–174.

Olneck, M. (2000). Can multicultural education change what counts as cultural capital. *American Educational Research Journal, 27*(2), 317–348.

Palinscar, A. S., & Brown, A. L. (1984). Reciprocal teaching of comprehension-fostering monitoring strategies. *Cognition and Instruction, 1,* 117–175.

Park, R. E. (1950). *Race and culture.* Glencoe, IL: The Free Press.

Payne, C., & Kaba, M. (2001). So much reform, so little change: Building-level obstacles to urban school reform. *Journal of Negro Education,* 2, 1–16.

Pease-Alvarez, L., & Schecter, S. R. (Eds.). (2005). *Learning, teaching, and community: Contributions of situated and participatory approaches in educational innovation.* Mahwah, NJ: Lawrence Erlbaum Associates, Inc.

Perry, P. (2002). *Shades of White: White kids and racial identities in high school.* Chapel Hill, NC: Duke University Press.

Perry, T. (2004). Up from the parched earth: Toward a theory of African-American achievement. In T. Perry, C. Steele, & A. G. Hilliard, III (Eds.), *Young, gifted, and Black: Promoting high achievement among African American students* (pp. 1–87). Boston: Beacon.

Phillips, S. (1972). Participant structures and communicative competence: Warm Springs children in community and classroom. In C. Cazden et al. (Eds.), *Functions of language in the classroom,* (pp. 370–394). New York: Teachers College Press.

Phinney, J. S. (1989). Stages of identity development in minority group adolescence. *Journal of Personality and Social Psychology, 65,* 186–198.

Polanyi, M. (1958). *Personal knowledge.* Chicago: University of Chicago Press.

Polanyi, M. (1967). *The tacit dimension.* New York: Anchor.

Pollack, W. (1999). *"Real boys": Rescuing our sons from the myths of boyhood.* New York: Random House.

Polletta, F. (2002). *Freedom is an endless meeting: Democracy in American social movements.* Chicago: University of Chicago Press.

Pollock, M. (2004). *Colormute: Race talk dilemmas in an American school.* Princeton, NJ: Princeton University Press.

Putnam, R. D. (2001). *Bowling alone: The collapse of revival of American community.* New York: Simon & Schuster.

Reid, E., & Henry, G. B. (2000, February). *Waiting to excel: Biraciality in the classroom.* Paper presented at the meeting of the National Association of African American Studies & National Association of Hispanic and Latino Studies, Houston, TX.

Roediger, D. R. (1999). *The wages of whiteness: Race and the making of the American working class.* New York: Verso.

Rogoff, B. (1994). Developing understanding in the idea of communities of learners. *Mind, Culture, and Activity, 1,* 209–229.

Rogoff, B. (2003). *The cultural nature of human development.* Oxford, UK: Oxford University Press.

Rogoff, B., & Lave, J. (Eds.). (1984). *Everyday cognition: It's development in social context.* Cambridge, MA: Harvard University Press.

Roth, W. M. (2004). Identity as dialectic: Re/making self in urban school. *Mind, Culture, and Activity, 11,* 48–69.

Rowley, G. C. (2004). Dissecting the anatomy of African-American inequality: The impact of racial stigma and social origins on group status and college achievement. *Educational Researcher, 33*(4), 15–21.

Sacchetti, M., & Jan, T. (2005, May 29). Gift of college proves a boon and a burden. *New York Times.* Retrieved May 31, 2005, from http://www.nytimes.com

Sadker, M., & Sadker, D. (1986). Sexism in the classroom: From grade school to graduate school. *Phi Delta Kappan, 67,* 512–515.

Sadker, M., & Sadker, D. (1994). *Failing at fairness: How America's schools cheat girls.* New York: Macmillan.

Sadowski, M. (Ed.). (2003). *Adolescents at school: Perspectives on youth, identity and education.* Cambridge, MA: Harvard University Press.

Saxe, G. B. (1991). *Culture and cognitive development.* Hillsdale, NJ: Lawrence Erlbaum Associates, Inc.

Schoenfeld, A. H. (1994). *Mathematics thinking and problem solving.* Hillsdale, NJ: Lawrence Erlbaum.

Scollon, R. (1976). *Conversations with a one year old: A case study of communication in early language development.* Honolulu, HI: University Press of Hawaii.

Scollon, R., & Scollon, S. B. K. (1981). *Narrative, literacy, and face in interethnic communication.* Norwood, NJ: Ablex.

Scribner, S., & Cole, M. (1986). *The psychology of literacy.* Cambridge, MA: Harvard University Press.

Searle, J. (1979). *Expression and meaning: Studies in the theory of speech acts.* Cambridge, UK: Cambridge University Press.

Sfard, A., & Prusak, A. (2005). Telling identities: In search of an analytic tool for investigating learning as a culturally shaped activity. *Educational Researcher, 34* (4), 14–22.

Siddle-Walker, V. (1996). *Their highest potential: An African American school in the segregated south.* Chapel Hill: University of North Carolina Press.

Siegler, R. S. (Ed.). (1978). *Children's thinking: What develops?* Hillsdale, NJ: Lawrence Erlbaum Associates.

Sleeter, C. E. (1992). *Keepers of the American dream: A study of staff development and multicultural education.* Washington, DC: Falmer.

Sleeter, C. E. (2000). Epistemological diversity in research on pre-service teacher preparation for historically underserved children. *Review of Research on Education, 25,* 209–250.

Sleeter, C. E. (2001). Preparing teachers of culturally diverse schools: Research and the overwhelming presence of whiteness. *Journal of Teacher Education, 52,* 94–106.

Sleeter, C. E., & Grant, C. (1988). Race, class, and gender and abandoned dreams. *Teachers College Record, 90,* 19–40.

Smitherman, G. (1986). *Talkin' and testifyin'.* Detroit, MI: Wayne State University Press.

Stanton-Salazar, R. D. (2004). Social capital among working class minority students. In M. A. Gibson, P. Gandara, & J. P. Koyama (Eds.), *School connection: U.S and Mexican youth, peers and school achievement* (pp. 18–38). New York: Teachers College Press.

Steele, C. (1997). A threat in the air. *American Psychologist, 52,* 613–629.

Steele, C. (2004). Stereotype threat and African-American student achievement. In T. Perry, C. Steele, & A. G. Hilliard, III (Eds.), *Young, gifted, and Black: Promoting high achievement among African American students* (pp. 109–130). Boston: Beacon.

Stevens, J. W. (2002). *Smart and sassy: The strengths of inner-city Black girls.* New York: Oxford University Press.

Stryker, S. (1968). Identity salience and role performance: The relevance of symbolic interaction theory for family research. *Journal of Marriage and the Family, 30,* 558–564.

Stryker, S. (1987). Identity theory: Developments and extensions. In K. Yardley & T. Honess (Eds.), *Self and identity: Psychosocial perspectives* (pp. 89–103). New York: John Wiley & Sons.

Tatum, B. (1997). *"Why are all the Black kids sitting together in the cafeteria?": A psychologist explains the development of racial identity.* New York: Kirkus Associates.

Tharp, R., Estrada, P., Dalton, S., & Yamauchi, L. A. (2000). *Teaching transformed: Achieving excellence, fairness, inclusion and harmony.* Boulder, CO: Westview.

Tharp, R. G., & Gallimore, R. (1988). *Rousing minds to life: Teaching, learning, and schooling in social context.* Cambridge, UK: Cambridge University Press.

Tharp, R. G., & Gallimore, R. (1991). *Instructional conversation: Teaching and learning in social activity* (Report from the Office of Educational Research and Improvement). Washington, DC: U.S. Department of Education.

Tomasello, M., Carpenter, M., Call, J., Behne, T., & Moll, H. (2005). Understanding and sharing intentions: The origins of cultural cognition. *Behavioral and Brain Sciences, 28,* 675–691.

Van Ausdale, D., & Feagin, J. R. (2002). *The first R: How children learn race and racism.* New York: Rowman & Littlefield.

Vernon-Feagans, L. (1996). *Children's talk in communities and classrooms.* Cambridge, MA: Blackwell.

Vygotsky, L. (1962). *Thought and language* (E. Hanfman & G. Bakar, Eds. and Trans.). Cambridge, MA: MIT Press.

Vygotsky, L. (1978). *Thought and language.* Cambridge, MA: MIT Press.

Weick, K. E. (1979). *The social psychology of organizing* (2nd ed.). Reading, MA: Addison-Wesley.

Weick, K. E. (1995). *Sensemaking in organizations.* Thousand Oaks, CA: Sage.

Wenger, E. (1998). *Communities of practice: Learning, meaning, and identity.* Cambridge, UK: Cambridge University Press.

Wertsch, J. V. (1985). *Culture, communication, and cognition: Vygotskian perspectives.* Cambridge, UK: Cambridge University Press.

Wertsch, J. V. (1998). *Mind in action.* New York: Oxford University Press.

Wiley, M. G. & Alexander, N., Jr., (1987). From situated activity to attribution: The impact of social structural schemata. In K. Yardley & T. Honess (Eds.), *Self and identity: Psychosocial perspectives* (pp. 105–117). New York: John Wiley & Sons.

Willis, P. (1982). *Learning to labor: How working class kids get working class jobs.* New York: Columbia University Press.

Wilson, A. N. (1978). *The developmental psychology of the Black child.* New York: Africana Research Publication.

Wink, J. (1997). *Critical pedagogy: Notes from the real world.* New York: Longman.

Wittgenstein, L. (1953). *Philosophical investigations.* Oxford, UK: Blackwell.

Wortham, E. F. (1994). *Acting out participant examples in the classroom.* Philadelphia: John Benjamins.

Wortham, E. F. (2001). *Narratives in action.* New York: Teachers College Press.

Wortham, E. F. (2003). Interactionally situated cognition: A classroom example. *Cognitive Science, 25,* 37–66.

Wortham, E. F. (2006). *Learning identity: The joint emergence of social identification and academic learning.* New York: Cambridge University Press.

Yon, D. (2000). *Elusive culture: Schooling, race, and identity in global times.* Albany: State University of New York Press.

Author Index

Subject Index